Henry James Coleridge

The Prisoner of the King: Thoughts on the Catholic Doctrine of Purgatory

Henry James Coleridge

The Prisoner of the King: Thoughts on the Catholic Doctrine of Purgatory

ISBN/EAN: 9783743397422

Manufactured in Europe, USA, Canada, Australia, Japa

Cover: Foto © Lupo / pixelio.de

Manufactured and distributed by brebook publishing software (www.brebook.com)

Henry James Coleridge

The Prisoner of the King: Thoughts on the Catholic Doctrine of Purgatory

PREFACE.

THE form in which these thoughts on the doctrine of Purgatory are put forth in this volume is accidental, and I am well aware that it cannot claim to present to the reader a well arranged treatise on the great subject with which it deals. Two or three years ago it fell to my lot, in conjunction with a dear friend and brother in religion, who is now, I trust, at rest with God, to preach during the Octave with which the Society of the Helpers of the Holy Souls is accustomed to celebrate the annual Commemoration of the Faithful Departed. It occurred to me that some of the miracles of our Lord might be usefully applied in illustration of the doctrine of Purgatory, and thus the substance of some few of the chapters of this book was put together. At the beginning of the present year I began a series of papers on the same subject in the *Messenger of the Sacred Heart*— a religious magazine the existence of which we owe to the zeal and exertions of the widely loved and valued priest of whom I have already spoken.

The work has grown under my hands, and it seemed better to finish it at once, in order that it might perhaps be of some little use in promoting the devotion of which it mainly treats during the month which Catholics constantly consecrate to the relief of the Holy Souls. About a third of the contents of this volume has appeared in the *Messenger of the Sacred Heart.*

Although the form in which this book is cast almost of necessity precludes the regular and orderly treatment of the doctrine of Purgatory, I am in hopes that no considerable point connected with that doctrine has been altogether passed over. I have found much help from two books which are not very widely known to readers on the subject— the two *Sagri Trigesimi* on Purgatory preached by Pope Benedict XIII. when Cardinal Archbishop of Bologna—in which the whole doctrine of St. Thomas is illustrated with great erudition—and the *Patrocinium Defunctorum* of Father Hautin. I have not thought it necessary to specify all my obligations to these and other writers, in a work the object of which is simply to promote intelligent devotion, written at intervals of time and under circumstances which forbade any unnecessary exertion.

What is new in this volume is chiefly the application of the successive miracles of our Lord to various points of the doctrine of Purgatory. Our Lord's miracles were almost universally acts of mercy as well as proofs of authority, and thus it is natural to find that they are full of teaching as to the various spiritual miseries of souls and His tenderness in succouring them. The Holy Souls are sufferers to a degree and in a manner which are but faintly pictured in the bodily maladies which our Lord so lovingly relieved, and they are sufferers whose case He has left very much to the charity of the children of the Militant Church. His Sacred Heart looked further than the outward disease or privation for which He used His healing or restoring power, and, if it is most natural to consider all bodily evils as shadows and images by which spiritual infirmities are represented, it is not any exaggerated extension of the same principle of accommodation to consider the sufferings of Purgatory, all of which are caused by sin or negligence, as included under it. And no phase or department of Christian devotion can ever lose by being connected in any way with considerations on the acts and sayings of our Lord.

H. J. C.

Feast of our Most Holy Redeemer, 1878.

CONTENTS.

PREFACE . . . . v—xii

PAGE

CHAPTER I.

The Desire of our Lord that the Holy Souls should be released from Purgatory even before the time.

(The Miracle at Cana of Galilee.)
St. John ii. 1—10.

1. Narrative of the miracle 1
2. Points illustrative of our subject . . 3
3. Part borne by our Lady 3
4. Our Lord's delight at her urgency . . 5
5. The Holy Souls and the banquet of Heaven . 8
   Their great needs . 10
6. God the Host at the banquet . . . 11
7. Virtue of obedience . 13
8. Our office of intercession 15

CHAPTER II.

Purity required by God in those who see Him in Heaven.

(The Cleansing of the Temple.)
St. John iii. 13—19.

1. Greatness of this miracle 17
2. Its circumstances . 18

PAGE

3. Our Lord's zeal for the purity of those who enter Heaven . . 21
4. Great need of purification . . . 23
5. Light thus shed on Purgatory . . 24
6. Effect of the zeal for Holy Souls on ourselves . . . 26

CHAPTER III.

The Devotion to Purgatory as an Exercise of Faith.

(The Healing of the Ruler's Son.)
St. John iv. 46—53.

1. Account of the miracle 28
2. Great faith required by our Lord . . . 30
3. Devotion to Purgatory an exercise of faith . 32
4. Great gain to ourselves 35

CHAPTER IV.

Gratitude of the Holy Souls for their deliverance from Hell.

(Our Lord's escape from His enemies at Nazareth.)
St. Luke iv. 28—30.

1. Our Lord at Nazareth . 37

PAGE

2. Immense gratitude of the Holy Souls. . 38
3. Reflected in the Psalms 41
4. Baffling of God's enemies . . . 42
5. Thanksgiving for the Holy Souls . . 44

CHAPTER V.

The Holy Souls and the Evil Spirits.

(The Demoniac in the Synagogue.)

St. Mark i. 23—29; St. Luke iv. 33—37.

1. The miracle in the Synagogue . . 45
2. Fearfulness of possession . . . 47
3. Opinions as to the presence of evil spirits in Purgatory . . 49
4. Probable truth . . 50
5. Sufferings of the Holy Souls . . . 52
6. Their regret . . 54
7. Profit of this truth to ourselves . . . 55

CHAPTER VI.

The Holy Souls and the Saints.

(Healing of St. Peter's Wife's Mother.)

St. Matt. viii. 14, 15; St. Mark i. 21—31; St. Luke iv. 38, 39.

1. St. Peter's wife's mother 57
2. Our Lord's regard to St. Peter . . . 58
3. Power of the Saints . 59

PAGE

4. Question as to their intercession . . 62
5. Gratitude of the Holy Souls to the Saints . 64
6. Our devotion to the Saints . . . 65

CHAPTER VII.

Promptitude in Assisting the Holy Souls.

(Cures wrought on the evening of the Sabbath.)

St. Matt. viii. 16—18; St. Mark i. 32—34; St. Luke iv. 40, 41.

1. The Sabbath evening . 67
2. Promptitude of the people of Capharnaum . . . 68
3. Value of promptitude . 69
4. Especially in justice, charity, and fidelity . 72
5. Application to Purgatory . . . 73

CHAPTER VIII.

The Church on Earth and the Holy Souls.

(The Miraculous Draught of Fishes.)

St. Luke v. 1—11.

1. The Church on earth and Purgatory . . 75
2. Miracles in Galilee . 76
3. The miraculous draught 78
4. Circumstances . . . 79
5. Work of the Church . 80
6. Success at our Lord's word 81

CONTENTS.

7. The Holy Souls committed to us . . 83
8. Fruitfulness of prayer for them . . . 84
9. Abundance of our means of grace . 86

CHAPTER IX.

Duration of the pains of Purgatory.

(The Healing of the Leper.)

St. Matt. viii. 2—4; St. Mark i. 40—45; St. Luke v. 12—16.

1. Miracle of the Leper . 87
2. Circumstances . . 88
3. Character of leprosy . 89
4. Duration of Purgatory 91
   Its reasons . . . 92
5. Arguments for it. . 93
6. Little that is done to shorten it. . . 94
7. Call on our charity . 96
8. Our assistance to them 96

CHAPTER X.

The Holy Souls and the Sacrament of Penance.

(The Healing of the Paralytic.)

St. Matt. ix. 1—6; St. Mark ii. 1—14; St. Luke v. 17—26.

1. Miracle on the Paralytic 98
2. Claim to forgive sins . 99
3. Paralysis of the Holy Souls . . . 101
4. Regret as to the Sacrament of Penance . 104
5. Efficacy of the Sacrament . . . 105

6. Indulgences . . 107
7. Profit from these truths 108

CHAPTER XI.

The application of our Suffrages to certain Souls in particular.

(Cure of the Man at the Probatic Pool.)

St. John v. 1—15.

1. Our Lord at Jerusalem 109
2. Miracle at the Pool . 110
3. Principle of selection . 112
4. To be adopted by us 113
5. Natural obligations considered . . 116
6. Length of suffering and loneliness . . . 118
7. Catholics in this country 120

CHAPTER XII.

The Holy Souls specially helped by Prayers on Festivals and Anniversaries.

(The Cure of the Man with the Withered Hand.)

St. Matt. xii. 2—14; St. Mark iii. 1—6; St. Luke vi. 6—11.

1. Miracles on the Sabbath 122
2. The withered hand . 123
3. Our Lord and the Sabbath . . . 124
   Festivals of the Church 125
4. Deliverance from Purgatory . . . 126

PAGE

CHAPTER XIII.

The Holy Souls specially helped by works for the Service of the Church.

(The Healing of the Centurion's Servant.)

St. Matt. viii. 5—15; St. Luke vii. 1—10.

1. The Centurion at Ca-
    pharnaum   .   . 129
2. His great faith   .   . 131
3. Works for the Church 132
4. Benefit to the soul   . 135
5. "Lord, I am not
    worthy"   .   .   . 136
6. Humility of the Holy
    Souls   .   .   . 137

CHAPTER XIV.

Our Blessed Lady and the Holy Souls.

(The Raising of the Widow's Son.)
St. Luke vii. 11—16.

1. The widow's Son   . 138
2. Our Lord's motive   . 139
3. Our Lady the Mother
    of Purgatory   .   . 140
4. Her interest in the souls 141
5. The Holy Rosary   . 143
6. Pilgrimages   .   . 144

CHAPTER XV.

Our Lord's Mission to Purgatory.

(The Miracles wrought before the Disciples of St. John the Baptist.)

St. Matt. xi. 2—6; St. Luke vii. 17—23.

1. Disciples of St. John . 147

PAGE

2. "He that was to come" 148
3. Our Lord and Pur-
    gatory   .   .   . 150
4. Antiquity of Suffrages 152
5. Their decay a sign of
    separation from our
    Lord   .   .   . 154
6. Our own duties   .   . 155

CHAPTER XVI.

The desire of the Holy Souls for the Society of Heaven.

(The Cure of the Dumb and Blind Demoniac.)

St. Matt. xii. 22, 23 (see St. Mark iii. 22, seq.).

1. Miracles on the dumb. 156
2. Calumny as to Beel-
    zebub   .   .   . 157
3. Sufferings of the dumb
    and blind .   .   . 157
4. Analogous sufferings in
    Purgatory   .   . 159
5. Partial consolation   . 161
6. Consideration for their
    relief   .   .   . 162

CHAPTER XVII.

Peace of the Holy Souls.

(Stilling the Tempest.)

St. Matt. viii. 23—27; St. Mark iv. 36—40; St. Luke viii. 22—25.

1. Our Lord and the
    powers of nature   . 163
2. Stilling the tempest   . 164
3. Calm of Purgatory   . 165
4. Confirmation in grace. 166
5. Love for God's law   . 168

PAGE

6. Peace from their interior
condition . . . 168
7. Freedom from un-
certainty . . . 170

CHAPTER XVIII.

*Contrast between Purgatory
and Hell.*

(The Casting Out of the Legion
of Devils.)

St. Matt. viii. 28—34, ix. 1 ; St.
Mark v. 1—21 ; St. Luke viii.
26—41.

1. Purgatory and Hell . 172
2. Miracle on the Legion
of Devils . . . 172
3. Characteristics of the
devils . . . 174
4. Suffering of loss in
Hell 176
5. Pain of sense . . 177
6. Company and despair. 178
7. Aversion from God . 180
8. Reflections . . . 181

CHAPTER XIX.

*The Sense of Shame in
Purgatory.*

(The Healing of the Woman with
an Issue of Blood.)

St. Matt. ix. 19—22 ; St. Mark v.
24—34 ; St. Luke viii. 42—48.

1. Narrative of the miracle 183
2. Characteristics of the
woman . . . 185
3. Shame in the Holy
Souls . . . 186
4. Sense of unfitness for
Heaven . . . 189
5. Simplicity and humility 190

PAGE

CHAPTER XX.

*The Pain of Sense in
Purgatory.*

(The Raising to Life of the
Daughter of Jairus.)

St. Matt. ix. 18—26 ; St. Mark v.
22—43 ; St. Luke viii. 41—56.

1. The daughter of Jairus 191
2. Possible effects on her
of the glimpse of the
next world . . 192
3. Impressions as to the
pain of sense . . 194
4. Its intensity . . 195
5. Testimony of the Saints 197
6. Objections to repre-
sentations of Pur-
gatory . . . 199
7. Importance of the
truth . . . 202

CHAPTER XXI.

*The Eternal Losses of the
Holy Souls.*

(The last Cures in Capharnaum.)

St. Matt. ix. 27—34.

1. Our Lord leaving Ca-
pharnaum . . 203
2. Last cures there . . 204
3. His denunciation of
Capharnaum . . 205
4. Eternal losses of glory 207
5. Intense sorrow of the
Holy Souls . . 209
6. Effect of not aiming at
perfection . . . 210
7. Great loss of glory to
God 211

PAGE

CHAPTER XXII.

Purgatory and Natural Piety.

(The Miracles wrought at
Nazareth.)

St. Matt. xiii. 54—58 ; St. Mark
v. 1—6.

1. Our Lord at Nazareth 214
2. Motives for His visit . 215
3. Natural piety in the
Holy Souls . . 216
4. Purity of their love . 218
5. Piety towards them . 219

CHAPTER XXIII.

*The Holy Souls and the
Sacrifice of the Altar.*

(The Feeding of the Five
Thousand.)

St. Matt. xiv. 13—21 ; St. Mark
vi. 30—44; St. Luke ix. 10—
17 ; St. John vi. 1—13.

1. The first miracle of the
loaves . . . 221
2. Effects of the Adorable
Sacrifice . . . 222
3. Ancient customs as to
Masses for the dead . 224
4. Some questions . . 226
5. Hearing Mass for the
dead . . . 228

CHAPTER XXIV.

*Pre-eminence of Charity to the
Holy Souls.*

(Our Lord walking on the Waters.)

St. Matt. xiv. 22—36 ; St. Mark
vi. 45—56; St. John vi. 14—21.

1. Our Lord walking on
the water . . . 230

PAGE

2. Contrast in the dis-
ciples' condition . 231
3. Case of the Holy Souls 232
4. Heroic donations to
them . . . 234
5. Profit to those who
make them . . 236
6. Conditions of such acts 237

CHAPTER XXV.

*Privileges of the Children of
God.*

(The Healing of the Daughter of
the Syrophœnician Woman.)

St. Matt. xv. 21—28 ; St. Mark
vii. 24—30.

1. The Syrophœnician
mother . . . 239
2. Teaching of the miracle 241
3. Who can be admitted
to Purgatory . . 243
4. Who cannot . . 244
5. Many may be, who
are not thought of . 245
6. Intellectual sins . . 247
7. Silence of Scripture . 248
8. Great calls on our
charity . . . 249

CHAPTER XXVI.

*Particular Punishments in
Purgatory.*

(Cure of the Deaf and Dumb in
Decapolis.)

St. Mark vii. 31—37.

1. The deaf and dumb
man 252
2. Particularity of the
healing . . . 253

PAGE

3. Particular sufferings in Purgatory . . 254
4. Use of the five senses . 255
5. Profit of mortification . 257

CHAPTER XXVII.

The Holy Souls relieved by Holy Communion.

(The Feeding of the Four Thousand.)

St. Matt. xv. 29—39; St. Mark viii. 1—19.

1. Second multiplication of loaves . . . 258
2. Holy Communion . 259
3. Its immense benefits . 260
4. Power of impetration for the Holy Souls . 262
5. Spiritual Communions 263
6. Presence of the multitude 263
7. General Communions for the Holy Souls . 264

CHAPTER XXVIII.

Degrees of Punishment in Purgatory.

(The Cure of the Blind Man at Bethsaida.)

St. Mark viii. 22—26.

1. Story of the Blind Man 267
2. Gradual nature of the cure . . . . 268.
3. Great differences in Purgatory . . 269
4. St. Paul on venial sins 270
5. Mortal sins forgiven . 271

PAGE

CHAPTER XXIX.

The Holy Souls helped by Prayer and Fasting.

(The Cure of the Lunatic Boy.)

St. Mark ix. 16—28.

1. The possessed boy . 274
2. Prayer and fasting . 275
3. Power of prayer . . 276.
4. Use of long prayers for the dead . . . 279.
5. Union of prayer and fasting . . . 281

CHAPTER XXX.

Union between the Holy Souls and our Lord.

(Our Lord paying the Didrachma.)

St. Matt. xvii. 23—26.

1. The tax for the Temple 282
2. Union of the Holy Souls with our Lord 283
3. As objects of mercy . 284
4. As representing Him . 285
5. They are one with Him 286
6. Effect of this truth . 288

CHAPTER XXXI.

The Pain of Loss. I. Loss of the Beatific Vision.

(The Cure of the Man born blind.)

St. John ix. 1—7.

1. The man born blind . 289
2. The Holy Souls and the Beatific Vision . 290.
3. The Beatific knowledge of God . . . 292
4. Effect of its loss . . 294

PAGE

5. Knowledge of God and the Holy Souls . . 295
6. Comparison of St. Catharine of Genoa . 297

CHAPTER XXXII.

The Pain of Loss. II. Loss of the Love of God.

(The Cure of the Mute Demoniac.)
St. Luke xi. 14—26.

1. The Mute Demoniac . 299
2. Faith and sight . . 300
3. Love of God of the Holy Souls . . 302
4. Its effects — Ecstasy — Union . . . 303
5. Absorption in God . 304
6. Peace of God . . 306

CHAPTER XXXIII.

The Pain of Loss. III. The Loss of the Joy of Heaven.

(Cure of a Woman with a Spirit of Infirmity.)
St. Luke xiii. 10—17.

1. Miracle on the woman 307
2. Circumstances . . 308
3. The joy of Beatitude . 309
4. Its subject-matter . 311
5. Sorrow of the Holy Souls for its delay . 312

CHAPTER XXXIV.

The Pain of Loss. IV. Causes of Sorrow to the Holy Souls.

(The Cure of the Man with the Dropsy.)
St. Luke xiv. 1—6.

1. The dropsical man . 314

PAGE

2. Causes of sorrow to the Holy Souls . . 315
3. The grace of God . 315
4. Consideration of sin . 317
5. Other causes . . 318

CHAPTER XXXV.

Visits to the Blessed Sacrament for the Holy Souls.

(The Healing of the Ten Lepers.)
St. Luke xvii. 11—19.

1. Miracle on the lepers . 320
2. Devotion to the Sacred Humanity . . 321
3. Our Lord in the Tabernacle . . . 322
4. Visits for the Holy Souls . . . 324

CHAPTER XXXVI.

Purgatory and the glory of God.

(The Raising of Lazarus.)
St. John xi. 1—44.

1. The miracle on Lazarus . . . 326
2. Its connection with God's glory . . 328
3. Purgatory glorifies God's justice and holiness . . 329
4. And His mercy . . 331
5. Fitness of its existence . . . 331
6. Honour to our Lord as Redeemer . . 333
7. God glorified by the virtues it occasions . 334

CHAPTER XXXVII.

Diligence in relieving the Holy Souls.

(The Cure of the Blind Man at Jericho.)

St. Matt. xx. 29—34; St. Mark x. 46—52; St. Luke xviii. 35, xix. 1.

1. The miracles at Jericho 336
2. Our Lord's unwearied charity . . . 338
3. Diligence in helping the Holy Souls . . 340
4. Blessings on this diligence . . . 341

CHAPTER XXXVIII.

The Angels and the Holy Souls.

(Miracles on Palm Sunday.)

St. Matt. xxi. 14—17.

1. The Angels and Purgatory . . . 344
2. Miracles on Palm Sunday . . . 345
3. Offices of the Angels . 346
4. Consolation . . 348
5. Intelligence of help rendered them . . 350

CHAPTER XXXIX.

Fasting and Almsdeeds.

(The Withering of the Fig-tree.)

St. Matt. xxi. 19; St. Mark xi. 13, 14, 20.

1. The Fig-tree . . 353
2. Fasting and Almsdeeds . . . 354

3. Satisfaction by penance 356
4. And Almsdeeds . . 358
5. Pious foundations . 359
6. Good works corresponding to faults . 359

CHAPTER XL.

Forgiveness of Injuries.

(The Healing of Malchus.)

St. Luke xxii. 51.

1. Miracle on Malchus . 362
2. Power of entire forgiveness . . . 363
3. Abstinence from judgment . . . 366
   Perfect contrition . 367
4. Other means of escaping Purgatory . . 367

CHAPTER XLI.

The Treasure of the Church.

(Our Lord's last Miracle on the Lake.)

St. John xxi. 1—19.

1. Our Lord's last miracle 369
2. Doctrine as to the Keys . . . 371
3. Impediments to the entrance to Heaven . 372
4. Indulgences . . 374
5. Applicable to dead and living . . . 376
6. Plenary Indulgences difficult to gain . 377
7. Indulgences and the glory of God . . 378

CHAPTER I.

The desire of our Lord that the Holy Souls should be released from Purgatory even before the time.

(THE MIRACLE AT CANA OF GALILEE.)

St. John ii. 1--10.

1. THE wonderful series of our Lord's miracles of mercy began, as we well know, at the marriage festival at Cana in Galilee, only a few days after the time when He had first called to Himself some few of His future disciples and Apostles, on the banks of the Jordan, where St. John Baptist had trained them in the school of penance, and spoken to them of the Lamb of God Who was to take away the sin of the world. The blessed Evangelist St. John, who was himself, we cannot doubt, one of these first disciples, and who must certainly have been present at the marriage-feast at which the miracle was wrought, has left us the history on which so many of the saints of God have meditated lovingly, seeing in it a great deal more than the narrative of a passing incident of our Lord's life. They have considered that the beginning of miracles, or "signs," as St. John calls it, must have been so ordained by God that all its circumstances must have very deep spiritual significance, and that the first action of our Lord of this kind which has

B

been selected for relation by the author of the last and most sacramental Gospel, must contain in itself prophecy and doctrine, as well as the external display of power and mercy. The Mother of our Lord was present, he tells us, at the marriage-feast, and our Lord and His disciples were invited. After a time the wine failed, and then our Blessed Lady, who was perhaps related to the bridegroom or bride, appealed to our Lord in the well known words, "They have no wine." Our Lord replied, "Lady, what is to Me and to thee?" Words which are not wrongly interpreted by the other version, "What have I to do with thee?" which conveys more pointedly the sense of a kind of acknowledgment of influence which our Lady was exerting over Him, without which He would not do what He was about to do. Our Lord added, "Mine hour is not yet come"—as if thus also to imply that the time for His first display of miraculous power had not arrived, except inasmuch as it was advanced and hastened on by her interference. Thus our Blessed Lady seems to have understood Him, for she told the servants who were waiting at the table, "Whatsoever He saith to you do, do it;" and thus it was that when He bade them fill the six water vessels, which stood by for purposes of purification, with water, they did so at once without hesitation. Then He bade them pour out the contents of the water-pots to the guests, beginning with the person who filled the office of the ruler of the feast. They did this, and the water was found to be changed into

wine, of so excellent a quality that the ruler of
the feast called the bridegroom, and told him
that people usually gave their best wine first, and
then that which was less good, whereas he had
kept the good wine for the last.

2. It is also clear that the obedience and simple
faith of the servants at the feast, who, without any
hesitation or question, filled the water-pots with
water, and then poured out their contents to the
ruler of the feast and others, had a certain part in
the miracle—a part which we find constantly required by our Lord on such occasions. It is not
our purpose to consider here all the circumstances
of the miracle, nor all the lessons which may be
drawn from it for our own instruction. But we
may select certain points in the conduct of our
Blessed Lady and others, and use them for our
own guidance and encouragement in the great
work of intercession and satisfaction for the Holy
Souls of Purgatory, the successful accomplishment
of which will give so much glory to God, so
much joy to our Lord and to His Blessed Mother,
and shed a glow of happiness over the whole company who are banqueting in the Marriage Supper
of the Lamb, far more intense and lasting than that
which followed at this feast of Cana, when the
water had been made wine for the satisfaction and
consolation of the hosts and their guests.

3. We may venture, then, in the first place, to
enter into the Heart of the Immaculate Mother of
our Lord, and ask ourselves what are the virtues
which she here practises, and what may have been,

in a more special way, her motives for this great act of clemency. We see at once that in her motherly care for the bride and bridegroom she anticipated their wants, and that in the mightiness of her faith she sought the remedy at the hands of our Lord, when nothing less than a miracle could supply it. Others might have hesitated, either as to His power to perform so wonderful a work, or as to the seemliness of appealing to Him in such a matter, or lastly, as to His willingness to use His Divine power, when asked, for so slight a cause. Again, we may see that our Blessed Lady was overflowing with zeal for the glory of God and for the honour of her Divine Son, for the manifestation of His power in such a way as to enlighten the minds and confirm the faith of His Apostles concerning Him, and that she discerned with a clear spiritual instinct how well all these great ends might be served by His working such a miracle, even upon this homely occasion, and in the midst of a number of simple country people gathered together for a wedding feast. Again, we may see in this tender condescending consideration of our Lady for the accidental defect of preparation for their guests on the part of those who gave the banquet, a lesson as to her extreme tenderness of heart for even the smallest spiritual needs and sufferings of her children. She was such a mother to those poor people that she could not bear to see them want their full measure of wine : and this lets us see how eager she must be that no one of those who had been redeemed by our Blessed Lord, and made her children by Him on the Cross, should lack the fullest measure of spiritual graces and blessings which He has destined for them. No temporal loss or sufferings, however great and poignant, can be compared to the least possible loss or suffering in the order of grace, and if she was so ready to exert her power at once at the sight of a slight material inconvenience, how can we ever fathom the depths of her all but infinite compassion for the needs of the soul, and the miseries which may issue in the eternal loss of God? Again, we may contemplate the marvellous prudence and humility of her prayer, the penetration with which she understood what our Lord meant when He pleaded that the time was not yet come, the confidence with which she expected the granting of her prayer, and her careful warning to the servants to do whatsoever He told them. In the whole scene we seem to see the great reverence which at this time waited on our Lord wherever He went, as the homage due to a Person as to Whom there was an indefinable instinct that He was more than man. But our Blessed Lady was anxious that the human part, the exercise of faith and obedience, which was essential for the working of the miracle according to the ordinary laws on which our Lord insisted, might not be wanting, and so the whole of her loving design for His glory and the relief of the poor couple might not be frustrated.

4. The respect in which they held our Blessed Lady, the reverence with which they regarded our

Blessed Lord, their own good-will to the bridegroom and bride, the simplicity of their faith and
their natural docility, aided, as we cannot doubt,
by the prayers of our Lady and the grace of God,
prevented the servants at the feast from falling
into the danger of not heeding the charge which
had been given to them. It was their business to
obey, even against all appearance of reasonableness
in the command which they received, and even
although they might have been exposed to mockery
and reproof if the miracle had failed in its effect.
They were told, " Whatsoever He shall say unto
you do, do it," and so they did not hesitate to fill
the six water-pots with water, and to bear them to
the ruler of the feast. Thus they had indeed that
part in the miracle which belongs to those who
obey against appearance of reason, and so fulfil
the conditions which, as has been said, our Lord
ordinarily exacted on such occasions. Our Lord,
then, in the great readiness which He always
shows in rewarding faith and obedience, as also in
His own very great compassion, greater, even than
that of His Mother, for human needs and miseries
of every kind, full also as He was of the desire to
see the Father glorified, to manifest His own Name,
especially to those who were, after Him, to manifest it to the world, rejoicing, moreover, interiorly
in the beauty of the graces shown in His Mother's
condescension and prayer, and desiring, among
other things, to exalt her name also and let it be
connected for ever in the history of His Kingdom
with the beginning of His chain of miracles,

brought about in His own sweet and prudent way
the wonderful change of the water into the wine,
so full of deep spiritual significance, especially as
to the marvellous Sacrament of sacraments which
He was afterwards to leave behind Him in the
Church. Although the time was not yet come,
that is, He was not then to have begun His
miracles unless the time had been anticipated and
forced on by the prayers and actions of His
Blessed Mother, still He is not so bound down to
times and reasons as that He cannot alter them ;
and in the infinite foreknowledge of God both
times are fixed, when things might happen, as well
as when they do happen, when the power of
Mary's intercession and of the prayers of the
Church are brought to bear upon them. For to
God all things are present, what might have been
and what might be, as well as what has been and
what shall be. It would indeed be very strange,
and inconsistent with true intelligence of our
Lord's Sacred Heart, to imagine that He wrought
this miracle unwillingly or grudgingly, or with any
other feeling than that of great joy at the deep
faith and ardent charity of His Blessed Mother,
which had, as we may say, loosened His hands
before the time, and enabled Him to grant for her
sake and to her prayer, and to the obedience of the
servants, what He would not otherwise have
granted to the needs of the bridegroom and bride.
On the contrary, our Lord loves to be constrained
by prayer, He delights in the importunities of His
children, and is grateful to them when they give

Him an occasion of allowing His justice to yield to His mercy by interposing the blessed influence of intercession, which has its lawful weight in His government, on account of His merits and of our union with Him. Thus it is equally true to say that God has appointed a certain course of things, as in the case of the chastisements which in this world or in the next He inflicts upon sin, and also to say that He desires that His arrangements may be modified and altered by the power of prayer, and that, taking that power and its exercise into account, He may appoint a certain other course of things in which those arrangements are so modified, with an increase of glory to Himself. For it is more to His glory that He should grant to prayer favours which He would not have granted without it, than that no prayer should be made to Him for the obtaining of those favours.

5. Let us now apply the instruction which is thus contained in the narrative of this miracle to the particular subject of these considerations, that is, to the Christian doctrine concerning Purgatory, both as to the lessons which we may learn for our own use therefrom, and as to the means which may be used for the relief of the sufferers there. Our desire is, to consider the case of those Holy Souls, or the decrees of our Lord as to their help, or the various manners in which they may be helped by us, as in some way, more or less, represented to us in each link of that beautiful chain of His miracles of mercy and power which has been woven for us in the narratives of the four Evangelists. The

miracle with which we are now concerned has
been left to the Evangelist of the Christian
mysteries to relate, and it stands, in a very true
sense, at the head of the whole series, placing the
prerogative of our Blessed Lady in the clearest
light, much as the sanctification of St. John Baptist
in the womb of his mother, at the sound of the
voice of Mary, stands at the head of our Lord's
works of interior grace. It is not at all difficult to
apply the main teaching of this wonderful miracle
to the doctrine of Purgatory. The persons who
were in need at the marriage supper at Cana, and
who were relieved by our Lord's condescension to
the prayer of His Mother, were the guests at the
banquet and, in the first instance, the entertainers
themselves, on whom might have fallen the sorrow
of being unable to give their guests what was meet
and right at the time. But, after all, what are
such human needs as these, when we compare
them with those which our faith represents to us in
the case of the holy prisoners in Purgatory! They
are souls who have a right, by virtue of the redemption which has been applied to them, their
adoption as children of God, and the grace in
which they have left this world, to a seat at the
eternal banquet of ineffable delights which is
spoken of in Holy Scripture as the marriage
supper of the Lamb. Their craving for this
enjoyment is far more intense than any hunger or
thirst which can be felt or even imagined in this
world. Their numbers are undoubtedly very great ;
or they include, not only the great majority of

Catholics who die in a state of grace, but an immense multitude whose magnitude can only be measured by that of the manifold mercy and compassionate wisdom of God, Who provides in so many ways, that far outrun our imaginations, for hundreds of thousands of souls who die outside the pale of the visible Church, in good faith, with true sorrow for their sins, or with only venial sins on their souls, and with a desire, which He accepts, to know and to do all His will, though unrevealed to them formally, or hidden from them by the clouds of education, false instruction, and misrepresentations of the Church. The Creator of all these souls has exercised a marvellous care over them in His Providence, shielding them from many dangers, leading them to the practice of many virtues, and, we cannot doubt, unlocking the more secret and marvellous stores of His mercy for them at the last. When we know how much may be gathered from the lives and revelations of the saints as to the length of time during which some souls may be detained in Purgatory, it is not easy to conceive of the number that may be there at any given time as anything but very large. Especially may this be the case with those whose friends do not believe in or do not practise the many holy methods of aiding the departed which are familiar to Catholics. And each generation in the Church may say to itself, that there are there its own more immediate ancestors and predecessors, those to whom it owes the transmission of the precious deposit of the Christian faith and the sacraments, and all the spiritual benefits which it enjoys. All these are so many thoughts which may spur us on to exertion in the cause of the deliverance of these "guests" of the Great Father of all from the prison in which His justice now detains them. Just as we hear nothing, in the narrative of the miracle before us, of any complaint or petition made by the guests themselves or by their hosts, so is it the rule of the justice of God that the Holy Souls of Purgatory cannot merit or pray for themselves. Their patient, intense, wistful, longing suffering is indeed a prayer which strikes on the mercy of God and the compassionate Hearts of Jesus and Mary with immense force. But their resignation also is perfect, and the union of their will with that of God: and so they leave it to others to say for them, "They have no wine"—simple words, which when we consider what it is from which they are debarred, how deep and burning is their thirst for it, have a depth and fulness of meaning which it would require a long contemplation to unfold.

6. We must also spend a few moments in considering who are the hosts in the marriage supper from which the Holy Souls of Purgatory are, for the time, excluded. We can imagine the deep joy and gratitude of the simple bridegroom and bride when they saw the miracle which had been wrought in their favour. The contemplative writers lead us to suppose that the great act of Divine power struck them so deeply, that they at once consecrated themselves to God in the way

that was open to them, vowing to live during their married life in the holy state of virginal continence. But in the banquet of eternity the Host is God Himself, the Father, the Son, and the Holy Ghost, and, wonderful as it seems to say so, we can make Him bound to us by a debt of gratitude far greater than that which bound the bride and bridegroom of whom we are speaking to those who brought about the miracle, by using the means which the Ever Blessed Trinity has placed in our hands of opening the door of the marriage supper to those who have a right to be there, but who are now excluded from it. In a thousand ways in His ordinary Providence, and also in the great economy of salvation through Jesus Christ, has God put Himself and the execution of the designs of His love into the hands of His children. In a very great measure indeed has He done this in the execution of the counsels of His mercy with regard to the suffering souls of Purgatory. He can feed the hungry and clothe the naked upon earth by the ministry of His angels, if He will, but He has intrusted them, in His ordinary Providence, to human charity. And, in the same way, He is not precluded from pardoning as He pleases the souls who are so dear to Him, still less from hearing in their behalf the prayers of His Blessed Mother, or the saints, or the guardian angels and others. But in a great measure He has left them, in the wisdom of His charity, to the good offices of the children of the Church, who are in their turn some day to take their places as sufferers in that blessed prison.

And as God is infinite in everything, in wisdom, in mercy, in justice, in power, so is He unbounded in His gratitude, and He will repay a thousand and a thousand fold the charity which He thus puts it in our power to practise, which rejoices so intensely His own Heart, the Sacred Heart of Jesus, His Blessed Mother, and the saints and angels, which adds so much to the glories and joys of Heaven, and of which He has given us the opportunity for the very purpose that it may flow back again upon ourselves, according to the laws of His eternal Kingdom, in over-abundant streams, according to our own needs, like that measure "heaped up and pressed together and running over" * of which our Lord speaks in the Gospel.

7. Again, there is much instruction for us, in connection with the subject of Purgatory and the charity which is exercised towards its inhabitants, in the part which is played by the servants in the marriage feast, and in the charge which is addressed to them by our Blessed Lady : " Whatsoever He shall say unto you do, do it." It is here that we shall find most practical teaching for ourselves. In the first place, it is clear that the accomplishment of our Lord's most loving purpose in the miracle depended in no slight degree on the ready faith and obedience of the servants. It is conceivable that if they had failed the miracle might have been deferred ; and it is, at all events, certain that in the case of the deliverance of the Holy Souls a very great deal does actually and continually

* St. Luke vi. 38.

depend upon the vivid faith of the children of the Church, understanding the needs of the Holy Souls and their own power of helping them, as well as on the activity of their charity in using that power to the utmost. As a matter of fact, it is probable that very few indeed of us are as much alive as we ought to be to our duties and opportunities of this kind, and that even fewer are as persistent and energetic in their exertions as God would fain have them be. It may be that many and many a soul would reach Heaven much sooner, but for the languor of our faith and the coldness of our charity, and the considerations which have been already urged might lead us to a practical self-examination as to our use of our manifold and rich opportunities of succouring the departed and so consoling the Sacred Heart of our Lord. In the second place, we may apply the words of our Lady to the servants in the sense of a special charge to ourselves with regard to the performance of our duties to the Holy Souls. Thus, " Whatsoever He shall say unto you do, do it," may mean to us that we are to follow out every inspiration that our Lord sends us as to this work of charity, that we are to consider, in their bearing on this matter, all the charges and promises which He has left behind Him as to charity to our neighbour in general, and that we are to use all the means of gaining Indulgences or performing works of satisfaction that fall in our way, without neglecting any. We are to endeavour to fulfil to the utmost the merciful counsel of our Lord in His Providence to us in this respect—to do every act of charity to the departed which He, seeing all our circumstances and opportunities, would have us perform. There is also another sense in which we may understand these words—a sense in which they may help us very much towards cancelling our own debt to the justice of God, as well as towards helping others in the same way. For, if we perform perfectly all the duties and obligations which our Lord lays upon us, if we faithfully and fully discharge the daily duties of our calling in life, we shall by this faithfulness to grace and duty heap up day by day a very considerable treasure in the way of satisfaction for our daily faults, and at the same time we shall gain power to aid Him, as He desires, in the accomplishment of His merciful intentions towards these Holy Souls. For every good work has, besides other qualities, a quality of satisfaction for sin, and the constant sacrifice to God for a perfect life according to our vocation is impetratory of immense graces and gives wonderful power to our prayers. All these things, the satisfactory character of our good actions of every kind, the increase of grace and favour with God which advance in perfection implies, and the power of intercession, when winged, as it were, with the soaring efficacy of a good life, may be turned by us at will to the help of the Holy Souls.

8. Above all, it is well to begin these our considerations on the doctrine of Purgatory with this reflection—that as surely as our Blessed Lady fulfilled her proper office in the Kingdom of her

Son by this act of intercession, whereby our Lord
was induced, or as we may say in other words,
enabled, to anticipate that beginning of His
miracles which must have been an object of very
great and longing desire to His Sacred Heart, so
surely do we fulfil our office and duty in the
Church by forcing on, if we may so speak, the
time of the deliverance of the Holy Souls, by
means of the suffrages, and prayers, and sacrifices,
and penances, and satisfactions, to which He has
been pleased to attach so great a power for this
very purpose. In one sense we may say of Him,
as to these Holy Souls, His time has not yet come;
but in another, He has made it depend on us
whether it has come or not. Indeed, the thought
that the time has not come for His justice to set
them free without the help of His children,
involves and contains the other thought, that the
time for our exertions, which He so much desires,
has come already, if we will but enter into the
counsels of His love. For His justice can be
satisfied by our charity as well as by their sufferings, and it is more for His glory that the
satisfaction should be made in the first way than
in the other. At the wedding-feast our Lord's
time had not come, but Mary's time had come—
and so in regard of the Holy Souls, our time for
relieving them has come, and is always present, as
long as their sufferings endure, and as long as we
have the power to lighten and shorten them.

CHAPTER II.

Purity required by God in those who see Him in Heaven.

(THE CLEANSING OF THE TEMPLE.)

St. John iii. 13—19.

1. THE cleansing of the Temple, an action which was twice performed by our Blessed Lord, at the beginning and at the very end of His Public Ministry, is not, strictly speaking, reckoned among His miracles. It was a moral, rather than a material, miracle, and the result was produced by the effect of His wonderful majesty and dignity, by the panic which fell upon the merchants in the Temple, produced, no doubt, in part by their own unquiet consciences and the reverence which they knew to be due to the Holy Place, and perhaps by other spiritual influences working upon them. And yet St. Jerome reckons this action as among the greatest of our· Lord's miracles, using the word in the widest sense which it usually bears. For certainly, few things could be more wonderful than to see a crowd of busy money-getters, bent on their own enrichment and tolerated by the authorities of the Temple, suddenly driven in fear and confusion from its courts by a single Man, armed with no authority but that inherent to His own

c

Person, with no visible assistance, and no weapon in His hand more formidable than a scourge of small cords. The malice and obstinacy of men, the hardness of heart which is produced by a life given up to sensuality or to the eager pursuit of wealth—these are forces which seem more difficult to tame and cow than the physical elements or the diseases which assail the body. In this sense, then, this action was a great miracle, and, being so, we shall find that it affords us more than one point which may be profitably studied by us in our considerations with relation to Purgatory, and which may help us both to avoid those punishments ourselves, and to deliver from them others who are now undergoing them.

2. St. John tells us, then, that soon after the miracle at Cana, our Lord went up with His disciples to the feast of the Pasch at Jerusalem. He found the Temple crowded, not only with worshippers from all parts of the Holy Land, and, indeed, of the Roman world, but also by other occupants who had established a custom which sanctioned their presence. "He found in the Temple those who sold oxen and sheep and the changers of money sitting." Upon this our Lord made a sort of scourge of small cords, "and drove them all out of the Temple, the oxen and the sheep also, and He poured out the money of the money-changers, and overturned their tables, and to those who sold doves He said, Take these things hence, and make not the house of My Father a house of traffic." St. John adds an authentic commentary on

this remarkable action of our Blessed Lord, when he says that His disciples afterwards applied to it the saying of the Psalmist, " The zeal of Thy house hath eaten Me up."* The motive, therefore, which prompted our Lord was the zeal for the purity and honour of the house of His Father,—as, indeed, is shown by His own words to the sellers of doves, " Make not the house of My Father a house of traffic"—words which are still further illustrated by what He said on the second occasion on which He cleansed the Temple, when He quoted the pro- phecy, that, " My house shall be called the house of prayer to all nations." † It was inconsistent with the reverence which was befitting a place in which God was so specially worshipped, and in which He vouchsafed to dwell with a peculiar kind of presence, such as was to be found nowhere else in the whole world, that traffic should be carried on in its courts, even though it was traffic which was, more or less, necessary on account of the sacrifices and offerings which were there made by the many devout persons from all parts of the world who came thither to honour God. Such persons required that the money which they brought with them should be changed for coin which could be offered in the Temple—many of the coins which they brought from abroad being idolatrous in their inscriptions—and also that they should find at some convenient place near at hand the victims which were prescribed for the various kinds of

* Psalm lxviii. 10.
† St. Mark xi. 17 ; Isaias lvi. 7.

sacrifices which their circumstances or their piety prompted them to offer. This traffic, therefore, was not in itself sinful, except in so far as it was carried on in an unjust spirit of extortion by the dealers whom our Lord drove out. But it was something profane in the place in which it was carried on—something inconsistent with the perfect silence and reverence, the spirit of worship, adoration, recollection, the intimate feeling of God's near presence, which became the courts of that solemn Temple, and our Lord's burning love for His Father's honour would not suffer it. It was now that was fulfilled of Him that prophecy of Malachias, which is also applied to His presence in the Temple at the Purification of His Blessed Mother, "Presently the Lord Whom you seek, and the Angel of the Testament, Whom you desire, shall come to His Temple. Behold, He cometh, saith the Lord of hosts. And who shall be able to think of the day of His coming? and who shall stand to see Him? For He is like a refining fire."* His zeal for God's honour made Him lay aside the meekness and gentleness which were His ordinary characteristics. They made Him take the law into His own hands, though in all other matters He refused to assume the office of a judge or of an executioner of justice. They made Him use a sort of violence, although even this was tempered by considerateness and equity, for He was less severe on those who sold doves, the offerings of the poor, and simply bade them remove the cages

* Mal. iii. 1, 2.

in which they were confined from the courts of the
Temple.

3. We have therefore, in this action of our
Lord, as has been said, an instance of His zeal for
the honour of His Father, and of His high sense
of the ineffable purity and holiness which must
be required in all that dwells or passes in His
sanctuary. Our thoughts pass very easily from
this consideration to that in which this significant
action becomes an image of the severity with
which our Lord's Heart must burn at the sight of
anything that is unworthy or unbecoming in those
who are to live in the presence of God, and in
whom He has, as the Scripture tells us, taken up
His abode. St. Paul tells us that our bodies are
the temples of the Holy Ghost, and we know from
many other passages in Sacred Scripture that the
hearts and souls of Christians are the chosen
sanctuaries in which God delights to dwell. If,
then, our Lord, when as yet His mission was one
of mercy, when He came in meekness, lowliness,
and humility, not breaking the bruised reed or
quenching the smoking flax, yet felt Himself
constrained to lay aside His gentleness in order to
cleanse the Temple with a scourge, how much
more terribly will His zeal for the honour of His
Father burn "like a refining fire" when He comes
to the soul which has been the chosen dwelling-
place of God at its last day, when He comes, not
as Saviour only, but as Judge, and when the very
reason of His coming, is that He may exact a
most minute account of all our shortcomings, and

punish with due severity everything which He finds unworthy of the presence of God? It is not a material temple, which is doomed to perish, which He will then come to cleanse and purge of all that He finds unbecoming in it. It is not a temple in which God will dwell for a time only, and then depart. The souls of Christians which are presented to Him by their Guardian Angels at the moment of Particular Judgment are intended by His immense mercy to live in His presence and sanctuary throughout all eternity, and He is to take up His abode in them and never to depart from them. They are to be for ever the homes of most holy thoughts, most burning affections of the purest and sublimest charity; they are to be filled with the supernatural knowledge of Him and of all His works and ways, and to be flooded, without being destroyed thereby, by the ineffable ecstatic love which is the fruit of the Beatific Vision. No presence of God in an earthly temple can be compared with the close and intimate union between Him and them in Heaven. How can He, Who was full of zeal for the external purity of the material Temple at Jerusalem, bear, in souls like these, which He has purchased with His own Blood and fed upon the graces which flow therefrom, with anything that is soiled, or crooked, or mean, or earthly, the miserable results of passion, or carelessness—with anything, in short, which may fairly move Him to anger on account of His zeal for the justice of God and the holiness of all that are to belong to Him?

4. On the other hand, when we consider what
we may well suppose to be true as to the state in
which many souls meet our Lord as their Judge,
souls which nevertheless die in His faith and in
His grace, we may well say to ourselves that He
must find in them far more things to offend His
most pure eyes and to provoke His anger than He
found on this occasion in the Temple at Jerusalem.
For such things are all the arrears of penance
undone for sins confessed and absolved; all the
penalties of sins, lighter in comparison with mortal
sins, but still very displeasing to Him in themselves, which through carelessness and want of self-
knowledge have never been retracted and made
the subject of sorrow—sins of habit, sins caused in
others by bad example or negligence, sins of others
in which we have shared, besides the immense
and overwhelming multitude of sins of omission.
The holy Psalmist cries out: "Who can understand sins? From my secret ones cleanse me, O
Lord, and from those of others spare Thy servant."*
No doubt many of these debts to the justice of
God may have been cancelled in various ways
before the moment of death; but here, again, we
are met by the thought of our extreme carelessness
in doing penance, in the practice of good works
which may satisfy God's justice, in gaining Indulgences, and the like. When we put together the
thought of the intense purity which is required for
God's presence and the thought of the blindness
and carelessness of many Christians as to the debt

* Psalm xviii. 13.

which they owe to His justice, we are certainly led
to the fear that our Lord, when, in this sense, He
comes to His living temples, will usually be obliged
to exercise very great severity, and we find it easy
to understand that those who pass from His
judgment-seat to their thrones in Heaven without
experiencing the pains of Purgatory are few indeed.

5. Indeed, if it were not for the blessed knowledge which our faith assures to us of the ineffable
mercy of God in the Incarnation of His Son and
the Redemption of the world through Him, the
thought of the infinite justice of God might well
make us wonder how any one can stand in that
terrible moment of the Particular Judgment.
And, in the same way, the glimpse of our Lord's
severity, in His zeal for the honour of His Father,
which is afforded us in this action on which we
are meditating, might very well help us to understand the teaching of Scripture and of the Saints
as to the very great sufferings to which the souls in
Purgatory are subjected, in order to the full expiation of their faults and that perfect purification
which is necessary to them to make them fit to
stand before God for ever. The more fully we
are enabled by the teaching of the Holy Ghost to
understand, in part at least, the holiness of God,
the more shall we be prepared to believe in the
intensity of the pains of Purgatory. But now—to
take up the thought which presented itself so naturally to us in the first of these considerations—
there is indeed no vestige in the sacred history on
which we are meditating of any help or even

encouragement furnished to our Lord in His work of purification by the bystanders or witnesses of His action of zeal. But, when we turn our minds to that other purification of which we are considering this cleansing of the Temple to have been a figure, we find that it is in our power very materially to assist our Lord, to share, as it were, His work with Him, and by so doing to gain His gratitude and the abundant blessings which flow from His Sacred Heart on all who in any way advance what He is engaged upon. Surely it would have been a most blessed work and a service to our Lord which He would have repaid in His own magnificent way, if the disciples, or the priests and officers of the Temple, had thrown themselves into the work which He had begun, and removed with their own hands the articles and animals which offended His eyes. This is what we can do. For we can make the accomplishment of the work of purgation of the Holy Souls more easy and more rapid by the many means which He has placed at our disposal of helping those blessed victims of His justice, who are, at the same time, the objects of His tenderest love. Their immense sufferings, far greater than any that we can either feel or imagine upon earth, may well enough move us to compassion, and make us exert ourselves for them as we do when we see our fellow-creatures in the agonies of death from hunger, or disease, or pain of any kind. At such a time we do not hesitate to sacrifice ease, comfort, our own resources, even what may now or hereafter be most necessary for ourselves—the extreme needs of those who are bound to us by so many ties of nature and grace overpower all other claims. But it is not compassion for the suffering souls alone which is suggested to us as the motive of our charity by the action of our Lord of which we are considering. It is also a desire to see His zeal for the glory of His Father and the holiness required in everything that belongs to Him, satisfied—a desire that everything that is unbecoming may be swept away at once from the sanctuary of God, that the temple, in which He is delighted to dwell for ever, may be at once made fit for His Presence, "not having spot, or wrinkle, or any such thing,"* as St. Paul says of the Church.

6. And, with regard to ourselves, it is impossible but that the kindling in our hearts of the flame of zeal for the purity of God's abode should very greatly help us to make our own hearts fit dwellings, as far as may be, for the Holy Ghost. The very consideration of the holiness of God and of the very great dishonour to Him which may be brought about by the careless and indifferent lives of those who belong to Him, must in itself furnish a powerful motive for the avoidance of such negligence on our own part, and for the immediate cancelling, by means of the holy sacraments, prayer, penance, almsdeeds, and the like, of the debt which we ourselves may have contracted to His justice. The consideration that the soul of the Christian is, in truth, the chosen temple

* Ephes. v. 27.

and abode of God cannot be deeply rooted in the soul, without, by the assistance of His grace, producing in us a readiness in that holy exercise of the Presence of God which is of such immense importance in the process of sanctification. These two fruits are, as it were, naturally engendered by the zeal and devotion for the relief of the Holy Souls. But we have not only to deal with the fruits which are given up to this devotion. We may also reckon on the bountiful goodness and graciousness of our Blessed Lord, Whose part, as it were, we take when we aid in the purification of these holy prisoners. We may also look for an especial blessing and assistance from His own Royal Mother, the Queen of Purgatory, the first, as we saw in the former meditation, to exert herself in a cause like that of the sufferers there. We may expect that their patron saints, and indeed the whole company of the Blessed, will assist us in keeping our own souls free from stain, or in getting rid of any stains which may now infect them, as well as on the intense and burning gratitude of the Holy Souls themselves— a gratitude only to be measured by their sense of the awful holiness of God and of the severity of His judgments.

CHAPTER III.

The Devotion to Purgatory as an Exercise of Faith.

(THE HEALING OF THE RULER'S SON.)

St. John iv. 46—53.

1. THE miracles which we have already considered in relation to the Catholic doctrine concerning Purgatory, have shown us the great claims which the Holy Souls have upon our charity, the great delight which our Lord takes in hearing our prayers for them, and the extreme severity of the justice of God in consequence of which they suffer as they do. The next miracle in the Gospel history adds another general consideration to those which we have already set before us, for it impresses on us very strongly the value which our Lord attaches to the exercise of faith, which has so large a part in all our thoughts and conduct concerning Purgatory, whether as to the relief of those who suffer there, or as to the pains which we may take to save ourselves from the same chastisements. This third miracle is related by St. John, in the place named above, and it took place within a few weeks of that visit of our Lord to Jerusalem at which He cleared the Temple for the first time. On His return into Galilee He went to Cana, where the first miracle had been performed, and while there He received

the visit of a man of rank and authority who
lived .at Capharnaum, whose son lay at the point
of death. The father had heard of the .wonders
which our Lord had worked at Jerusalem, and
came to beg Him to come and visit his son,
hoping that He would cure him, as He had
already cured so many others. Our Lord, as
we know, was always full of the most gracious
condescension in such cases, and allowed Himself
to be called hither and thither by those who had
need of Him for themselves or others. But on
this occasion He did not at once comply, just as
He had not at once complied with the prayer of
His Blessed Mother at the marriage-feast. He
put the father off, as it were, with the remark,
"Except you see signs and wonders, you will not
believe !" This was not a simple reproach—it was
at least half a question. It was a hint to the
father's faith, by means of which our Lord sought
to raise it higher than it was—to make it as firm
and penetrating as the faith of the centurion
afterwards, who may have been a friend of the
ruler, and who, instead of begging our Lord
to come to him and heal his servant, told Him
that he was himself unworthy that He should
enter under His roof, and that if He only spoke
the word his servant would be healed. The ruler
does not seem at once to have understood our
Lord, and he renewed his prayer that He would
come down to Capharnaum ere his child was
dead. But our Lord's first words had no doubt
stimulated his faith, and had been accompanied

by grace which raised it to a higher level. So, when our Lord told Him to go, that his son was living and restored to health, he believed, as St. John says, the word that Jesus said to him, and went his way. He was met on the road by some servants of his household, who told him of his son's recovery at the very time when our Lord's words had been spoken. And the fruit of his faith and gratitude was greater than it might otherwise have been, for he became a believing disciple of our Lord with all his household.

2. The characteristic, then, of this miracle is that it is a practical lesson of that same truth which our Lord afterwards expressed in His words to St. Thomas, "Because thou hast seen Me, thou hast believed; blessed are they that have not seen and have believed." * If He had not wished to lead the father, in the miracle before us, on to this more blessed grade of faith, He would probably have granted his request at once, and gone with him to Capharnaum. We see here, then, the great joy which our Lord takes in the higher degrees and forms of faith, inasmuch as He took the pains to lead this anxious suppliant on at the cost of the trial which the first apparent denial of his petition must have involved. And we cannot doubt that the miracle is recorded for us with this intention, among others, that we may understand and practically use the truth of the immense importance to our souls of all the highest exercises of faith of which we are capable.

* St. John xx. 29.

It is better to believe without sight, than to see
and believe. The most profitable exercise of this
holy virtue is that in which there is the least
sensible evidence — that in which we have the
Word of God for what we believe, and nothing
else but the Word of God. It is in this spirit that
the Church, when she commends the soul of a
departing Christian to God, pleads for him his
faith in the highest mysteries of the Creed, "for
although he has sinned," she says, "yet he has
always firmly believed in the Father, Son, and
Holy Ghost;" and in the same way the great
Sacrament of the Altar, by means of which the
greatest grace of all is conveyed to us, is essentially
and pre-eminently the mystery of faith, of which
St. Thomas sings—

> Sight and taste and touch are all in Thee deceived,
> But the hearing only safely is believed,

—the merit of faith being all the greater in proportion as the thing which we believe is not only
simply difficult to nature and sense, but even, as
its seems, contrary to them. We know, on the
other hand, how often our Lord had to complain
of the want of a perfect and, as it were, full-grown
and robust faith, even in the Apostles and in
others who were not His enemies. The unbelief
of the Nazarenes stopped the full flow of His
gracious miracles in His own town.* When
He was asleep in the boat during the storm, and
His disciples woke Him up in alarm, He rebuked

* St. Matt. vi. 5.

them for their want of faith.*   When St. Peter
attempted to walk on the waters, and began to
sink, he also was chidden as one of little faith.†
And in these two last instances our Lord seems
to find fault with His Apostles for the absence of
a very high degree of faith, such as might hardly
have been expected in them as a matter of course.
The very high promises which He makes elsewhere
to faith in prayer, and such expressions of His as
that in which He told them that if they had faith
as a grain of mustard-seed they should move
mountains, may be also cited as a proof towards
the same conclusion.   And, indeed, it seems only
reasonable that God should give immense privileges
to the exercise of faith, by which the intellectual
part of our nature, the most excellent quality
which we possess, is brought into subjection to
Him at the command of a loving will.

3. It seems to follow from this that we may
expect a special blessing upon devotions and acts
of virtue in which the exercise of faith has a
specially larger part and influence, in which the
things of sight and natural considerations are
less mixed up than in others.   Many beautiful
sayings are found in the writings of holy men
in special commendation of the devotion to the
Holy Souls in Purgatory, on account of the
excellence of the charity which manifests itself
in that devotion, and the like.   But the point
which, more than any other, belongs to the
subject before us in the miracle now under

* St. Matt. iv. 40.   † St. Matt. xiv. 31.

consideration, is that which relates particularly to the very great exercise of faith which that devotion implies. In the case of the corporal works of mercy, and in others of the spiritual works of the same virtue, we have before our eyes the sufferers for whom we exert ourselves. Their miseries appeal to us sensibly, and a hard heart indeed is required to enable us to steel ourselves against the appeal to our natural compassion which is made by the sight of the hungry, the sick, the prisoners, and the many kinds of affliction which the providence of God brings home to us in such cases. Again, there is a sensible satisfaction and pleasure in the act of giving such relief and help as are in our power to bestow. We see the misery, and we see and feel the healing of that misery which the act of charity brings about. We may, indeed, be able to resist the temptation to self-gratulation, which sometimes arises at such times, and our intention may be so pure, and our Christian prudence and humility so well grounded, as to make it easy for us, if we do not escape the praises of men, at least to be indifferent to them. We may accustom ourselves to turn all these acts of charity into exercises of faith and of love to our Blessed Lord, Who has so tenderly committed misery in all its visible forms to our care, and tells us that whatever we do to the least of those who belong to Him is done to Himself. But in the compassion which we practise towards the holy suffering Souls, there is nothing visible or

D

sensible at all to move sympathies, and there is
no danger at all that the mercy which we work
should fall under the eyes of men, and so, in
some measure, have its reward here. The doctrine
concerning Purgatory is not against reason—on
the contrary, it is the natural offspring of a right
and reasonable conception concerning the justice
and holiness, as well as the mercifulness, of God.
But it is faith that teaches us the truth of what
we might conjecture as reasonable concerning
the existence of Purgatory. It is faith that
teaches us what we know concerning the pains
which are there suffered, and the expiation which
is wrought out by means of those pains. It is
faith that teaches us that we possess, by God's
infinite mercy, the power of relieving those pains
by means of our own prayers, suffrages, sacrifices,
and satisfactions, and the great benefits to ourselves
which we may earn by this exercise of charity.
The results which we may obtain by this devotion
are as unseen as the sufferings themselves which
we strive to relieve; and although our hearts
are naturally moved to aid this or that particular
soul which is dear to us on account of the ties
of nature or love, we still cannot tell what the
state of that soul may be, whether it is in need
of our assistance or not. We have no visible
success to encourage us, nothing tangible to be
the reward of our toil. In these and other
particulars the prayers and penances and alms
and Indulgences which we offer for the Holy
Souls are a constant exercise of faith, in a

manner and degree which cannot be affirmed of the other works of compassion and mercy.

4. It is clear that one great object which our Lord had in view when He seemed to decline the request of the father in this miracle, was not so much the good of the child that was sick as that of the father himself and of his family. He sought to procure for them the spiritual reward of a higher exercise of faith, and not only to find an opportunity of relieving the poor suffering child from the disease which affected him. We may see that there is the same end to be gained in the exercise of faith which our Lord requires of us in the devotion to the Holy Souls. It is pre-eminently a spiritual devotion—one which blesses those who practise it as well as those for whose sake it is practised, and especially in the way of perfecting their faith, and giving them, as it were, a firm hold of its truths and a clear perception of the realities of the unseen world. Those who are drawn especially to this devotion live in an atmosphere in which the great truths of the holiness of God, the heinousness of sin, the keen penetrating severity of the Divine justice, the purity which is required for Heaven, the value of time and grace, the power of prayer, the unfailing efficacy of the Precious Blood, the Sacraments, the Holy Sacrifice, and the Cross, are seen more clearly and more nearly, with none of the clouds of earth, the mists of sense, or the false lights of the world, to veil them or distort them. Many persons have learnt the true emptiness and nothingness of the

world, its pleasures and gains and honours, by being forced either to suffer themselves, or to devote themselves to the care of the sick or afflicted who have claims upon them. The truth of the miseries of our present condition is borne in upon them with wonderful power, and they are enabled to walk along the common paths of life with a new sense, as it were, of what it is. It is less easy for such men to be deceived by the emptiness and hollowness which impose upon the frivolous and thoughtless worldlings around them. There is something analogous to this in the case of those who live very much in the habitual thought of the sufferers in Purgatory, of the claims which they have on our charity, and of the means which are so abundantly supplied to us in the Church of satisfying those claims to our own immense advantage. It is impossible but that such Christians should gain daily in delicacy of conscience, in familiarity with spiritual truths, in courage under suffering, in love of the Cross, and in charity for souls. They must grow in knowledge of God and of His ways, in contempt for the things of sense, in keenness of discernment as to the pettiness of many things which are commonly hindrances to perfection, and of the immense power of sacramental grace, and in the spirit and habit of prayer. Thus a silent change comes over them, and, in reward for their charity, which has so little that is sensible to feed on, they insensibly acquire spiritual instincts almost as keen as those of the holy sufferers themselves.

CHAPTER IV.

Gratitude of the Holy Souls for their deliverance from Hell.

St. Luke iv. 28—30.

1. VERY soon after the miracle of the healing of the nobleman's son, who was ill at Capharnaum, we find that our Lord went to His own home at Nazareth, and there taught in the synagogue on the Sabbath day. This is not the place to explain at length how it came about that, after charming His whole audience by the gracious words in which He commented on the passage of Isaias, in which His own mission as the Messias was described, He offended them grievously by telling them that He was not about to perform wonderful miracles to gratify them, as if they had a sort of right in Him, and by reminding them how the great prophets, Elias and Eliseus, had been guided by Providence to work miracles in favour of Naaman the Syrian and the widow of Sarepta, rather than their own people. The Nazarenes were "filled with anger," as St. Luke tells us, "and rose up and thrust Him out of the city, and brought Him to the brow of the

hill whereon their city was built, that they might cast Him down headlong. But He passing through the midst of them, went His way." The Evangelist does not tell us in what manner it was that the malice of these Nazarenes was baffled, and how our Lord delivered Himself out of their hands. There is a spot shown at Nazareth which is traditionally said to mark the place where our Blessed Lady looked on in agony while her Son was being taken to the "Mount of Precipitation," —and we may feel sure that her tender heart must have been torn with anguish at that time, somewhat like that which she had afterwards to endure at the foot of His Cross. And in proportion to the pain and anxiety which she then suffered must have been her relief and joy when she knew that our Lord was safe, and that no one had any power to hurt Him in the least. This thought will be enough to supply us with matter for meditation in accordance with the general subject which we have set before us.

2. We cannot suppose that the deliverance of our Lord from His enemies, in whatever manner it may have been effected, can have come to Him as a matter of surprise, or as something for which He had not hoped. But nevertheless it would have been an occasion for Him to give thanks to His Father for the care with which He watched over Him, and the Psalms, which represent so wonderfully to us the affections of the Sacred Heart, are full of expressions of gratitude for such deliverances. The lives of the Saints were to be

full of such escapes and instances of God's protection, and for this reason among others, it may
be, that our Lord chose to have experience of the
like in His own life. We may pass on at once
to that which is the special subject of these
chapters, and find something in the doctrine of
Purgatory which may be illustrated from this
incident. It is certain that at the moment of
death the soul has a sudden light flashed upon it,
which may be considered as an essential part or
condition of the Particular Judgment, by which it
is enabled to see in the light of truth the whole
of its past life, and to form a right estimate as to
each particular incident of it. Then it sees what
God has done for it, and what it has in return
done for or against God—the devices of His
ineffable mercy and unwearied faithfulness, its
own faults and shortcomings, the dangers which
it has escaped, and the opportunities of grace
which it has missed. The light which then
streams in upon the mind will reverse and cancel
all human judgments and estimates which it may
have formed of these things. We must not
consider it as entirely engrossed by any one of the
vivid impressions and feelings which will then be
brought home to it, to the exclusion of others, and
we must always remember that the souls which die
in grace are confirmed therein for ever at the
moment of death, and that the love of God will
take possession of the heart as the queen and
ruler of all other affections. Still, we may consider
one of these affections by itself, for the purpose of

enhancing our own conceptions of its truth; and so in this way we reflect on the feeling of gratitude with which the soul will then be filled at the sight of so many dangers, of which it was either entirely ignorant or only half aware, averted by special Providence, and favours of which also it had but little thought. Many souls will then wake up, as it were, like persons who have been walking in their sleep along the brink of a precipice, by a narrow winding path, with death on every side of them, and be appalled and aghast at the sight of what that path has been. They will see the dangers of what they thought almost harmless, the snares in which they almost of their own accord entangled themselves, and the malice and cunning of the enemies who were besetting them with temptations, from which they hardly cared to turn away. On the other hand, they will see the immense care of God, either in guiding them away from danger, or in giving them the means and the opportunities of repairing the injuries which they may have done to Him and to themselves; they will understand the power of sacramental grace, the efficacy of angelic guardianship, the might of Christian intercession in Heaven or earth, of the Communion of the Saints, what it is to have been made members of Jesus Christ and "partakers of the Holy Ghost." Especially in the case of those who have even sinned mortally, will there be a most keen sense of what it is to have deserved Hell after having been made heirs of Heaven, what it is to have been saved over and over again,

as we may say, from the eager hatred of the
enemies of God, in whose power they had placed
themselves. It would seem as if this one thought
would be enough to generate a love and gratitude
to God intense enough to extinguish all desire of
shrinking from the temporary punishment which
the justice of God has yet to exact from them.
The effects of this true view of what their life has
been will abide throughout the whole of their time
of purification, giving a special intensity to their
love of God, even if the details of the picture then
presented to them are not allowed to remain upon
their memory with undiminished vividness.

3. The consideration which is here suggested
may be used to help us to feed our devotion with
regard to Purgatory and God's great mercy as
displayed there. It will be found that a great
number of passages in the Psalms, especially in
those which are used in the Office for the Dead,
or again, the other Gradual and Penitential
Psalms, as well as those which are full of thanksgiving, such as the hundred-and-second and the
hundred-and-sixth, will seem wonderfully full of
meaning if they are looked on as utterances of the
Holy Souls in Purgatory, or of the Church in their
name. And although such Psalms contain a
great number of penitential and sorrowful expressions, of complaints, as it were, of suffering
and the like, still the dominant tone in many
is full of confidence, hope, and especially thankfulness. This may help us to understand the
truth of which we are now speaking—the immense

gratitude of the Holy Souls for their deliverance from the terrible punishments of Hell which they may have deserved, punishments the very worst part of which is that they are not accompanied or sweetened by any love of God or any hope in His mercy. Another feature of the passages of which we speak is the frequent reference to the enemies from whom the Psalmist has been delivered, to their malice and to their power, which have nevertheless been defeated by God's goodness. We shall have occasion to speak of the enemies of God and man from whom the Holy Souls have been delivered, in the next chapter, but it may be well to add here a few thoughts concerning the way in which they are so frequently baffled and disappointed, contrary to all their hopes and desires.

4. St. Paul, in the Epistle to the Colossians, speaks in marvellous language of the triumph of our Lord over the evil angels by means of the Cross, on which He took away and cancelled, as the Apostle tells us, what was a sort of title which they had over us on account of our sins. He speaks of our Lord as " blotting out the handwriting of the decree that was against us, which was contrary to us; and He hath taken the same out of the way, fastening it to His Cross, and despoiling the principalities and powers, He hath exposed them confidently in open show, triumphing over them in Himself."* His words remind us of the image which our Lord used on more than one occasion,

* Coloss. ii. 14, 15.

of the "strong armed man," who keeps his court
and his goods in peace, until a stronger than
he comes upon him and overcomes him, and takes
away all his armour in which he trusted, and distributes his spoils.*   The intense pride and arro-
gance of the devils made it most difficult for them
to understand how they were to be conquered and
baulked by the humiliations of our Lord, and, in
the same way, they are for ever being disappointed
and spoiled of their prey in the case of Christian
souls which are rescued from their very jaws by
the grace which is the fruit of those humiliations.
These victories tend immensely to the glory of
God and of our Lord, and are perpetual occasions
of fresh discomfitures to His enemies.   Thousands
of souls, for instance, are saved from them by the
last Sacraments duly received, even after a long
course of sin ; thousands more by interior graces,
such as the power to make an act of contrition
at the last moment, which are, no doubt, special
favours on which no one could be so foolish as
to reckon without almost certainly, by that very
presumption, debarring himself from them, but
which still are granted in a measure of which we
have no knowledge to many sinners who would be
lost without them, on account of the intercession
of our Lady or the Saints, or in reward for some
good work or service to God and the Church
done long before, it may be, by the person or by
some one to whom he belongs.   Again, it may be
considered as certain that God takes the soul out

* St. Luke xi. 21, 22.

of the world at a moment when He sees it to be merciful to do so, knowing that if it lives on it will not be better, or that if its life is not shortened it may be worse. For the moment of the death of each one of us is entirely in the hands of God. In these and in other ways the malice of the enemies of our souls is constantly defeated, to their great indignation and confusion and disappointment, and to the great glory of God. All this part of His Providence, in their own case, is clear to the Holy Souls of Purgatory. This knowledge must be the foundation of most intense acts of love and gratitude, such as we find expressed in the passages of the Psalms to which reference has been made.

5. It must certainly be their wish, and also to the glory of God, that we should help them to discharge this debt of gratitude, by mingling thanksgivings for their deliverance with our prayers for their perfect and speedy purification. It is possible, also, that in many cases a want of thankfulness to God for benefits of which they were conscious, and a general unfaithfulness as to the full discharge of the duty of thanksgiving, may be among the causes of their detention from Heaven. When St. Paul instructs his disciple, St. Timothy, as to the practices to be observed in the Church over which he was set to rule, he says, " I desire, first of all, that supplications, prayers, intercessions, and thanksgivings, may be made for all men,"* and although the last-mentioned kind of prayer may

* 1 Tim. ii. 1.

more especially signify the offering of the Holy Sacrifice, this would certainly not take away the force of the injunction as to making thanksgiving in all other ways also for all men. We certainly learn from the Psalms the lesson of uniting thanksgiving with supplication, and we may help, as well as gladden the Holy Souls, by giving earnest thanks to God for His great mercies towards them.

CHAPTER V.

The Holy Souls and the Evil Spirits.

(THE DEMONIAC IN THE SYNAGOGUE.)

St. Mark i. 23—29 ; St. Luke iv. 33—37.

1. Two of the Evangelists, St. Mark and St. Luke, place at the beginning of our Lord's public preaching in Galilee a series of miracles—of which some are related by St. Matthew also—and which were worked by Him on the Sabbath day in Capharnaum, the city in which, more than any other, He dwelt during His Public Ministry. It is impossible not to be struck by the contrast between the events of this Sabbath and those of that which may have immediately preceded it in order of time. Our Lord had almost openly declared to the people of Nazareth that He was not sent to them to work miracles, but to the inhabitants of Capharnaum. It is often found in the lives of His saints that a

great danger and a signal deliverance are the immediate antecedents of great exertions on their part
for His glory, and of remarkable successes in His
service.   Something of this kind may be noticed
as to the wonders which occurred on this Sabbath,
which came so soon after the attempt made on our
Lord's life by the Nazarenes.   The first of these
miracles attracted very great attention, and was
the immediate cause why His name came to be
published abroad throughout the whole of the
region of Galilee.   This miracle is that which was
wrought on the demoniac in the synagogue.   The
case does not appear to have been one of those
in which the demoniac was ordinarily so violent
as to make it impossible for him to remain in his
usual home and among the society of men, such
as we meet with afterwards in the account of our
Lord's visit to the country of the Gadarenes.   He
was allowed to attend the services in the synagogue,
and this is enough to show that he was not in the
habit of disturbing them.   But the great majesty
and authority of the teaching of our Lord produced
an unusual impression on all who heard Him, an
impression for good or for bad as the case might
be, according to the state of their hearts.   To the
impure spirit who had been allowed by the permission of God to possess himself of this poor man,
the presence of our Lord was altogether intolerable.
His hatred of God and of all God's creatures, above
all, his hatred of any thing or person that bore a
close connection with the great mystery of Redemption, made him writhe in extreme spiritual

tortures at the near presence of the Incarnate Son
Who had come to work out the salvation of the
world. So the rage of the devil overpowered him,
and he broke out while our Lord was teaching in
a loud voice, using the organs of the poor man
whom he possessed : " What have we to do with
Thee, Jesus of Nazareth ! art Thou come to destroy
us ? I know Who Thou art, the Holy One of God."
Our Lord, Who so constantly forbade the persons
whom He healed to make Him known, would not
allow the enemy of God and man to bear witness
to Him in this way, so "He threatened him, saying :
Speak no more, and go out of the man ! And the
unclean spirit, tearing him and crying with a loud
voice, having thrown him in the midst ;" as St. Luke
adds, " but without doing him any harm, went out
of him."

2. The great astonishment of the congregation
who witnessed this display of our Lord's authority,
of which each of the Evangelists speaks, shows that
they were entirely unaccustomed to such exertions
of power. We know that instances of possession
were by no means uncommon, either among the
Jews or among heathen nations, and that there
were exorcisms occasionally used by the Jews to
which our Lord referred when He was accused of
casting out devils by the power of their own prince.
But, even though exorcisms were more frequent
among them than we can suppose, there would still
be something far more striking about the authority
of a Teacher Who in His own name, and without
any prayers or ceremonies, cast out the devils at

His word. This seems to have been the impression produced upon the people, of whom St. Mark tells us that "they were all amazed, insomuch that they questioned among themselves, saying, What thing is this ? What is this new doctrine ? for with power He commandeth the unclean spirits, and they obey Him." It is difficult to think that even those who might live with frequent experiences of these horrible phenomena could soon become so accustomed to them as to be without terror and consternation at such sights. For such facts bring home to us in the most appalling manner the truth that we live exposed to the assaults, and to a certain extent in the power, of malignant and relentless spirits, far more intelligent and far stronger by nature than we are, who hate us with a hatred which has no parallel in the creation of God, and who could at any moment inflict on us the most fearful physical evils, if they were permitted to exert all their forces against us. When they are allowed, in God's inscrutable providence, to usurp that all but entire dominion over human beings like ourselves, which is seen in the case of possession, we might be tempted to think that our Creator had altogether abandoned His creature, and handed it over to its most deadly enemies, whom it has no chance of escaping or power of resisting. Faith tells us that this is not the case, and that even in possession the will may remain unbent and unconsenting to the awful wickedness which the devil may put into the mouth, or the terrible mischief for which he may use the hands. Still, we can

imagine nothing in nature more absolutely appalling than the sight or hearing of a human being
under the influence of possession. And then, when
all this fearful tempest of diabolical passion is
calmed at a word, and the seemingly irresistible
might of the evil one is paralyzed in a moment, so
that he becomes at once weaker than 'a child, and
reduced to the most abject obedience, the power
of God is certainly shown in a way which has few
parallels, and we receive a most wonderful assurance
of His loving care and protection over us. We
might think and know less of His absolute sovereignty over the spiritual creation, if we had not
experience of the temptations, obsessions, and
possessions, which He sometimes permits to His
enemies and ours, all of which are quelled by a
word from Him, or from His saints, or by the
ordinary and appointed rites of the Catholic
Church.

3. The consideration of this miracle, therefore,
naturally suggests to us the whole large subject of
the extent to which God allows us to be assailed
and tried by our spiritual enemies, the greatness
of their natural powers, and the victories which He
gains over them in the weakness and humility of
His children. The whole mystery of the Incarnation, and of Satan's defeat thereby, is the typical
instance of a victory of this kind, and we know
how much this thought of our great deliverance
from our spiritual enemies seems to occupy the
mind of our Blessed Lady and of St. Zachary in
the *Magnificat* and the *Benedictus.* But we are

E

now to ask ourselves what bearing the points of doctrine which here rise to the surface, as it were, in our consideration of the miracle before us, may have upon the special subject of the sufferings of Purgatory. Does the permission which God accords to the evil spirits in this life, to molest and annoy us, extend to the world beyond the grave? Are they to be our tormentors in Purgatory, as they are allowed to be the tormentors of the lost souls in Hell? It has been thought by some Catholic writers that the presence and sight of the devils form a part of the sufferings of the Holy Souls; indeed, it seems to have been held by some that the devils had a part in the infliction of these torments. We have no certain authority speaking on these subjects, although the lives of the saints and the chronicles of religious orders contain several visions which seem to support this view. On the other hand, other writers have thought it best altogether to deny that God will permit His enemies either to afflict, or insult, or distress by their presence and their blasphemies against Him the souls which are in that holy prison. These writers rely on the dignity of the souls there detained, and on the immense love with which God regards them, for arguments in support of their opinion. They say that the Holy Souls are, after all, victors in their conflict with the powers of evil, and that it is not becoming that the vanquished foes should be allowed to insult or annoy their conquerors.

4. Perhaps the truth may be that, as we shall

have occasion to consider hereafter, there are very
many and very great differences between various
classes of souls in Purgatory, as, indeed, there are
great and wide differences between various souls in
Heaven and in Hell. In the case of those who
have been saved by a late penitence, assisted by
the sacraments of the Church, after a long period
of sin, during which they have been, more or less,
led captive by the devil at will, as the Apostle
speaks, it need not be thought impossible that the
devils should be allowed to be visible to them
during their detention in Purgatory, perhaps to
upbraid and revile them, or to afflict them by the
blasphemies which they are continually hurling
against God. The torment caused by their presence
alone would be very great and intense. Some of
the saints, as St. Catharine of Siena, have been
allowed for a moment to see the utter deformity
and hideousness of these enemies of God, and the
effect has been that they have felt that they would
rather walk along a path of fire until the Day of
Judgment than again endure such a sight. Inasmuch as Purgatory is the place of God's justice, a
justice which is most particular and accurate and
discriminating in allotting to every offence the
punishment which it deserves, it does not seem
unnatural that, as everything which has been used
as an instrument or an occasion of sin is here made
an occasion or instrument of punishment, the devils
also may be made in some special manner such
instruments to those who have been their willing
dupes and slaves during life. There are some sins

which are in a manner more diabolical than others, such as pride, calumny, blasphemy, and the many various forms of unlawful intercourse with the unseen world. Even if we consider that the mercy of God shields other sufferers in Purgatory from the terrible anguish of such sufferings, it may be supposed that in such cases as those mentioned it is not always so.

5. At the same time it may be remembered, that even although the visible presence and activity of the evil spirits may not be among the ordinary pains of Purgatory, there is a sense in which all who are there detained may have to suffer intensely on their account. For among the pains which are there suffered those are certainly not the least which are the results of the neglect of grace, the misuse of opportunities, the yielding to temptations, and the like. The souls who are there suffering have been enabled to look upon the whole of their former lives and on the course of God's providence towards them in the light of truth, caught from the close presence of our Lord at the Particular Judgment. Conscience then wakes up, and discerns everything as it has never discerned anything before, and if they have an altogether new intelligence concerning the mercies and the bounties of God towards them, they have the same new intelligence as to the means of grace, the value of the opportunities of merit, the importance of every moment of time, which have been vouchsafed to them. The same clear light must of necessity show their sins and negligences and omissions in colours of

heinousness such as they did not before perceive;
and it will be by a gleam of the same illumination
that they will understand, not only the true malice
and hatefulness of the spiritual foes who have
assailed them, their intense activity and cunning,
the perseverance with which they have plied their
work, but also the treachery and disloyalty of their
own want of vigilance and faithfulness in the service
of the Master Whose sovereign goodness was
assailed in every temptation and evil suggestion
with which they were themselves beset. They are
enabled thus to see that what seemed at the time
the promptings of natural weakness or indolence
were in truth the suggestions of the evil spirits,
who despise nothing in their warfare against men,
and count it a gain worthy of all their exertions if
they can make Him be served imperfectly by those
whom they cannot persuade to offend Him openly
and grievously. In proportion as the Holy Souls
are filled with His love and raised above the
delusions of the world of sense, in the same
measure must the thought of having so often been
the occasion of unholy triumph to His enemies
have grieved and cut them to the heart when it
was presented to them at the moment of their
judgment, and of their confirmation in the grace
in which they have left this world. The saints of
God, even in this life, have a wonderful quickness
in discerning the action of the evil spirits in matters
in which no thought of them at all occurs to less
enlightened Christians. It is Satan's great desire
to hide himself, and he is content not to be known

if he can only be successful. At the moment of death, at all events, the veil which has so often concealed him will be torn away, and it cannot but be an intense grief to those who suffer there to see how often he may have deceived them.

6. Thoughts of this kind may enable us to understand that everything that is a source of grief to the Holy Souls, in consequence of the details of their past lives, may be connected in their sorrow with the evil spirits, who have always gained something whenever they have themselves failed in perfect faithfulness to God, and whose malignity and loathsomeness they have learnt for the first time fully to conceive. We may elsewhere have to draw out more in particular what some of the chief sources of their regret may have been—a regret based not merely on the offences which they may have committed, but also on the loss of grace which has entailed an eternal loss of degrees of glory to which they might have attained. God's goodness is so great that in Heaven every one feels the most absolute contentment with his own lot, though it may not be the highest lot to which he might have attained. The Holy Souls are confirmed in charity, and they too are so perfectly united to the will of God that their state is one of content. But the love of God which penetrates them does not destroy their pain, which is founded on the knowledge which lit up their minds at the hour of death and judgment as to their own sins against that Infinite Love. To deliver them altogether from this pain by hastening on their perfect

purification is one of the great acts of charity which it is in our power to accomplish by our prayers and by the other means which are given to us of helping them. And we shall certainly advance our own claims on the mercy of God and on their gratitude very greatly by labouring for them in this way, while the thought of the pain which they may be suffering at the recollection of the miserable satisfaction which they must, from time to time, have given to the evil spirits, cannot but make us more watchful, more discerning, more ready to meet their attacks, more perfectly awake to the truth of which the Apostle speaks when he says that our warfare is not "against flesh and blood, but against principalities and powers, against the rulers of the world of this darkness, against the spirits of wickedness in the high places." *

7. It would indeed be well for us if we could gain, as a reward for any exertions which we may make or pains which we undergo for the sake of the relief of the Holy Souls, something like the keen perceptions which they possess of the truths and facts which surround our spiritual existence and our state of trial. This would be an increase of faith, both in intensity and in the range of truths which it embraces, such as that which the Apostles once begged of our Lord. The knowledge with which theology supplies us as to the power and malice of the evil spirits, of the extent to which they are permitted to try us, and of their extreme activity and cunning, would then become a practical

* Ephes. vi. 12.

influence on our daily conduct, giving us a manliness, a courage, a disregard of trifles and frivolities, a readiness to suffer and even an eagerness to fight, such as become soldiers of Jesus Christ who have no time for softness, for effeminacy, for dalliance with the things of sense and with anything that can weaken us or fetter us in the warfare in which we are engaged. This is the true fruit which we ought to draw from the consideration of the great power and malignity of our spiritual enemies, when that consideration is balanced by the other truths which God has made known to us as to the assistance which He will afford us in the conflict. Taken by itself, the knowledge that we are the constant objects of the hateful machinations of the citizens of Hell might well appal us; but we know also that we have Him on our side of Whom it was said that, "With power He commandeth even the unclean spirits, and they obey Him." Thus it is that after the words which have just been quoted from St. Paul as to the "spirits of wickedness in the high places," we find the Apostle breaking out into his famous exhortation about all the weapons with which the Christian warrior is to arm himself. St. Paul is speaking, as it appears, in the first instance to the clergy of the community to which he is writing, but his words are applicable to all Christians. "Therefore, take unto you the whole armour of God, that you may be able to resist in the evil day, and to stand in all things perfect. Stand, therefore, having your loins girt about with truth"—the continual meditation of the great truths—"and

having on the breastplate of justice"—the practice
of all Christian virtue—"and your feet shod with
the preparation of the gospel of peace"—for the
preaching and advancement of the Gospel is the first
duty of all Christian priests, and, in their degree,
of laymen also—"in all things taking the shield of
faith, wherewith you may be able to extinguish all
the fiery darts of the most wicked one"—using
faith as a shield against all temptations—"and take
unto you the helmet of salvation and the sword of
the Spirit, which is the Word of God, by all prayer
and supplication praying at all times in the Spirit,
and in the same watching with all instance and
supplication for all the saints."*

CHAPTER VI.

The Holy Souls and the Saints.

(HEALING OF ST. PETER'S WIFE'S MOTHER.)

St. Matt. viii. 14, 15 ; St. Mark i. 21—31 ; St. Luke iv. 38, 39.

1. IMMEDIATELY after the miracle by which the
devil was driven out in the synagogue from the
man whom he had possessed, the Evangelists tell
us how our Lord, when the congregation had
broken up and the people returned to their homes,
went Himself to the home of St. Peter and St.
Andrew, taking with Him St. James and St. John,
and there healed the mother of St. Peter's wife of
a violent fever which had attacked her. The

* Ephes. vi. 13—18.

circumstances which are specially mentioned as to
this miracle are these : that the disciples told our
Lord of the case, and entreated Him to heal the
sick woman; that He went in to the place where
she was lying, stood over her, took her by the
hand, commanded the fever to leave her, and lifted
her up in such perfect health and strength that she
was able at once to minister to our Lord and His
companions at the meal which followed.   There
are many points in this simple narrative on which
the meditative soul may well delight to linger, such
as the perfection of the cure, the condescension of
our Lord in His Incarnation, and the necessity of
communion with Him, as taught by the power
of the touch of His hand on this woman, and the
like.   But, as it is our business here not to attempt
to exhaust all the holy teaching which may be
found in each one of our Lord's miracles, but to
fasten more particularly on some point in each
which may help us in our charity towards the Holy
Souls and in our own preparation against Purgatory, we need go no further than the first circumstance which meets us as we consider the story in
detail.

2. All the Evangelists who relate this miracle
especially mention the connection between St. Peter
and the person who was healed by our Lord, and
it seems unlikely that this would have been the
case unless there had been in their minds the
thought that the favour was granted, in some
measure, out of regard to St. Peter, as the favour
at the marriage-feast at Cana had been granted

out of regard to our Blessed Lady. Our Lord
may have desired in a particular manner to encourage and deepen the faith of His Chief Apostle,
and He may also have intended the miracle as a
mark of His favour towards him, and as a reward
for the faithfulness with which he had hitherto
followed Him at His word. He was about to set
forth on the morrow of this day on the first of His
great missionary circuits throughout Galilee, and
He was about to require the attendance of at least
the four of the future Apostles who are named in
the history of the miracle. The home which Peter
and Andrew were to leave behind them was in
distress and anxiety on account of the alarming
illness of the mother-in-law of the first-named
Apostle, and it was in keeping with that immense
tenderness of consideration which our Lord showed,
at the very same time that He showed His master-
ful authority and absolute power in commanding
those whom He chose to follow Him without
delay, to leave that home of the Apostles full of
joy and gratitude in the place of sorrow and
mourning. Thus, if we pass from this particular
instance of our Lord's most thoughtful and grateful
mercifulness to the consideration of that mercifulness in general, the circumstances of this miracle
suggest to us how great is the love which our Lord
bears to His saints and His servants, and how
ready He is to lavish His more extraordinary
bounties out of consideration for them.

3. The power which God has accorded to His
saints in Heaven, the great glory which He desires

to derive from the honour which is paid to Him, through and in them, the importance in the scheme of His Kingdom which belongs to the "Communion of Saints," and the charity which is, as it were, its life-blood, and the immense benefits which He intends to impart to the members of the Church who are not yet in Heaven by means of those who are reigning there, would furnish subjects for far longer meditations than any for which we can find space.   The language which is so constantly used by our Lord in His Parables and in other parts of His teaching concerning the reward of His faithful servants is enough to assure us of all these truths, at least when that language is taken in connection with the belief and practice of the Catholic Church in all ages.   For our Lord constantly speaks of power and authority conferred as the reward for faithful service.   In one of His parables the faithful steward is to be "set over all that his Lord possesseth."*   In another, that of the talents, the servants who have trafficked well with the sums confided to them are not rewarded in kind, as it were, by riches, but by the promise, "I will set thee over many things; enter thou into the joy of thy Lord."†   In another, that of the pounds, it is the same thing; the servant who has gained ten and the servant who has gained five are both rewarded, not by having more pounds intrusted to them, but by power. "Thou shalt be having power over ten" or "five cities."‡   In another place, our Lord

---

* St. Luke xii. 44.   † St. Matt. xxv. 21.
        ‡ St. Luke xix. 17—19.

describes the reward of His servants by saying
that their Master "will gird Himself, and make
them sit down to meat, and passing will minister to
them."* And thus we find that the memories of
the Saints were presented to God from the first,
even in the Holy Sacrifice of the Altar, and that
their names are repeated before Him in the sacred
Canon itself, as if He would have His own peculiar
honour accompanied by honourable mention of
their names also. We come to the same conclusion
as to the immense power of the Saints from the
consideration of the Calendar of the Church, whose
offices and services day after day throughout the
year are almost uniformly connected with them,
the only breaks in such uniformity being the great
feasts or seasons which commemorate the most
important mysteries of the Life, Death, Resurrection, and Ascension of our Lord Himself, the
coming of the Holy Ghost, and the great mysteries
of the life of our Blessed Lady. For the offices
and liturgy of the Catholic Church are framed,
indeed, with a view to our instruction and edifica-
tion, by the examples of our Lord and the Saints
which are successively set before us, and by the
continual commemoration of the mysteries of our
Redemption. But they also are framed so as to
honour God in the way which is most acceptable
to His Supreme Majesty, and we should not be
taught by the Church on earth to honour Him so
continually in His Saints, if the Church in Heaven
were not honouring Him perpetually in the same

* St. Luke xii. 37.

way, with adoration and homage and thanksgivings of which ours here below are but the faintest echoes.

4. A question has been raised among Catholic theologians of various schools, as to the extent to which the Saints in Heaven use their powerful intercession in favour of the Holy Souls of Purgatory. To most Christians it would seem a strange announcement that there could be any doubt on such a matter, inasmuch as we know that the whole Church, whether in Heaven, on earth, or in Purgatory, is the kingdom of charity, and that one of the laws of that kingdom is that each member feels most intensely, according to his capacity and condition, for all and each of the rest, and exerts himself to the utmost of his power which God gives him for the relief or help of those who are in any way in need of them. We shall see that one of the reasons adduced on the negative side is founded on the immense force of this charity on the parts of the Saints, as if their prayers for the Holy Souls would continually empty Purgatory, if there were not some restriction to prevent it. The chief argument, however, is that the Saints cannot perform any works of satisfaction, and that therefore they cannot in this way help the holy prisoners of Purgatory. It is undoubtedly true that the Saints cannot satisfy for sin in the way in which the children of the Church upon earth can do this. But they can impetrate mercy and forgiveness, and the merits which they have accumulated in their lifetime may enable them to do so with

greater efficacy. Besides this, their prayers can move God to accept for the Holy Souls the satisfaction of living persons; they can move Him to inspire the living to help the departed, and give them powerful grace to do so; they can obtain from the Divine Mercy that the time of the detention of the Souls in Purgatory may be shortened, perhaps by the pain being made more intense. Moreover, the satisfactory works of the Saints during their lifetime, of which they have themselves no need, may be applied at their prayers to the Holy Souls in Purgatory. Certainly the offices of the Church, and the prayers in use among her children, imply that the power of the intercession of the Saints for the Souls in Purgatory is beyond all question. The difficulty about the emptying of Purgatory is easily answered, for the prayers of the Saints have no power of satisfaction, which is what is chiefly and most directly needed for the relief of the Holy Souls, and, moreover, the Saints, like the Holy Souls themselves, are confirmed in grace and perfect in charity, and therefore can desire or ask nothing that is not in perfect conformity with the ordinances of God. But, as has been already said in the chapter on our Lord's first miracle, it is often the especial desire of God that the ordinances of His justice should be overridden by those of His mercy, which is set in motion by prayer.*

* See on the subject of this paragraph, Benedict XIII. *Trig.I.* *sopra il Purgatorio*, Sermon xxiv., where the references to Soto, St. Thomas, Suarez, and other writers will be found.

5. Although we cannot be certain to what extent the holy suffering Souls are already illuminated as to the glories and happiness of Heaven, still we may well suppose that they are able to see, in some measure at least, the innumerable blessings and mercies which they have received in the course of their life from the good providence of God, and among these, the many benefits which He has granted to them by means of the intercession and protection of the saints. They have also seen at the time of their judgment, how many more favours might have been won by them from God if they had been more devout to His servants reigning with Him, whose power to help us is so often made to depend for its exercise on the faithfulness with which we invoke them and honour God in them. In this way, while the Holy Souls are filled with immense gratitude to their heavenly patrons, and are burning with desire for the moment when they are to become their companions in the enjoyment of the Beatific Vision, in that ineffable charity which unites all the blessed to God and to each other in Him, and in the great work of praise, adoration, and intercession on which they are for ever occupied, they have also been grieved and pained at the little use which they have made of the charity and power of the saints, to the glory of God and the perfection of their own souls. The regret which they have felt at their own neglect of all the means of grace causes intense sorrow to these holy sufferers, because they know that it has deprived God of so much glory, and themselves of

so much grace, that it has delayed their entrance into Heaven, and that it has made them for ever incapable of reaching that high place there which they might have attained by greater faithfulness. In this sense, even the saints and angels, and the Blessed Mother of God herself, and our Lord Jesus Christ, have been causes of pain to the Souls in Purgatory—pain made up of a sense of ingratitude to benefactors so powerful and so loving, of the knowledge of their own immense loss, and that the measure of the joy and love which they are to give and receive in that blessed companionship in Heaven is for ever shortened by their fault. This is a pain which must be very keen to noble, generous, grateful, and loving hearts—a pain which, in the case of which we speak, may not be entirely cured till they enjoy that perfect contentment and ineffable love of God which reigns in every single soul that sees His face, whether its place in Heaven be high or low.

6. We may very well make this regret of the Holy Souls a reason for an increase, both in fervour and in frequency, in our own devotion to and honour of the saints of God. All Catholics, by God's mercy, know what it is to honour the saints, and very few indeed can be found who have not experienced the tenderness of their charity and the greatness of their power in various ways. But so it is with this as with the other means of grace—there may be few good Catholics who do not use them at all, and there may also be very few, who use them to the full extent to which God

F

intends them to be used; and thus the glory of God and of His saints is curtailed, and our own souls are deprived of countless blessings and graces. A great, thorough, intelligent, and familiar devotion to any one of the saints is a rare gift, which produces untold benefits to the soul; and the saints whom God would have us honour and love, and whom the Church proposes to our veneration and imitation, are multitudinous in number as well as indefinitely various in the special character of their sanctity and in the powers which they may exercise with God.   A duty such as that which is here set before us—for our duties to the saints flow naturally from the position towards God and us, which He has allotted to them in His Kingdom—should not be left to accident, but be a matter of study and consideration, and it is for this reason, as we may suppose, among others, that the Church raises them to her altars, and sets saint after saint before us as the days of the year pass on.   The names we bear, the places or countries in which we are born or are educated or live, the paths of life which we follow according to our several vocations, the lines of our studies or professions, even what seem the accidents of our career, which bring us to this shrine or to that, or make us need this or that particular grace—these, and a score of other circumstances, are so many suggestions on the part of God's providence to attach our devotion to one or other of His saints. The ways, too, in which they may be honoured are many and various, such as invoking them, imitating them, visiting their shrines, venerating their relics, propagating the charities to which they have been specially devoted, helping the orders which they have founded, or making known any works which they have left behind them. All these things vary according to the circumstances of their lives and the peculiar services which God has received from them. In all these, and in other ways, we must pay to them the debt of gratitude and reverence which the Holy Souls have owed, as well as that which we owe to them ourselves, and we may thus secure their powerful intercession and protection in their favour as well as in our own.

CHAPTER VII.

Promptitude in assisting the Holy Souls.

(CURES WROUGHT ON THE EVENING OF THE SABBATH.)

St. Matt. viii. 16—18 ; St. Mark i. 32—34 ; St. Luke iv. 40, 41.

1. THE miracles wrought in the deliverance of the demoniac in the synagogue, and in the healing of the mother of St. Peter's wife, do not exhaust the gracious works of mercy which made this first Sabbath of our Lord's preaching at Capharnaum so memorable in the Gospel history. The Evangelists tell us that, in the short evening of that day, after the sunset, "they brought all to Him that were diseased, and that were possessed with devils : and

all the city was gathered together at the door."
St. Luke, speaking of the sick, says that "He, laying
His hands on every one of them, healed them."
As to the demoniacs, St. Matthew says that "He
cast out the spirits with His word;" and St. Luke
and St. Mark add that, when the devils cried out,
"Thou art the Son of God, He rebuked them, and
would not suffer them to speak."

2. These miracles have one characteristic circumstance, which each of the Evangelists mentions,
and which will be sufficient for our present consideration. In each narrative we are told that these
poor sufferers were brought to our Lord as soon as
it was evening, after the sun had set. The reason
for this, in the minds of the people of Capharnaum, was that the rest of the Sabbath lasted from
sunset to sunset, and that they were consequently
free to do so much of work in the way of charity
as was required for the bringing of the sick, some
of whom no doubt had to be carried on beds or
pallets to the door of the house in which our Lord
was, as soon as the sun had set. The twilight in
those countries is usually very short, and there was,
therefore, very little time for the transport of the
sick from one part of the city to another, and for
the leisurely healing of them by our Lord, as He
laid His hands on each one singly. But the charitable zeal of the good people of Capharnaum would
not wait for the morning, and it may have been
that this wonderful exercise of our Lord's mercy
was carried on when, but for that, the whole city
would have been wrapped in sleep, under the

bright light of the summer moon, and it must
have lasted far into the night ere the last poor
sufferers had been relieved. And it was well for
them that their friends had been so eager, and
even so impatient to procure their speedy cure.
For we are told by the Evangelists that very early
indeed on the following morning our Lord rose
and went out of the city into a desert place to
pray. He was pursued by Simon Peter and the
other disciples, who entreated Him to return, as
every one was seeking Him. But He bade them
come with Him on the journey which He at once
began, to go through the other cities and villages
of Galilee preaching, and it does not seem that
He even went back for a moment into Capharnaum. As it appears, the sufferers would have
been unrelieved but for the eagerness and promptitude of their friends, who would not delay a
moment in bringing them to our Lord, notwith-
standing the lateness of the hour and the great
throng at the door, so great that St. Mark, speaking
from the recollection of St. Peter, an eye-witness,
says that "all the city" was collected there. It
was probably a warm summer night in June, and it
cost them but little to wait patiently for their turn
in that immense crowd, and when in the morning
they learnt that the wonderful Teacher and Healer
was already far on His way to other places, they
must have thanked with all their hearts the quick
charity which had taken them at once to His feet.

3. These people of Capharnaum, therefore, are
in this narrative set before us as examples of

promptitude in acts of mercy and charity, and we cannot be surprised if our Lord, in His joy at their faith and eagerness, poured out for them a very large measure of His bounty. The language of the Evangelists would almost justify us in saying that He left no one unhealed who could be brought to Him, and that a very large number of the sick and the demoniacs that were there to be found were brought to Him. It was the beginning of the great display of miracles by which His public preaching throughout the country of Galilee was heralded, and it is often the way of God to give at the beginning of His merciful dispensations more freely and largely than afterwards, in return for the fresh ready faith with which those dispensations are welcomed. However the facts of the case may have been, it is certain that the conduct of the people of Capharnaum, which was met by our Lord with so rich and magnificent a series of miracles, may be taken as a typical instance of that very beautiful virtue of promptitude which is so dear to God. Like other graces, it has a natural representative and image in the natural quickness in which some persons excel others so much—a quality not always virtuous, but which enables those who possess it to do so much more in the business and conflict of life than others who are by nature slower. The promptitude which is a grace of God, and which may be said in some measure to reflect His own rapid way of working great effects and changes in a moment, is accompanied with the most perfect calm and tranquillity, which also are qualities which characterise the most mighty and the most instantaneous works of God. In some respects God appears to us to be infinitely patient and deliberate in His works, biding His time, as we say, and letting years or centuries pass away until the moment which He has chosen arrives. And then—swiftly, silently, and in a moment—His works are done. We are to imitate His patience and deliberateness, so to speak, by never acting until our path is plain and until we are clear as to His will, and then we are to reflect His swiftness in brooking no further delay, and carrying out at once the good work which we have conceived. For all that we have to do must be done in time, and time is a thing which we can never command—the moment passes away, the opportunity is lost. All the good that we can do depends for its performance and for its perfection on the assistance of His grace, and grace is another thing which we can never depend upon at a future moment if we do not use it while we have it. We cannot bid it wait or come again to-morrow. Thus, one of the great beauties in the perfection of the work of the saints is the swiftness and promptitude of their actions, which are guided by Him of Whom a Father says—"Nescit tarda molimina Spiritûs Sancti gratia." This quickness runs through the whole range of their virtues, and con- sists in perfect correspondence to Divine grace in the use of the occasions of virtue which present themselves. It has nothing of impetuosity or hurry or fussiness about it. For just as the good use of the tongue consists as much in silence as in speech, so swiftness and promptitude consist as much in not doing things before their time as in doing them at the right time, and not later. The Preacher counsels us—"Whatsoever thy hand is able to do, do it earnestly,"* as if we had nothing else to do for the time but that; and our Lord bids us "take no thought for the morrow," as if to do so were to occupy our minds anxiously on things which have not yet come to our hand, and as to which we are not certain that they ever will come.

4. Among all the exercises and acts of virtue which are to be done swiftly and at once, after the pattern of God's works, there are some which fall under this head in an especial way, such as works of justice, of charity, and of fidelity. Thus not to pay wages or debts at the right time, to delay the fulfilment of a promise which we have made, or to put off an act of charity which concerns God, our own souls, or our neighbour's good, are acts on which the failure of promptitude may have very serious consequences. Thus we find St. James reproaching the rich and threatening them with severe punishment for keeping back the wages of their labourers.† Any debt that we owe to man or God, such as the debt of penance and satisfaction, or of a vow or promise, and the like, comes under that urgent instruction of our Lord in the Sermon on the Mount, where He bids us "be at agreement with thy adversary betimes, whilst thou art in the way with him: lest perhaps the adversary

* Eccles. ix. 10.   † St. James v. 4.

deliver thee to the judge, and the judge deliver thee
to the officer, and thou be cast into prison. Amen,
I say to thee, thou shalt not go out from thence till
thou repay the last farthing."* And we know that
when our brethren are in need or in pain, and it is
in our power to relieve them, we are bound in all
charity not to delay a moment, if possible, to
relieve their affliction. To delay help is at all
events to increase their suffering, to add to its
duration, and to run the risk of not relieving it
at all.

5. These thoughts very naturally lead us to the
application of the lesson here set before us as to
our duties in regard of the Holy Souls of Purgatory. For in the first place, very many of them
may be suffering there for a lack of this promptitude in the discharge of obligations, whether of
justice or of charity, of which we have spoken.
Many an act of devotion, or of charity, or of
restitution, or of satisfaction for sin, may have been
delayed by them, and death may have found them
with that debt undischarged. It is impossible
that persons who have not habitually this grace of
promptitude and exactness should have nothing to
make up in the next world in consequence—and
when we remember that death, however much it
might have been looked forward to in an ordinary
way, is unexpected when it actually comes to the
majority of Christians, we may be certain that most
men will be found, in this sense, unprepared for it.
But, putting this consideration aside, it is certain

* St. Matt. v, 25, 26.

that our charity to God, and to the Holy Souls, and to ourselves, binds us, even when there is no obligation of justice, not only to assist them in all the ways in our power, but also to assist them as quickly as possible. The obligation of justice, of course, is still more serious, as binding those who are children or heirs of the departed, those who have received benefits and kindness from them, those whom they have instructed and helped, the priests who have received alms in order that they may say Mass for them, or any who have lived upon the foundations which they have made. But where the obligation is strictly an obligation of Christian charity, the circumstances of the case of the Holy Souls plead for their help without a moment's delay. It is a very great difference indeed whether God is deprived or not of His glory by their complete deliverance even a little later or a little sooner. If it was an immense gain to one of these poor sufferers from disease or demoniacal possession at Capharnaum to have been healed or set free by our Lord on that Sabbath night rather than on the next day, much more is it an incalculable gain to a soul in Purgatory if its detention in that prison be cut short even by an hour or by a minute. It is not the certainty that they will be delivered some time or other that is enough to satisfy the charity of any one who is at all enlightened as to the pains of sense and of loss which are to be undergone there. We count it very poor charity indeed, in the case of human sickness or affliction of any kind, that is content with the knowledge that, after an indefinite period, that affliction will cease. And when we remember that our Lord has told us that we shall be dealt with by Him as we have dealt with others, we may be quite certain that, if by His merits and mercy we escape the flames of Hell, it will still be a terrible aggravation to our lot in the fires of Purgatory if we have any slowness or delay in relieving others with which to reproach ourselves.

CHAPTER VIII.

The Church on Earth and the Holy Souls.

(THE MIRACULOUS DRAUGHT OF FISHES.)

St. Luke v. 1—11.

1. THE two preceding chapters have shown us the truth that, although the saints of God in Heaven are so full of charity and also so powerful in His Kingdom, as to appear almost to share His almightiness, they are yet in a certain way fettered as to the exercise of their influence in favour of the Holy Souls in Purgatory, by their inability to use that which is the most direct way of relieving those sufferers, because they are unable to make satisfaction for them. We also saw, in the last chapter, the special importance to them of seizing without delay every opportunity which may occur for their relief. We may use the next miracle of our Lord

in illustration of a further and kindred truth, the thought of which is suggested by the foregoing considerations. What the Saints in Heaven cannot do for the Holy Souls, in the way of satisfaction, which is their most direct need, that the Church on earth alone has the power of doing. It seems from many truths which meet us in these considerations, as if it were no exaggeration to say that the Holy Souls are in a special and direct manner commended and even left by God to the charity of the Church on earth, all of whose children have the power of aiding them by prayers, penances, almsdeeds, fastings, and by the offering of the Holy Sacrifice of the Mass for them, while her Pontiffs have also the power of applying the treasure of the satisfactions of our Lord and the Saints to them by way of Indulgences. Much as the saints and angels can do for them, still the official duty of their liberation, if we may so speak, rests upon the Militant Church rather than on the Triumphant Church, and the time during which they can be helped by us so efficiently, as well as with so wonderful benefit to ourselves, is just this short time of our life here, while we are in the possession of the means of grace and merit. This is the arrangement of God and our Lord in His Kingdom, and that it is so is a great and urgent reason for us to exert ourselves to the utmost in their behalf. We may use, as has been said, the next in order of our Lord's miracles as enabling us to draw out this truth.

2. It was mentioned in the last chapter that our

Lord, immediately after that Sabbath at Capharnaum, which He made so notable by the many
and various miracles which He had wrought on
that day and on the following night, left the city
and proceeded, with a few followers, some of the
future Apostles, on the first of His great missionary
circuits throughout the region of Galilee. His
chief occupation, during the busy weeks and
months that ensued, was preaching, instructing,
comforting, and guiding the many souls who came
to Him, either in crowds or singly, for the precious
lessons which He was commissioned to deliver.
Great multitudes always thronged to hear Him,
and large crowds, it is probable, followed Him
from city to city, and formed a sort of continual
pilgrimage that waited upon Him. It was to such
a multitude as this that, after He had been for
some considerable time employed in His missionary work, He delivered His great discourse
which is known to us as the Sermon on the Mount.
But although our Lord's chief employment at this
time was the discharge of the office of Teacher
and Healer of souls, He never neglected the
exterior works of mercy and compassion. His
miracles at this time were probably countless and
very magnificent, but they were of necessity more
or less of the same kind everywhere, and thus they
have not been specially recorded by the Evangelists. Thus it is, that in our attempt at tracing
His great recorded miracles one by one, we have
to pass over this long period of activity, or, at
least, the greater part of it. The next miracle, the

circumstances of which we find specially recorded, is that which has been named above—the first of the two which our Lord wrought on the Sea of Galilee, is what is commonly called the miraculous draught of fishes.

3. The future Apostles were not at this time, as afterwards, collected into a sort of religious community, so as never to be separated from our Lord and from each other. Thus it was that at some short interval in the course of our Lord's active missionary labours—very probably after the delivery of the Sermon on the Mount—St. Peter and St. Andrew, with St. James and St. John, had spent the night in their former occupation as fishermen, and had taken nothing in their nets. On the morning after this our Lord came to teach the people by the sea-shore, as was sometimes His habit, and finding that the pressure of the throng was very great, He had entered one of the fishermen's boats, and delivered His instruction from the water at a distance of a few yards from the land. When the time of teaching was over, He bade Simon Peter, the owner of the boat, to launch out into the sea, and let down his nets. St. Peter replied that they had already laboured in vain all night, but that at our Lord's word he would let his nets down. The result was that the nets now inclosed an immense multitude of fishes, so great that the nets were in danger of breaking, and when the partners of Simon Peter and his brother, St. James and St. John, whose boat was also close by, were called to help, both the boats were so laden

with the fishes as to be near sinking. St. Peter turned
to our Lord in his deep astonishment, awe, and
thankful humility, with the famous words : " Depart
from me, Lord, for I am a sinner." Then our Lord
answered him : " Fear not : from henceforth thou
shalt be catching men. They drew their boats to the
shore, and left all, and followed Him." That is, as
it appears, they once more started in His company
on a great expedition over the country, the object
of which was the preaching of the Gospel.

4. This miracle has many very remarkable
features, and it is not our purpose at present to
dwell on them one by one. It is one of the
unsolicited miracles of our Lord—in which, for
that very reason that they were unsolicited and
unexpected, we naturally look for some deep
prophetical meaning and instruction. Indeed, it
is clear that our Lord's object was to encourage
His Apostles, and especially St. Peter, for the work
which He was about to commit to them. The
failure of their toil during the whole night before,
when they had not our Lord with them, and did
not let down the nets at His word, was provi-
dentially arranged in order that the success
of their fishing when these circumstances were
changed might strike them more forcibly. The
connection between our Lord's preaching to the
crowds and the fishing of the Apostles was also
providential, and the miraculous draught showed
in a figure how fruitful and multitudinous was the
effect of His Divine words on the souls of His
hearers. He shows Himself, in the multitude of

the fishes, as the Master of the whole creation, possessing power and dominion which nothing can gainsay, and disposing of His irrational creatures according to the behests of His sovereign will. In the spiritual truth which is represented by this external dominion, He is seen as the Lord and Master of the human heart, which it has been His will to make free, and to endow with the responsibility on which its eternal lot is to hang, and which yet is in His hands to draw as He chooses when He addresses it with the solicitation of His interior grace, and the external ministrations by which He chooses to work upon it. In both cases we see Him arranging, according to His absolute will, both the material and the spiritual creation; and thus we are led to the remembrance of the wonderful wisdom and lordly freedom with which He has ordered the whole of the universe, and the various functions and offices and mutual relations of the beings, His creatures, who compose it.

5. This order of the universe is one of the marvels the contemplation of which furnishes endless delight and instruction and thankfulness to the Blessed in Heaven, who understand how everything is in its place, how all creatures serve Him, how each contributes in its own way to the carrying out of the eternal counsel which He has decreed to follow. At His word all things were made, on His word the angels wait to perform their various tasks, on His will the whole creation depends. So at His word Peter let down the net, certain that He could give no command which was

not the command of a Sovereign whom all things
are bound to obey. It is His word and decree
that has endowed the Church on earth with the
great array of powers which she possesses for the
benefit of the holy departed, and when we do all
that lies in us to make this array available and
fruitful, we are but carrying out His behests, with
His word for the guarantee that we shall not
labour in vain. He has committed this work to
the Church, which has always been considered as
represented by the barque of Peter, and with His
word to encourage us, we may venture to undertake what is not in the same way committed to
angels or saints in Heaven, just as to them it is
not committed to consecrate the Adorable Sacrifice or to absolve men from their sins in the
Sacrament of Penance.

6. One point in the miracle on which our
thoughts may fasten in connection with the subject
which runs through all these considerations, may
be that which filled the future Apostles with deep
astonishment and awe, so as to frighten them by a
close sense of the presence of Divine Power in our
Lord, as it were, touching them, and by its very
nearness casting them down at His feet, in the
consciousness of their own unworthiness to be
assisted and blessed by the Pure and Ineffable
Majesty of His Godhead. It was the prodigious
multitude of the prey which had fallen into their
hands, that caused this effect, and the immediate
connection between His simple word of command
and the success which rewarded their obedience.

G

This wonderful and preternatural efficacy of the labour undertaken at our Lord's word, when contrasted with the utter barrenness of their former exertions, struck them, as it were, to the heart, and was, we cannot doubt, a most efficacious lesson in preparing them for the Apostolical labours which were foreshadowed in this fishing. For success in all such labours, of whatever kind, depends altogether, not on any human exertions, though these must not be wanting at the very utmost of our power, that we may not do the work of the Lord negligently—but on the word or will of our Lord, Who reserves it to Himself either to prosper the work or not, according to His own inscrutable counsel. But there is one security for His prospering it, and that is to be found in His command. Now the commands of our Lord are expressed to us in various ways—sometimes by the injunctions of our Superiors in the Church, and sometimes by the ordinary instructions and rules and practices of that Church, all of which come from Him. To know that He has attached certain graces and promises to prayer or good works for a particular object in His Kingdom, which cannot but be very dear to the Sacred Heart, is to know that He desires and enjoins us, in the degree in which it lies in our power, to labour for that end with the prayers and good works which He has so blessed. And in the case of the Holy Souls we have so far an injunction from Him to do this—though it may not be expressed in so many words in any one place—

that consciously to neglect it can hardly be less than an act of disloyalty to Him.

7. Our faith tells us that the holy realm of Purgatory never gave up its prisoners to the enjoyment of the Beatific Vision in Heaven until after our Lord's Passion and descent into Limbus. In this respect we may compare the great work of the full deliverance of the Holy Souls, to the draught of fishes which rewarded the faith and obedience of the Apostles, when our Lord bade them cast their nets, and we may contrast that success with the comparative fruitlessness of all efforts that might have been made before the accomplishment of the work of Redemption on the Cross. It is only at the word of our Lord that this work of zeal and charity can be carried out, because it is by the merits of His Passion alone that the gates of Heaven are thrown open to the faithful departed. The pious prayers which were made for the dead under the older dispensations of God might profit them so far as to procure their relief from the pain of sense, and their translation to the peaceful abode in which our Lord found the saints of the Old Covenant, when He descended among them from His Cross. But they could not win for them that perfect deliverance which it is now in our power to procure for them, and which in His providence He mainly looks to us to procure, because good works wrought on earth have a power of satisfaction which does not belong even to the prayers of the saints in Heaven. To know this Catholic doctrine is to know the power which our Lord has

placed in our hands with regard to the holy dead, and to know our power is the same thing to know that He wishes us to exercise it. Thus, then, the word has been spoken to us by our Lord to let down our nets, to labour in every way that is in our power, systematically, continuously, thoughtfully, seriously, and at the cost of any [sacrifice to ourselves, in the great ransoming of souls so dear to Him. He bids us all, according to our opportunities and capacities, to take up this work, not as a spiritual superfluity which we may indulge in or not, according to our tastes, but as a duty imposed upon us by the great law of charity, and by the special power which He has placed in our hands for its performance. St. John says, "He that hath the substance of this world, and shall see his brother in need, and shall shut up his bowels from him, how doth the charity of God abide in Him?"* And on the principle of this argument it may be said, that the knowledge of the need of the Holy Souls on the one hand, and our special power of helping them on the other, make it imperative on us, if we have the love of God, to labour in the great work of their release.

8. But the Apostles were amazed and struck dumb, as we may say, on the occasion of which we are speaking, not simply at the fact that their labours when undertaken at our Lord's bidding were successful, but at the amount and marvellous abundance of the prey which they had taken. Now there are good reasons for thinking that the

* 1 St. John iii. 17.

great abundance which rewarded them in their
fishing would seem as nothing if it were placed by
the side of the multitudinous fruitfulness which, by
God's blessing, will attend the labours of those
who give themselves with all their heart to the
great work of Christian charity of which we are
speaking.   In the first place, the prayers which are
made for the relief of the Holy Souls are not
impeded in their effect by any indisposition on the
part of those for whom they are made.   Such
indisposition is the great reason why prayers for
the conversion of sinners or heretics, or for the
advancement of those who are already serving God
to a higher kind of service and greater spiritual
perfection, are often rendered comparatively fruit-
less in those for whom they are made.   In the
second place, every good work of every kind has
a quality of satisfaction belonging to it, and as this
may be applied, if we so choose to offer it, for the
benefit of the Holy Souls, they may receive daily
and hourly succour from us, and our whole
Christian life may be continually fruitful in this
holy work.   Again, the number of works which
may be specially directed to this object is very
great indeed, and very various, and embraces all
the chief acts and duties of our religious life,
fasting, mortification, almsgiving of every kind,
prayer, the Holy Mass, Communion, the Rosary,
the Litanies, meditation, the Divine Office, or the
Office of the Dead, and a thousand other such
good deeds.   And besides the direct power of
impetration and satisfaction which belongs to all

these good works as such, the Vicars of Jesus Christ, especially in these later centuries, have been moved by the guidance of the Holy Ghost to endow almost every Christian work of the kind of which we have been speaking with very rich and copious Indulgences, which are generally declared to be applicable to the holy departed.

9. When we consider the abundance of the means for this work which are thus placed in our hands, and which, by that very fact, we are plainly encouraged to use, we may well suppose that a faithful Christian who has made it one of his daily aims to help the Holy Souls to the best of his power by good works, prayers, and the gaining of Indulgences for them, may be seized at the Last Day with a holy and most blessed astonishment, like that of St. Peter in the boat, when he sees the multitudes upon multitudes of happy souls in whose deliverance he has had a share. Nor will he need, then, to ask our Lord to depart from him as one unworthy. For the charity with which he has laboured for the glory and content of God, and for the happiness of these Holy Souls, will surely have covered a multitude of his own sins, or perhaps have won for him the still higher grace of escaping from their committal. Nor will he have to be told that from henceforth he shall be catching men and not fishes, for the prey which he will have brought into the net of God's ineffable and entrancing love will be the noblest of the human race, the souls for whom our Lord

became incarnate and died, and to whom He has, in His infinite charity and wisdom, decreed that the full fruit of His atoning sacrifice should be applied by means of men like themselves— whose love will be rewarded by a never-dying and most tender gratitude from Him as well as from them, which will abide as a special bond between them, even among all the joys and glories of eternity.

CHAPTER IX.

Duration of the Pains of Purgatory.

(THE HEALING OF THE LEPER.)

St. Matt. viii. 2—4 ; St. Mark i. 40—45 ; St. Luke v. 12—16.

1. AFTER the miracle of the draught of fishes, our Lord, as it appears, left Capharnaum and its neighbourhood again for a time, in order to preach in other parts of Galilee. We have only one incident preserved to us by the Evangelists which seems to belong to the period of this new missionary expedition. But this one miracle was very remarkable indeed, both in itself, in the effect which it produced upon the people who heard of it, and in its spiritual and doctrinal meaning. Without attempting here to draw out all that it signified with relation to our Lord's Person and powers, we shall, as before, shortly

relate it, and then draw from it the lessons
which seem most appropriate to the great range
of truths concerning Purgatory and the Holy
Souls there detained.

2. The miracle before us has been related by
the three historical Evangelists, whose narratives
supplement each other so as to give us a full
picture of the incidents. It is remarkable, also,
as illustrating the great importance of this
miracle, that St. Matthew selects it as the first
of a long chain of miracles of various kinds,
by relating which he evidently intends to point
out how our Lord showed His marvellous healing power on every possible form of disease,
on persons afflicted by demoniacal possession,
on the elements of matter, as in the case of the
stilling of the tempest, and even over the maladies
of the soul; for such is the great lesson, as we
may see hereafter, of the healing of the paralytic.
The position which St. Matthew thus assigns to
the miracle on the leper, of which we are now
speaking, shows that the Evangelist considered it
as of very exceptional importance and significance.
Our Lord was in "one of the cities," St. Luke tells
us—one of those through which He passed in His
tour of preaching—"and behold a man full of
leprosy, seeing Him, and falling on his face,"
"bending his knee, and adoring Him," as the other
Evangelists say, "besought Him, saying, Lord, if
Thou wilt, Thou canst cleanse me!" Our Lord
"had compassion on him, and stretching out His
hand, touched him, saying, I will, be thou cleansed!"

The leprosy "immediately departed from him." Our Lord then laid on him a very strict injunction, which St. Mark tells us He enforced even by threats. He was to tell no one of the cure which had been wrought on him, but to go at once to the High Priest—who could only be found at Jerusalem—show himself to him, and then make the offerings and sacrifices which the Law ordained in such cases, in order that the fact of his cure might be established by the surest of testimonies. It does not belong to our present purpose to draw out the intention with which our Lord gave this strict command-ment. But the poor leper who had been healed was unable to keep his cure to himself. The blessing was too great, too sudden, too perfect, his gratitude too deep and intense, for him to be able to hold his tongue. So he began, as soon as he left our Lord's presence, to proclaim and spread about everywhere the miracle which had been wrought upon him, and in consequence of the notoriety which thus surrounded him, our Lord was obliged for a time to keep away from the cities, and remain in the less inhabited and cultivated parts of the country. Even there multitudes came to Him from all parts, while the rest of the time, which remained to Him from preaching to and healing them, was spent by Him, as St. Luke tells us, in prayer.

3. It is clear that the healing of a man from the terrible malady of leprosy, was considered by the people as an instance of supernatural power even

greater than that which our Lord showed in the
cure of other diseases. Leprosy was, and is,
where it still exists, a disease belonging, in certain
respects, to a class of its own, and it had a kind
of sacred character among the Jews, on account of
the merciful and significant provisions which had
been made for it in the Law of Moses. To heal
it was not only to do what was ordinarily impossible to medical science—as, for instance, to give
sight to a man born blind—but to cure a disease
which was considered as especially an infliction of
God, and, as such, reserved by Him to Himself
to alleviate or take away. Thus it seems to have
been that this, the first instance of the healing of a
leper by our Lord, was considered as a sign of His
Power more wonderful than the miracles which
had preceded it in point of time. The peculiarities
of the disease of leprosy, which made it so particularly fitted to be the special type of sin, were
many, and have been spoken of by many Christian
writers on this place. It was, for instance, a
disease which proceeded from within, and affected
the whole part of the body where it existed, making
it outwardly hideous and loathsome from its
corruption as well as the seat of a latent evil.
In consequence of this, and of the other circumstance, that it was incurable and yet often lasted
for many years before death ensued, being, in short,
a kind of living death, it involved a more complete
separation from the usual homes and friends of the
patients afflicted by it than was the case with other
diseases. We need go no further than these

particulars in order to find a very useful lesson for ourselves in regard to the truths which we believe concerning Purgatory.

4. We are often very much startled by the manner in which the sufferings of Purgatory are represented to us in the writings of ascetical authors, or in the visions which are recorded of the saints and servants of God. The reason why we are so startled lies, perhaps, in great measure, in our neglect to take in the whole of the teaching which is thus set before us, one part of which is needed in order to balance another; and it lies partly also in our forgetting that visions must of necessity take the form of pictures addressed to the eye of the mind, in which every detail has to be filled up in harmony with the principal point as to which it is the purpose of the vision to convey instruction to us. The points in the common teaching concerning Purgatory which are the most difficult for us to take in, are the extreme severity of the pains of sense—which are often represented in visions by the most painful pictures—and the very long duration of those pains. It is with regard to this latter point that the case of the leper may help us to understand the justice of God in dealing with the Holy Souls. The great misery of-the leper consisted in his loathsomeness to his fellows, to the members of his own family, his wife, brethren, sisters, and children, in the separation from them which was made necessary, whether by that loathsomeness alone or also by fear of infectiousness in the

disease ; and in the great length of time, often the greater number of years in a long life, during which his affliction lasted.   In all these respects the leper may be considered as an image of the Holy Souls of Purgatory, especially if we consider the doctrine which St. Thomas has laid down concerning the duration of the pains which are endured there. The Angelical Doctor teaches that the severity of the pains of Purgatory answers to the quantity of the faults which are to be there expiated, but that the length of time during which these pains last answers to the greater or less degree of what he calls the " radication " of the fault in the subject —that is, the degree to which the soul has been attached to an unlawful object, and to which that love has been engrained in the soul.   And thus, he tells us, it may be, that one person may be punished for a longer time than another, and yet to a less degree, and the converse.   For the soul is more attached to some venial sins than to others, and thus some have to suffer a longer time than others, because when there has been greater adhesion to what is wrong, then there is a slower purgation.*   This doctrine certainly explains to us how it is that many persons who die in a state of grace may have to remain a long time in Purgatory, even when the sins for which they are there detained are not more than venial.   For the lesser faults to which we are inordinately attached are those which are habitual to us, those as to which we often hardly think of making a serious

* St. Thomas *in Sent.* 4, dist. 21, qu. i. art. 3.

resolution of amendment when we confess them, and yet from the fact that they are habitual, they must amount to a very large number in the course of a long life. And yet these venial sins, though far greater in number than the mortal sins which have been confessed and absolved, are still not so heinous in the eye of God, nor deserving of so severe a punishment in the prison of Purgatory.

5. It may be useful to sum up very shortly the chief arguments which have been adduced by the writers who take the more severe side as to the question of the duration of the pains of Purgatory. Some of these have argued from the famous and very difficult passage in the First Epistle of St. Peter,* in which the Apostle speaks of our Lord's preaching to the spirits in prison, whom they suppose to have been the Antediluvians, who disbelieved the warnings of Noe. These must have been for very many hundreds of years in Purgatory. But it is easy to see that in any case this preaching of our Lord must have been addressed to those who were in Purgatory, if at all, before His Passion. Moreover, the greater length of human life before the Flood must have made it possible to accumulate an immense amount of sins to be expiated there. Another argument which has more force is that drawn from passages in ancient Liturgies, in which prayers are offered for all who have died since the beginning of the world, and from the practice of the Church of allowing and encouraging the foundation of Masses for the souls

* 1 St. Peter iii. 19.

of those who have been very long dead. Again,
the same conclusion is drawn from the great length
of the public penances inflicted in ancient times
upon sinners while alive; and, again, from the very
large Indulgences which have sometimes been
conceded. These Indulgences, of course, correspond to so much canonical penance, and so
are a fresh witness to the idea in the mind of the
authorities who granted them, as to the length of
penance that might be necessary for forgiven sins.
The same writers argue also from the great intrinsic
enormity of any single mortal sin, which deserves
eternal punishment, and they conclude from this
that when its guilt is forgiven, it cannot be
wonderful that its punishment in Purgatory should
be very long indeed. They add that many souls
may pass out of this life in a state of grace, after
living for a long time in a state of sin, and so with
a great accumulation of mortal sins on their souls,
which may have to be expiated in Purgatory.
Then, each venial sin requires some punishment,
and of these there may be almost a countless
multitude, making up an all but endless debt to
the justice of God.

6. They ask, in the last place, what is to be
thought as to the question, whether the great
majority of Christians do much or little while alive
to cancel the debt which they thus owe? It is not
likely that persons who lead careless lives, who
make almost an open profession of thinking it
enough to aim at, to keep out of mortal sin who
approach the sacraments but seldom, and then

without perfect dispositions, who hardly ever think of doing penance or making up for their sins by almsdeeds and prayers and acts of charity, can do much in the ordinary course of things towards paying the debt of satisfaction which will otherwise be exacted from them in Purgatory. It seems as if the souls who pass out of this world without having some debt still to pay are very few indeed, and there are a great many revelations among the lives of the saints which seem to imply that many, who are thought very perfect here, by reason of their state of life or of their devotion to good works and the service of God, are yet found by the Just Judge of all, before Whom they stand, to be in need of great purification, lasting for a long time. There are doubts as to the power of attrition without the Sacrament of Penance to cancel venial sin, and satisfactions do not apply to sins which have never been retracted. The ordinary manner of Confession of venial sins, especially of the lighter sort, and of those which are habitual, is often very much wanting in sorrow, even in the case of persons who approach the sacraments frequently. And there are many common defects in the use of the sacraments, both of Penance and of Holy Communion, which prevent those great fountains of remission from producing their full effect upon the soul. And the same may be said of the great treasure of Indulgences, which also are only applied to sins which have been in some way positively withdrawn and retracted. All these arguments tend to show that there may frequently be a very long Purgatory indeed awaiting persons who are not simply sinners reclaimed to God at the last moment and saved by the sacraments of the Church, but who have spent their lives more or less in the practice of Christian virtues and the service of God.

7. Such pictures as that which is suggested by the foregoing considerations require to be balanced, as it were, by others, which might represent to us the manifold provisions of God for the remission of sins in its fullest sense, provisions which are within the reach of men while yet on earth, and which also operate most powerfully—by His gracious arrangement, moving the hearts of His children to the charity towards the departed which it is the great object of these pages to promote—in favour of those who have been careless as to their own best interests during their lifetime. Let the reasons for thinking that Purgatory is often very long indeed be as powerful as they are represented to be, they are only all the more imperative calls on our charity towards those who now cannot help themselves.

8. We may therefore consider the sufferings of these Holy Souls as figured to us in the case of this poor leper, especially in those circumstances of his case which have been mentioned—the loathsomeness and disfigurement which have passed over the soul, so beautiful by nature and so far more beautiful by grace ; the pain of separation from the homes to which they belong, where they are loved and longed for with an affection which

far exceeds anything that can be found upon earth, and the extreme and weary length to which their banishment may be protracted by the justice of God. It is quite certain that unless that justice be settled in some other way, the sentence of our Lord, that they are not to come out "until they have paid the last farthing," must be executed. It is certain also that there are many very startling statements made by the Saints and the ascetical writers as to the length of time during which many very good souls are sometimes detained. We have already mentioned that some Catholic writers have said that our Lord does not allow to the intercession of the Saints the power which it might have, if the laws of His justice and their own intense love for all that He has ordained were not opposed to the immediate and constant emptying of Purgatory by means of their prayers. But it is certain also that our Lord has as great a goodwill towards them, and far greater, than that which He showed at the prayer of the poor leper, and that His Heart is constantly saying of them, "I will that they may be set free." Only in this case it is not the sufferers themselves that are to make the petition, for they cannot ask for themselves. It is by means of our prayers and good works offered for them that this yearning desire of the Sacred Heart for the abridgment of their long time of banishment, of that living death which they lead in Purgatory, is to be brought about. And here again comes in the consideration of our own great advantage, which is involved in the charity for

H

which the present life is the appointed time. The exercise of this charity may well win us the grace to be so careful in our own service to God, as to incur but little debt to His justice, or to cancel at once what we do incur. And our Lord will certainly remember His own promise, if He sees us suffering long in Purgatory, by returning to us in abundant measure the mercy which we have shown to others.

_____

CHAPTER X.

The Holy Souls and the Sacrament of Penance.

(THE HEALING OF THE PARALYTIC.)

St. Matt. ix. 1—6 ; St. Mark ii. 1—14 ; St. Luke v. 17—26.

1. THERE seems to be little doubt that the miracle of which we are now to speak, followed very soon after that of the healing of the leper. And the former miracle may have been intended, in the Providence of God, to prepare the minds of those who witnessed it or heard of it for the next great wonder which was to display, in a still more marvellous manner, the power with which the Sacred Humanity of our Lord was endowed. This miracle is one of the most remarkable in the whole glorious cycle of the works of power and mercy displayed by our Blessed Lord—not so much on account of the actual difficulty of the cure which was wrought, as on account of the circumstances

which attended it, both on the part of those who
procured the miracle by their faith, and on the
part of our Lord, Who made the marvel which was
evident to the eye a symbol and a proof of the
other wonder which was wrought in the soul of the
poor sufferer, who was brought to have his body
delivered from paralysis, and who went away, not
only in perfect health of body, but also with the
sins, by which his soul had been stained, forgiven
and absolved.

2. The circumstances to which we refer are
stated by the three Evangelists thus. Our Lord
had returned, after an absence of some time, to
Capharnaum. He was teaching in a house—not,
as it seems, the synagogue—and St. Luke describes
the occasion as one of unwonted solemnity. He
sat teaching, and " there were also Pharisees and
Doctors of the Law sitting by, that were come out
of every town of Galilee, and from Judæa, and
Jerusalem, and the power of the Lord was to heal
them." It may perhaps have been the case, that they
had heard of the new Teacher, or even of the miracle
on the leper, which had attracted so much notice,
and some of them may have been deputed from
Jerusalem to examine into the claims He had
advanced. "And behold," four men "brought
in a bed a man who had the palsy, and they sought
means to bring him in and lay him before Him.
And when they could not find by what way they
might bring him in, because of the multitude, they
went up on the roof, and let him down through the
tiles with his bed in the midst before Jesus." Our

Lord, "seeing their faith, said to the man sick of the palsy, Be of good heart, son, thy sins are forgiven thee." This was a claim hitherto unheard of among the Jews. The priests of the Old Law could offer sacrifices for sin, and purify the people from ceremonial defilements—they could expiate external transgressions of the Law, they could examine the leprosy, which was so perfect a type of sin, as we have seen, and declare it to be healed—but they had no power to cleanse the soul and absolve the sinner. Nor is there any ground for thinking that the bearers of the paralyzed man were any different from the rest of the multitude assembled to hear our Lord teach, as to their belief on this point. It does not seem that they had any thought of what our Lord would do, when they laid the poor sick man before Him, with so much faith. Nor need it be thought that he himself expected more than the relief of his bodily ailments. The words of our Lord alarmed and half scandalized the Scribes and Doctors who heard them, but there was not at this time any open and pronounced opposition to Him on their part, and it seems that they said nothing except in their own hearts: "Who is this that speaketh blasphemies? Who can forgive sins, but God alone?" It was for the very purpose of showing them that God had given to the Son of Man power to forgive sins—a power which He was to leave behind Him in His Church, to be administered for the benefit of the faithful by men like themselves—that our Lord had used words which were so startling to them: "Which

Jesus presently knowing in His spirit, that they so thought within themselves, He saith to them, Why think you these things in your hearts? Which is easier to say to the sick of the palsy, Thy sins are forgiven thee, or to say, Arise, take up thy bed and walk? But that you may know that the Son of Man hath power on earth to forgive sins, He saith to the sick of the palsy, I say to thee, Arise, take up thy bed and go into thy house. And immediately he arose, and taking up his bed went his way in the sight of all, so that all wondered and glorified God, saying, We never saw the like," or as St. Matthew puts it, "glorified God that gave such power to men."

3. This great miracle contains so many heads of sacred doctrine, that it would be impossible for us to attempt to exhaust its teaching in a few pages. But, as before, we may select one or two points which have a special bearing on the general subject of these chapters. In the first place, then, it is clear that if the disease of leprosy represents the state of sin in the respect of the loathsomeness which it brings with it, the length of time during which its punishment may be continued in the justice of God, and in the distressing separation, which it inflicts upon those who have to suffer for it, from their homes in Heaven and the loving society which awaits them there, this affliction of paralysis may well be taken as a figure of the state of sin in other respects—especially that of the loss of the power of motion and sensation which it induces, reducing its victims to that helpless con-

dition which is represented here by the man who
could not move himself to seek the aid of our
Lord's merciful power, so that he had need of the
charity of others to make him capable of receiving
the benefit which he required.   This is especially
true of the effect of sin unatoned for in this life,
and which has to be paid for in the fires of
Purgatory.   For it is a part of God's just decree
concerning such sufferers, that they cannot even
pray for themselves.   We therefore are the bearers
of these blessed souls of whose aid they have need,
in order that the mercy of God may be extended
to them.   And indeed their state may well be
called a state of paralysis, inasmuch as they live
indeed to God, and have a number of wonderful
capacities of enjoying Him and exercising the
functions of the life which is that of the saints and
angels in Heaven, and yet they are for the time
as dead persons, incapable of motion or sensation.
All the glorious operations of the state of beatitude
are theirs as it were in germ, and yet they are not
allowed to develope their powers or to enter on
their possession.   And if it moves us to compassion to see a man in the full bloom and beauty
of his age, struck down by paralysis, and fastened
in utter helplessness to a sick-bed, unable to move
or use the limbs and faculties which yet remain
in their entirety to him, surely it is much more
pitiable to see souls that might be enjoying God
and glorifying Him by that full and perfect intensity
of spiritual activity in which the life of the Saints
consists, unable to move or feel, as it were, them-

selves deprived of so much strength and enjoyment, and making the whole company of Heaven
wait for the glory which God is to derive from
their entrance into the state of beatitude which
He has prepared for them. We may surely well
call those four bearers blessed, who by their faith
enabled our Lord to work this miracle, so beautiful
in itself and so full of spiritual and doctrinal
teaching. And yet is their blessing greater than
that which is within the reach of us all, who have
so many means of bringing these helpless but
most dear victims of God's justice within the range
of His merciful indulgence, ever so ready to pour
itself out upon them, if we give it the opportunity?
Some pious persons, who are moved especially
to give themselves to the relief of the Holy Souls,
make it a rule, if possible, to exert themselves in
favour of these prisoners of the justice of God in
four several ways, as if to honour our Lord by
commemorating the four bearers in this miracle—
they remember the Holy Souls by offering for
them at least a part of the satisfaction of the Mass
which they say or hear, or the Holy Communion
which they receive, they give them a share in their
prayers, in their good works or almsdeeds, and in
their penances or sufferings of whatever kind—
under which head Indulgences may be included—
voluntary or involuntary. And in this way they
do something every day towards performing this
work of mercy, of which we have so beautiful an
image in the act of faith of these four bearers of
the paralytic.

4. But it must be remembered that the great object of our Lord in the performance of this miracle seems to have been to unfold to those who witnessed it, many of whom were among the appointed teachers of the holy people, the great doctrine of the power of the remission of sins, which had been conferred on His Sacred Humanity by God the Father. We should not, therefore, apply to the subject of Purgatory the peculiar lesson of this miracle, unless we considered the bearing of that doctrine on the state and sufferings of those who are detained there. We have already said that a great part of the interior sufferings of the Holy Souls must probably consist in their deep regret for the many opportunities of grace which they have let pass without availing themselves of them. Their love of God makes them grieve over all that has separated them from Him, and especially over every neglect of which they have been guilty of His tender provisions for their spiritual benefit. And certainly to none of the blessed ordinances of God can this regret apply with greater force than to the holy Sacrament of Penance. Well indeed may the people who witnessed the miracle, when they considered the power of which it proved the existence, have given glory to God Who had given such power to men! For it is certain that a right and perfect use of the holy sacrament of which we are speaking would enable us to obtain such absolute forgiveness of our sins, in the sense in which our Lord used the terms, as to reduce to very little indeed the claims

of the justice of God against us in the next world.
When we meditated on the miracle of the Healing
of the Leper, we had occasion to remind ourselves
of the great number of lighter sins, as we count
them, of which we daily make ourselves guilty, and
of which we do not receive pardon here in the
sense of remission of the pain due for them,
because they are sins of habit or character, hardly
noticed or not seriously retracted and repented of.
For there must be some sorrow where there has
been any wilfulness in the sin which is confessed,
some distinct and true desire and intention to
refrain from it for the future, if it is to be cancelled
entirely, both as to its guilt and as to the penalty
due to it.   But what is the reason why these sins,
which we call venial, are not got rid of altogether
as to their debt to God's justice by persons who
are frequently approaching the sacraments, especially the Sacrament of Penance?   It is because
that sacrament is not perfectly used, because it is
shorn of some of its effects and the power which
our Lord has imparted to it, on account of the
careless or hasty or otherwise imperfect manner in
which we use it.

5. It may be well to insist on this with ourselves.
It is quite possible that every confession which is
made may be so made that the sins which are
then brought to the sacred tribunal may be
entirely cancelled, not only as to their guilt,
but also as to their pain.   It is the intention
of our Lord that so it should be, partly by
virtue of the intensity of the sorrow which is

applied to the sins confessed, partly by virtue of the absolution, and the satisfactory power which is communicated to the works enjoined by the priest by way of penance, which power is greatly extended by the general words with which the form of absolution concludes, by which whatever good we do, and whatever evil we bear with patience, are raised, as it were, to the rank of satisfactory works. If persons who have been in the habit of frequenting the sacraments find themselves with a great debt to pay to the justice of God, it must be on account of the difficulty of using the sacraments perfectly, which comes from our own dulness and want of fervour, and of our neglect to make very frequent and very fervent acts of contrition, and to use the many means, short of the Sacrament of Penance, which God has given us for obtaining the remission of lighter sins. If a man who had daily access to the treasury of a most wealthy king had only taken each day so small a quantity therefrom as just to keep himself alive, instead of taking what might pay off all his obligations and make him altogether free from the debts of the past, he would only have himself to blame, if on a sudden emergency he found himself liable to accumulated demands without the power to meet them. Such a man would be a very inadequate image of the Christian soul which has been constantly using the sacraments, and yet has never taken their full benefit. And yet this is the reproach which the Holy

Souls of Purgatory must in so many cases have had to make against themselves. They have seen that a little more care in self-examination, a little more earnestness in their contrition for the sins which they confessed, a little more particularity and sincerity in their resolutions against the smaller faults which were habitual to them, a little more zeal in the performance of their satisfactions, and in suffering patiently the chastisements which the hand of Providence brought home to them day by day, would in the course of time have made an immense difference in diminishing gradually and surely the amount which they owed to the justice of God, Who is now forced by them, rather than by His own will, to punish them for a long time and with much severity in Purgatory, for sins which they might most easily have expiated altogether by their familiar use of the Sacrament of Penance.

6. There is also another point, connected with the Sacrament of Penance, to which it may be well to turn our thoughts for a moment while we are meditating on this miracle, although we shall probably have to speak about it at full length in a later chapter. The power of the Church to apply to the cancelling of the pain due to sin the satisfactions of our Lord and the Saints, on which power the whole system of Indulgences depends, must be considered as included in the words of our Lord, when He said that the Son of Man had power on earth

to forgive sins; and when Catholic theologians
treat of the Sacrament of Penance, they do not
conclude the subject without speaking of Indulgences. We may therefore add this thought to
those which have been already hinted at—the
thought how deeply the Holy Souls must regret
the little use which they may have made of this
immense benefit, the small space which the goodness
of God in allowing it may have occupied in their
minds, the scanty gratitude which they may have
rendered to Him for it, and the very slight efforts
which they have made to understand and appreciate
it, and to enrich themselves from the treasury which
is thus laid open to them.   This is one of the points
as to which there is the most difference between
the estimate of things which is formed in Purgatory
and that which is common even among good
Christians on earth.   And if the Holy Souls are
filled with sorrow and compunction at any neglect
of God's merciful provisions of which they may
have been themselves guilty, it is clear that their
sorrow must extend to the little thought which
they may have given to their own power, while
alive, of relieving others, then in Purgatory, by
this wonderful means.

7. Thoughts like these help to show us how
very profitable to our own souls is the devotion
which has for its object the relief of the sufferers
in Purgatory.   It is hardly possible for any one
to take their case to heart without being moved
strongly to greater care for himself.   The Holy
Souls, whom we aid to the best of our power,

will also aid us, both when they reach Heaven and before, and in this way also, our charity will turn to our own great benefit. They will pray for us, that we may have greater grace to be most careful in our approaches to the sacraments, and every step that we make in the more perfect use of the means of grace will make us more powerful to aid them, because we shall be nearer and dearer to God, and so able to win more from His ineffable love and mercy.

CHAPTER XI.

The Application of our Suffrages to certain Souls in particular.

(CURE OF THE MAN AT THE PROBATIC POOL.)

St. John v. 1—15.

1. IT appears that, not long after the miracle which has last been mentioned—the healing of the paralytic man who was let down in his bed. into the inner court of the house in which our Lord was teaching—He went up to Jerusalem for the celebration of the feast of the Pasch. It was now, then, just a year since He had taken on Himself publicly the office of Teacher and Prophet in the Holy City itself, by the wonderful exercise of authority which had been shown in the act of cleansing the Temple. By far the greater part of

this year had been spent by Him, as we have seen, in Galilee, at a distance from Jerusalem—from the neighbourhood of which He had retired, in order not to provoke too soon or too much the enmity of the Jewish authorities. At the time, however, at which we have now arrived, our Lord was following what we should call a bolder course, and was claiming for Himself, both by act and word, an authority which was not likely to be at once recognized by men so full of ambition and pride as the Chief Priests and Pharisees at Jerusalem. A notable example of a claim to authority hitherto unheard of, is that on which we meditated in the last chapter—His claim to forgive sins upon earth. The miracle of which we are now to speak is another such instance, at least in so far as it asserted an entire independence of the usual interpretation put by the Jews and their teachers on the law of the Sabbath. When our Lord came to explain, in answer to His accusers, the grounds of His conduct, we shall see that He put forward claims which went far beyond this.

2. It was, then, at this great feast, the second in the course of His Public Ministry, that our Lord went on the Sabbath day to a famous pool of water at Jerusalem, around which there were five porticoes or colonnades, under which a large multitude of sick persons, suffering from almost every form of disease, were lying, in expectation of an opportunity which might possibly lead, in the case of any one, to his relief. For an angel went down at certain times into the pool, and moved the

water, and then the first person who stepped into it after the movement was healed of whatever the disease might be which afflicted him. It was but a chance, for only one among so many could be healed, and we may well imagine how that large collection of sufferers must have moved the tender and compassionate Heart of our Lord. If it had been in Galilee they would probably have all called on Him with one voice to aid them as soon as He appeared; but in Jerusalem He was very little known, and He seems to have entered the place quietly and without any crowd of companions which might attract notice. The miracle which He was about to perform was altogether unsolicited. He did not require prayer or faith, except so far as the latter was implied in the obedience of the man whom He selected as the subject of His miraculous cure. This miracle, then, like many others, was wrought by our Lord for a special purpose of His own, just as He had turned to a like purpose the incidents of the last-mentioned miracle, and made the faith of the bearers of the paralytic give Him an occasion for proving His authority as to the forgiveness of sins. Thus, He did not heal all or many of those who lay around this pool at Jerusalem, but He selected a single sufferer as the object of His compassion. Again, He did not simply heal him, and then pass away; He laid on Him a special injunction to take up his bed and carry it to his home—an act which was certain to attract attention at any time, but which on that particular day was also certain to cause a kind of scandal, inasmuch as it was an act which was considered to be forbidden, and a breach of the Divine commandment. This act had the effect which our Lord must have foreseen. It brought upon Him the complaints and hostility of the Jewish rulers, and gave Him an occasion for setting forth to them the proofs of His Divine Mission in a long discourse which St. John relates, and for the sake of which, according to his usual principle in the composition of his Gospel, it seems to have been that he inserted the account of the miracle itself.

3. The particular truth which our Lord meant to assert by means of this miracle does not concern us at this moment, for we are engaged in the consideration of His miracles only as far as they may be used as illustrations of the Catholic doctrine of Purgatory. But there is one particular circumstance about the miracle which will furnish us with abundant matter for thought in respect of that doctrine. It has already been said that our Lord, Who might, if it had so pleased Him, have healed at a word the whole of the crowd of sufferers who were waiting for the movement of the waters, chose one only as the object of His special compassion. We have no right at all to think that this one person was more deserving of so high a favour than many others, on account of any special sanctity, or resignation to God's will, or contrition for the sins, which may have been punished by his Providential affliction. But two circumstances in the case are mentioned, one by himself, and the

other by the Evangelist, which seem to distinguish him from the rest of the crowd; and, as these circumstances are specially mentioned, it is not presumptuous to suppose that they may have had weight in his favour in the mind of our Lord Himself. In the first place, St. John tells us that he had been afflicted by his infirmity for as many as thirty-eight years, and that our Lord saw him lying there, and knew that he had been a long time. In the second place, the sick man himself furnishes us with another circumstance, when he tells our Lord that he had no man, when the water was troubled, to put him into the pool. Thus he had been a sufferer for a very great number of years, and he was also remarkably helpless and left altogether to himself. It may have been the case that our Lord selected him from the crowd on account of both these circumstances; certainly, it seems as if St. John meant us to understand that the first of them influenced the merciful tenderness of His Sacred Heart. Thus we have in this miracle both the principle of a selection of one from among many for the objects of Christian charity, and also the grounds on which, among others, preference may be given to this or that particular case—the length of time during which the suffering has been protracted, and the helpless and friendless state of some individual sufferer. From each of these heads we may derive some instruction as to the application of our spiritual alms in favour of the Holy Souls who are suffering in Purgatory.

4. In the first place, then, it is certain that the

I

satisfactions which may be applied to the relief of these holy sufferers are limited in their efficacy, either in themselves, as is the case with works which are simply our own, though wrought through God's grace, or in the decrees and arrangements of God Himself, as is the case with the satisfactory power of the Holy Sacrifice, infinite in itself, but not so in its application. Thus, when we visit in spirit this pool of holy punishment, by which so great a multitude of souls are lying, as it were, waiting for the movement of the refreshing waters of God's mercy, we may feel like persons who have but one boon to give, and who should therefore be guided in its application by some reasons of justice or wisdom. Our Lord, if He had chosen, might have healed at once all that suffering crowd ; but He did not so choose. In like manner, the application of His meritorious satisfactions to the Holy Souls, which is intrusted by Him to us, is limited by His own decree. The choice as to their application is left by Him very much in our hands for many wise and Divine reasons. All these reasons we need not attempt to fathom. It is enough to say, out of other things which might be said, that the thoughtful and careful application of our good works to particular intentions is a thing very pleasing to Him. It helps on devotion, it fosters charity, it gives us many opportunities of making reparation, or of showing gratitude and love, and every such act strengthens in the soul the virtue of which it is an act, while at the same time it forms a new link in that

marvellous chain of charity by which our whole
life is in His intention bound together, the full
effect of which is to knit us one to another in the
Communion of Saints. It is not contrary to this
truth that it is often our best wisdom to pray in
general for the conversion of sinners, or the advancement of the good in perfection, or for the
Souls in Purgatory, without any specification of this
or that person. These practices work in the same
way, and Christian piety has room both for one
and for the other. The Church teaches us to be
always honouring God in His great mercies to us
through our Lord, but she also sets before us one by
one the mysteries of His Life and Passion, and of
their fruits. She teaches us to honour all His Saints
in one great festival, and day by day throughout
the year she sets before us, one by one, the same
Saints in order, as if for the moment our desire
was to be to honour that particular Saint alone. We
gain in devotion if we offer Masses or Communions
or Indulgences or good works for the Holy Souls
in general, or for those in particular for whom we
are especially bound to pray, or for those whom
it may please our Lady or some one of the Saints
that we should especially succour in this way; and
in this last case we knit ourselves each time by
a fresh tie of love, not only to the souls for whom
we intercede, but also to our Blessed Lady or to
the Saints in whose honour we offer that good
work. Thus the whole spiritual doctrine of the
value of spiritual intentions in all that we do for
the honour of God or the good of souls is brought

before us by this instance in which our Lord selected one poor sufferer, out of so large a multitude, as the subject of the work of mercy which He was about to do in the course of that great series of manifestations of Himself which was so essential to the accomplishment of His work in the world. It was in accordance with the counsels of His wisdom that one single person should be selected; but He did not, as an ordinary man might have done, take the first person on whom His eyes might fall and work the miracle on him. He made a selection according to the instincts and judgments of His own ineffably wise and loving Heart.

5. Before we proceed to examine what may have been our Blessed Lord's principle of selection, so to speak, on this particular occasion, we must remind ourselves that we are not always free as to the choices which we have to make in this respect. There are often considerations of justice or of natural equity which may come in to guide us imperatively in this matter. There are souls to whom we owe more than to others; our parents, our near relations, our teachers, those who have laboured for and waited on us, those who have set us good example, those who have had to suffer on our account, those whose benefits and good works we inherit, as the founders of colleges, those who have given alms and made pious foundations of other sorts by which we profit, those, in short, whose debtors we are in any of the almost numberless ways in which such obligations can

arise. We need not speak of such obligations as constitute a strict debt of justice, for in that case the obligation could not be neglected without sin. But there may be others who have claims upon us in the sight of God, for whom He would have us pray, as showing thereby the virtue of gratitude which is so extremely pleasing to Him ; or again, charity in a particular manner, as our enemies, or even because in some cases we have been responsible in His sight for some of the acts which cause them suffering now. Thus, if we have ever neglected any duty of example or warning or correction, if we have ever connived at faults, or occasioned them, by provocations to anger or any other sin, delayed others in their conversion to a better life, or encouraged them to pay little attention to some Divine call, to put off the settling of some matter of conscience which was urgent, or, as happens frequently in the case of persons approaching the Church, used human motives or the pressure of earthly interests to keep them back from any sacrifice which God requires of them—then indeed we have a debt to them which we are bound to repay to our utmost. Many a high vocation has been lost, many a call to the relinquishment of schism or heresy has been corresponded to when it has been almost but not quite too late, in consequence of the thoughtless way in which people act to one another when in difficulties of this kind. And, to turn to another head, we have great obligations, accruing in the course of our lives, to a great number of persons of whom perhaps we think but little in our prayers —men whose books, or whose sermons, or whose example, have done us good and helped us on, and who may now be in need of our assistance in their time of suffering and expiation. Thoughtfulness in all this matter cannot but be very pleasing to God—and at all events we may be sure that it will be well sometimes to offer our Masses or our satisfactions for those for whom God would have us offer them, in order that we may practise this virtue of repaying as best we can the blessings we have received.

6. Having thus far reminded ourselves of the obligations under which we may lie, and which may guide our selection in the allotment of the spiritual alms which we have to distribute, we may return to the lesson which our Lord gives us, not only as to the thoughtfulness in general with which this selection should be made, but also as to the particular motives which seem to have influenced Him on this occasion. The two circumstances, already mentioned, which were peculiar in the case of the sick man who was selected as the subject of the miracle, were the length of time during which he had suffered, and his entire want of human aid. If we apply this thought to the case of the Holy Souls, we are at once struck with the ease with which the lessons of which we are in search are furnished to us. Something has already been said, in the chapter on the Healing of the Leper, of the great length of time to which the suffering in Purgatory may be extended, and the

books of holy writers on the subject are full of
very grave warnings upon this point. Thus;
Christian devotion has often felt itself moved
in a special manner to the relief of the souls which
have been the longest in Purgatory, or of those
who owe the longest debt to God's justice, unless,
it be cancelled otherwise than by their own
sufferings. "Woe is me, that my sojourning is
prolonged!" is the cry of such souls, and we
cannot think of such words without remembering
at the same time that even a comparatively short
period of suffering there is felt as immensely long,
on account of the intensity of their pain, or of the
burning desire which they feel for the enjoyment
of God. Both these circumstances have the effect
of making what is already long seem even longer
than it is. Again, the touching words of the sick
man in this miracle, "Lord, I have no man!"
apply very beautifully to the case of others among
the holy prisoners of Purgatory. It is very sad to
know, as we do by experience, how very soon the
memory of the departed fades away from the
hearts of men. It may be one of the things at
which the angels marvel most. The deadening
effect of the impressions of present and sensible
interests upon the traces left on our hearts even by
the deepest of our affections and the strongest
claims on our gratitude, is a thing which makes us
sometimes wonder whether we have hearts at all.
Sometimes, again, our own want of remembrance
of the departed who have claims on our assistance,
may be allowed in the just Providence of God to

act in our own case, when our time of need may
come, in turning away from us the thoughts of
those whom we may leave behind us. With the
same measure which we have used towards others
will the aid which we ourselves need so much be
meted out to us.

7. But, to conclude with a practical suggestion,
there are often other circumstances which may
produce the same effect on the holy sufferers in
Purgatory without so much of cause in faults of
their own as of others. For they may pass away
into the next world at a time or in a place where
many of the ordinary means of help to the departed
are comparatively wanting. Thus, for instance,
the Catholic parents of the generation in this
country which witnessed the change of religion
from Catholicism to Protestantism, must have been
largely defrauded of what may be called their
natural rights in this respect. The same may be
said of our own Catholic forefathers during the
centuries of persecution, when there were so few
priests in the country, and when it was so difficult
for Catholics to hear Mass or to approach the
sacraments. To such persons we owe the incalculable debt which their constancy in keeping to the
faith has entailed upon us; but they could have
had little aid, ordinarily speaking, from those who
came immediately after them in the inheritance of
that faith. The same thing may be said of a great
number of persons who are secretly converted to
Catholicism, perhaps on their death-beds, while
their families and friends remain Protestants. The

same is true of the number of souls, known to God alone, who die outside the visible pale of the Church, but who have been baptized, and have by His mercy either been preserved from mortal sin, or visited with interior grace sufficient to enable them to reconcile themselves to Him by adequate sorrow before they die, and whose good faith makes them, as the Fathers say, belong to the soul of the Church, though not to its body. In all these cases there are no suffrages offered for the departed. Their friends and kinsfolk may not forget them, but they have never been taught how much they stand in need of prayer. For it is the invariable device of Satan in the introduction of false and imperfect creeds, to shut the eyes of men as much as possible to the claims of God's justice, as well as to the provisions of His mercy for the relief of misery of every kind. These thoughts are sufficient to indicate a number of other cases in which the words of the sufferer in this Gospel narrative, "Lord, I have no man!" are true of certain among the Holy Souls of Purgatory, and thus to point them out as especial objects of the compassionate and thoughtful charity of the children of the Church.

CHAPTER XII.

The Holy Souls especially helped by prayers on Festivals and Anniversaries.

(THE CURE OF THE MAN WITH THE WITHERED HAND.)

St. Matt. xii. 9—14 ; St. Mark iii. 1–6 ; St. Luke vi. 6—11.

1. WE have seen that our Lord healed the poor man whom He found lying in one of the porches of the Probatic Pool on the Sabbath day, although the lesson with regard to the doctrine of Purgatory which was drawn from that miracle did not refer to the particular point. The student of the Life of our Lord will be aware that, just at the period of which we are speaking, He took occasion, more than once or twice, to assert very clearly, by word and action, that the Jewish tradition which seemed to forbid the exercise of good works on the Sabbath, if they were ever so little laborious in themselves, was a false tradition, and one by which He was not Himself in any way bound. It was soon after the miracle at the Probatic Pool that the disciples were blamed by the Pharisees for plucking the ears of corn and rubbing them in their hands on the Sabbath. On this occasion our Lord again defended Himself for permitting this, as He had defended Himself most formally and

at great length at Jerusalem after the working of
the miracle lately mentioned. It seems also to
have been a little later, after His return to
Galilee, that He worked the miracle on which we
are now to comment, with the same purpose of
enlightening men as to the observance of the
Sabbath, and with the result—which appears to
have been the reason why the three historical
Evangelists all mention the occurrence—of driving
His enemies to the mad and impious step of
making a plot against His life.

2. One circumstance is found the same in all
the miracles wrought by our Lord on the Sabbath
day—that is, that He worked them unasked, except
so far as the simple presence of the poor sufferers
was a silent but eloquent prayer to His Sacred
Heart. He worked them in different parts of the
country, as if it had been a special object with
Him to draw attention everywhere to the doctrine
which He taught and the authority which He
claimed about the Sabbath. In their narratives
of the miracle of which we are speaking, the
Evangelists tell us that He went into the synagogue
on the Sabbath, and that there was then present
a man who had a withered hand. The Pharisees
and others watched Him to see what He would
do, for the question raised by His act at Jerusalem at the Probatic Pool had already made a
great stir. St. Matthew tells us that His enemies
actually put the question to Him, whether it was
lawful to heal on that day. This must refer to
some few of the party, for the other Evangelists

only mention that they watched Him, and that
He knew their thoughts, and asked them the
question Himself, whether it was lawful on the
Sabbath to do good or bad, to save life or destroy
it? They were silent, and then He probably
added, as St. Matthew tells us, the words which
imply His own answer, asking them which of
them would not help out a sheep which had fallen
into a pit on the Sabbath—how much better was a
man than a sheep ! St. Mark tells us that He looked
round with anger, being grieved at their blindness of
heart. Then our Lord bade the man with the
withered hand stand in the midst, and asked
them the same question, as if to show that He was
about to answer it by deed as well as by word. He
bade the man stretch forth his hand; he did so,
and it was made whole.

3. It is not our business here to draw out our
Lord's reasons, as far as we can divine them, for
thus insisting, in the teeth of opposition, on the
Christian liberty of doing good on the Sabbath
day. But we may gather from it a very profitable
and practical head of instruction as to our own
special subject of Purgatory, by reminding ourselves that the Sabbath day, in our Lord's Life,
represented to Him the great chain of festivals, the
anniversaries of His mysteries, and the like, which
was afterwards to exist in His Church, and that
He was about to enact, as it were, the law of the
Sabbath in a new form, in the institution of all the
ecclesiastical festivals and solemnities with which
we are so familiar. The Church, acting by the

authority over the Sabbath which belonged to Him as the Son of Man, was to transfer the observance from the seventh day of the week to the first, as well as to spiritualise the mode in which the precept of the Sabbatical rest was to be obeyed. Our Lord was looking forward to this feature in His Kingdom in all that He did and said with regard to the Sabbath. It seems to have moved Him even to anger and indignation when He saw His critics so blind of heart as to object to the performance of works of active mercy on that day. But we may venture to think that He might not perhaps have acted or spoken so strongly in opposition to the religious prejudices of the Jews, unless He had meant to insist on a principle which directly contravened those prejudices—the principle that feasts and holy days and religious solemnities and commemorations were to be times of rejoicing and of spiritual activity, great occasions for the exercise of mercy and charity on the part of Christians, and for the bountiful diffusion of graces and spiritual gifts on the part of God. Thus Christians have always considered that they might hope for special and large gifts of grace on occasion of the great solemnities of the ecclesiastical year, the days on which the chief mysteries of our Lord or of His Blessed Mother or of the Saints are commemorated. The Church encourages this belief in a number of different ways, one of which, which has especial relation to our own subject, is the connecting her greater Indulgences with the more solemn feasts. Thus it may be said to be a principle of the new Kingdom of our Lord, that the great acts and mercies of God, whether in the life of our Lord Himself, or in the lives of His Saints, or in the history of the Church, should have each their special commemoration, as the great consummation of the work of Creation had its special commemoration in the observance of the Sabbath. But the observance of the Sabbath was not a simple commemoration, it was also an institution full of benefit to mankind for many various reasons. Indeed, there can be no such institution in the Kingdom of God as a simple commemoration of past mercies, which is not also an occasion for the obtaining of fresh benefits from His inexhaustible and ineffable goodness.   And, in the same way, the festivals of our Lord, His Mother, and the Saints, which are occasions of intense joy to the Church in Heaven and on earth, are also intended by God to be opportunities which He may take, in His infinite bountifulness, of pouring out ever fresh and fresh blessings upon those who celebrate them devoutly.

4. There are many reasons for thinking that, among the many ways in which we may please God at such times, that of praying especially for the deliverance of the Holy Souls is not the least. This act of mercy belongs, it may seem, as of right to the great moments of triumph in our Lord's history, and to the anniversaries which celebrate them. It is thought by many holy writers that, on Holy Saturday, after our Lord's descent " into the lower

parts of the earth," as St. Paul speaks, He not only set free from their captivity the Saints who were detained in Limbus, but that He also made His presence felt in Purgatory by the deliverance either of all the souls which were then suffering pain, or at least, as St. Thomas seems to think, of all those who by their faith and devotion while alive had merited that He should so deliver them. St. Vincent Ferrer says that if the number of the delivered from Purgatory on that occasion were measured by rigorous justice, it would not extend beyond these last mentioned; but that if it were measured by the sweetness of God's mercy, all would have been set free. It is also the opinion of many Doctors that, when our Blessed Lady was dying, she obtained from her Son the liberation of all that were then in Purgatory, who accompanied her to Heaven in the triumph of her glorious Assumption. It is said by some that she exercises her loving power in favour of the souls in Purgatory on every feast of her Assumption, and even on all her feasts, and on those of the Nativity and Resurrection of her Divine Son. We find also privileges of the same kind attributed by holy writers to some of the Saints, as St. Lawrence, who delivers a soul every Friday, and St. Francis of Assisi, who is allowed to deliver his own religious children on his annual feast-day. The number of instances in which some such privileges are mentioned in the Lives of the Saints and in other such books, seems to show us that it is according to the mind of the Church to think that these privileges exist, and that it is usual for the favourite servants of God to be allowed such powers at the times of their feasts. If we put by the side of this the other fact, already mentioned, of the habit of the Church to attach special Indulgences to works of piety on such days, we have quite enough to encourage us to hope that it is greatly pleasing to God that we should make such days occasions for exerting ourselves in some special manner for the relief of the Holy Souls. We may say to ourselves those words of our Lord, " How much is a soul better than a sheep ; " and if at times of rejoicing, and on occasions which remind us of mercies which we have received even in the natural order—birthdays, wedding days, and the like—we think it well to give alms, or to exercise the rite of hospitality, or the duty of visiting the sick and the afflicted, we may surely hope with great confidence that God will hear our prayers and accept our thanksgivings more readily, if we make it a point never to let a holy day or festival season pass away without endeavouring to make the Saints and the Holy Souls partakers in our feast, the latter by the prayers or good works or Masses which we offer for their deliverance, the former by the accidental glory which redounds to them when such offerings are made in their honour, and when their glorious company in Heaven is increased by fresh arrivals from Purgatory.

CHAPTER XIII.

The Holy Souls specially helped by works for the Service of the Church.

(THE HEALING OF THE CENTURION'S SERVANT.)

St. Matt. viii. 5—15; St. Luke vii. 1—10.

1. THE next of our Lord's miracles in order of time, after the miracle in the synagogue of which we spoke in the last chapter, seems to have been the healing of the centurion's servant. This took place after an interval of at least some weeks, during which our Lord was absent from Capharnaum, and in which we must place the great event of the delivery of His Sermon on the Plain, and the still more important event which immediately preceded it—the election of the twelve Apostles. It is natural to suppose that after some time spent in His usual course of missionary preaching our Lord returned for a short rest to Capharnaum. Here, as the Gospel narrative tells us, He was applied to by the chief Jews, the rulers of the synagogue, and the like, in favour of a person who was too modest to come to Him himself, partly on account of his sense of unworthiness, partly because he did not belong to the sacred nation. He was a Gentile officer, probably a Roman, in command of some small force in the

J

city, and it seems that he must have been a
dweller there for some time.   He had become
acquainted with the Jewish society of the place, he
had taken an interest in their religion, to which he
had probably become a proselyte, and he had
shown his attachment to it and to them by more
than one good work, especially by having built
them their synagogue at his own expense. He had
heard of our Lord—it is very likely that he had
heard of Him as a teacher, and not only as a
worker of miracles, for the story of his application
to our Lord seems to show that he knew the
nobleman whose son our Lord had healed at
a distance, before the formal beginning of His
Galilæan preaching, and had caught from him the
special lesson of faith which had been insisted on
in his case.   If this is so, it is not likely that the
nobleman would have been backward to speak to
him of his own belief as to our Lord's Divine
Mission. The centurion, however, was now anxious
about the health of one of his servants, of whom
we are not told whether he was or was not a Jew.
The servant was lying under a violent attack of
paralysis, in great pain, and not far from death.
Under these circumstances the master went to the
chief Jews, as has been said, and asked them to
intercede for him with our Lord.   This they did
very willingly, representing that he was a lover of
their nation, and had built them the synagogue. We
need not go through the whole series of details
which are related by the two Evangelists. Our
Lord said at once that He would come and heal

the sufferer, but He was met on the way, first by
some friends sent by the centurion, and then by
the centurion himself, begging Him not to put
Himself so much out as to come, for he was well
aware of his own unworthiness to receive Him
under his roof, and also that our Lord could heal
as well by a word as by His presence, at a distance
as well as on the spot. He was himself, he said, a
man both under authority and also with some
authority of his own over his inferiors; he knew
what authority was, and he was quite sure that our
Lord had only to exercise His authority over
disease and health in any way that pleased Him,
in order to produce the effect which He desired.
"Only say the word, and my servant shall be
healed."

2. We need not pause to dwell on the intense
delight which this display of faith, and of humility
founded on faith, caused in the Sacred Heart of
our Lord. In some respects this centurion was
an earnest and foretaste to Him of the multitude
of souls who were to follow him in his ready and
generous faith, and to come, as He said to His
disciples, from the east and west, and sit down
in the Kingdom with Abraham, Isaac, and Jacob.
These considerations belong to another time. At
present we shall find abundant food for thought
in two things which seem to stand out from the
story, and to illustrate in very different ways the
doctrine to which these chapters are devoted.
These two things are suggested, the first by the
recommendation with which the Jews sought to

move our Lord's compassion in favour of the
centurion, when they said that He loved their
nation and had built them their synagogue, and
the second by the beautiful words of the centurion,
which the Church has made her own by taking
them into her own mouth at Holy Communion,
"Lord, I am not worthy that Thou shouldest enter
under my roof."

3. The first of these heads contains the whole
doctrine, so to speak, of the immense value of
good works done for the Church and her children
as such, and especially of the particular good work
of building churches and raising altars for the
worship of God and the honour of His Saints.
When the Jews put this forward as their special
ground of recommendation to our Lord in favour
of the petition of the centurion, they may perhaps
have thought that they ought to meet the objection
which might be made that the subject of their
petition was an alien to the holy people. They
may have meant to say that although he was a
Gentile, still he had deserved well of the Jewish
community. If they meant no more than this,
then we may take their words as having more
force on our Lord's Heart than they expected.
To love the holy nation of the Church, and
especially to show that love by raising the
sanctuaries of God, gives a higher title to our
Lord's goodwill than simply to belong to the
holy people. The rewards which our Lord
confers on any service done to His Kingdom or
to the worship of God, are determined and

measured by His own most magnificent liberality. He says in His charge to His Apostles,* that any one who receives a prophet in the name of a prophet shall receive the reward of a prophet— that is, he shall be dealt with by God as if he had himself done the work of the prophet whom he receives. These words indicate the law of the gratitude of God, if we may so speak, for any services of the kind of which we are speaking. They are of immense consolation to all those who have the means and the goodwill to advance the service of God by the use of wealth, influence, position, authority, and the like. Such persons have opportunities which others have not, of gaining the friendship of the saints and of our Lord Himself, and their opportunities amount to nothing less than the power to gain a share in all the good works for which they open the way by their munificence. Let us take the case, for instance, of a person who uses his wealth to build a Christian church in which the Holy Sacrifice is continually offered to God, in which the Gospel doctrine is constantly preached, in which the sacraments are administered, in which the Blessed Sacrament dwells on the altar day and night, in which prayer is almost unceasing, and in which a thousand hidden graces are imparted, hour after hour, by our Lord to His faithful worshippers. Let us take the case of a person who founds a convent in which the chosen souls of the Church may retire from the world, and give themselves

* St. Matt. x. 41.

up without interruption or distraction to that
"attendance on our Lord," of which St. Paul
speaks;* or a college in which the highest
mental culture is imparted, under the guidance
and blessing of religion, in which learning is
pursued for the sake of elucidating Scripture and
theology, in which missionaries are trained for
the glorious work of carrying the Gospel into
heathen countries, and of supplying the wants of
the sacred ministry in countries where priests are
comparatively few. In all these cases the person
who makes this holy use of the worldly goods
which God has given him, has a share, according
to our Lord's rule, in all the good that is done to
His honour in the church or convent or school
or college, or in any other work of a like kind,
which he has helped to found. And as the work
goes on for generation after generation, the founder,
or the souls to whose benefit he may wish to apply
its satisfactory power, will continue to enjoy his
share. If he be in Heaven, he will have an
accidental increase of joy for all that is done;
if he or they be in Purgatory, it cannot be
doubted that his soul or theirs will be greatly
and continually relieved, and the time of their
deliverance hastened on, by the service to God
which is daily and hourly accruing in such places
as those of which we have been speaking. God
Himself, and all the Court of Heaven, the
Blessed Virgin and the saints and the angels, as
well as the Church upon earth and her children,

* 1 Cor. vii. 35.

are his debtors, who will certainly not forget
their obligations, and who are very powerful in
their means of payment and very prompt in
using them. The best works that can be done
for the Church are those which most directly
contribute to the worship of God and the preaching of the Gospel, and those also which last on
generation after generation. We see in all this
the holy wisdom and considerate charity and
prudence of ancient times, when the foundation
of convents or colleges or schools, or the building
of churches or of chapels in churches, was a
favourite work of piety, very often indeed undertaken with a distinct and definite purpose of
providing for the relief of the souls in Purgatory.

4. Here, then, is a very practical point of
teaching concerning the way in which we may
benefit those dear to us, for whose souls we
are anxious to obtain the speedy mercy of God.
The erection of an altar in their memory, or the
foundation of Masses, or the contribution to the
maintenance of a priest, especially in parts of
the world where the Church is most in need
of support from a distance, and in countries
where it is possible for a very small annual
sum to keep a mission alive, and so to contribute
to the service of the altar under circumstances
which promise exceptionally large returns for
any labour or alms that are spent upon them—
these and other similar ways of helping the holy
sufferers are suggested by the miracle before us.
It must be remembered that any one who procures

the celebration of a Mass which would not otherwise be celebrated, does not benefit alone his own
soul or the soul for whom the Mass is offered or
that of the priest who offers it, but the whole
Church of God in Heaven, on earth, and under
the earth. This is a good deed which rejoices
God and the saints and angels, as well as the
living and the dead, and it is no wonder if the
prayers and interests of such a person are assisted
by the intercessions of all Heaven.

5. But there is another and very beautiful lesson
to be learnt from this good centurion, which illustrates one of the most suggestive points in the
whole doctrine concerning Purgatory and its
prisoners. This lesson is contained in the words
to which reference has already been made : " Lord,
I am not worthy that Thou shouldest enter under
my roof, but only say the word, and my servant
shall be healed." These words should be put by
the side of other expressions of the same kind,
which are among those breathings of the Holy
Ghost which seem most clearly to interpret the
words of St. Paul, when he says that the Holy
Spirit of God prays in us and moulds, as it were,
our petitions, so as to make them the prayers
which are acceptable to our Heavenly Father.
They are to be set by the side of the cry of the
publican of whom our Lord speaks, who would
not so much as lift his eyes to Heaven, but
smote his breast, saying, " God be merciful to
me a sinner." They belong to the same class as
the words of St. Peter in the ship—" Depart

from me, for I am a sinful man, O Lord." They
remind us of the answer of the Syrophœnician
woman, "Yea, Lord, the dogs eat of the crumbs
which fall from the master's table." These are
the petitions which have so much power over
our Lord's Sacred Heart. We are told by holy
writers on the subject of Purgatory, especially
by St. Catharine of Genoa and those who have
followed her, that the Holy Souls have so deep
a sense of their own unworthiness to meet the
eye of God in Heaven, before they are perfectly
purged from the imperfections which are consumed in the fire of Purgatory, that they would
shrink back from His Presence if it were offered
them to pass into their destined Beatitude before
the time. So intense is their love of God, and
so entirely does that affection overrule or absorb
any other, such as the desire of their own
happiness, that for His sake and for the sake
of the holiness which becometh His courts, they
cannot bear to think of anything that is unfit
being presented there.

6. We cannot doubt that this beautiful humility.
of the centurion made our Lord all the more
ready and eager to help him ; and that it was
one of the fruits of his very keen and penetrating
faith, which made him see the dignity of our Lord's
Person far more clearly than many others who
approached Him with similar petitions. So in
the same way, the intense humility of the Holy
Souls, which is founded on their charity, is one
of the causes for which our Lord's Sacred Heart

yearns after them with so extreme a love. We may, then, add this to the other motives which we have already considered as incentives to our own charitable exertions for the relief of these Holy Souls, which all tend to their speedier purification and to the hastening of the moment when the desires of our Lord's Heart may be satisfied in them.

CHAPTER XIV.

Our Blessed Lady and the Holy Souls.

(THE RAISING OF THE WIDOW'S SON.)

St. Luke vii. 11—16.

1. NOT long after the miracle on the centurion's servant, of which we spoke in the last chapter, our Lord exercised, for the first time of which we have any record, His power over life and death, by raising the dead to life. Although we have but three instances recorded for us in the Gospels in which He raised the dead, we cannot doubt that He used this power much more frequently. In the same way, although this is the earliest of these instances given by the Evangelists, we cannot be certain that no other instance, unrelated by them, had preceded it. But St. Luke had, evidently, a particular reason for inserting it here, and we may fairly consider it, for purposes of meditation, as the first. The story is so familiar to us that it hardly needs repetition. Our Lord, with His

disciples and a considerable multitude of followers, was on the road near a city called Naim. Just as He came near the gates of the town, a funeral procession met Him. The corpse was that of a young man, the only son of a widow, and a great number of her fellow-citizens were accompanying it and her to the grave. Our Lord was touched with pity at her bereavement, and bade her not to weep. Then He went up to the bier, touched it, and while the bearers stood still, He bade the young man rise up, and "he that was dead sat up, and began to speak," and our Lord "gave him to his mother."

2. The manner in which we are applying these considerations to the state of the Souls in Purgatory and the methods which may be used for their relief and release, allows us frequently to leave aside the more obvious and direct teaching of a miracle, in order to dwell upon some truth which may be represented rather than directly conveyed by the circumstances of the case. In this anecdote of the raising of the widow's son, it appears that the motive which acted on our Lord's Sacred Heart was that of compassion for the widowed mother of the young man. Our Lord may have had other motives besides this—but this it is which is specially mentioned by St. Luke. We are told nothing of any intercession, as in the case of the centurion's servant, nor indeed, is it certain that the throng who came forth from the gates of the city to follow the young man to his grave had the faith which was requisite in order to make them

intreat our Lord to work so great a miracle. The bearers of the bier "stood still," but even this does not show more than a certain amount of deference and reverence to our Lord. The miracle, like so many others, was a most wonderful manifestation of power, and, as such, was an act which suited well the purposes of God in showing to this world the dignity of His Incarnate Son and the power with which His Sacred Humanity was endowed. Many other miracles were wrought by our Lord for the purpose of this manifestation. But in this case we have the one motive assigned—the compassion of our Lord's Heart at the sight of the widowed mother following to the grave the body of her only son.

3. If we turn our thoughts from the scene set before us by St. Luke, to the subject which has become so familiar to us in these chapters, that of the condition of the suffering souls in Purgatory, we naturally ask ourselves whether there is in their case any call on the compassionate Heart of our Blessed Lord which may be compared to the claim made on His mercy by the sorrowing widow at Naim. And we see at once that every Christian soul, and in a special way every soul in Purgatory, on account of its helplessness and of the lot of suffering to which it has been sentenced, may be considered as the child, in a different sense, of two mothers—the Catholic Church and our Blessed Lady. It is a serious truth, and not merely a poetical or fanciful image, that our Lord takes note of this claim on His compassion, and

that each poor Christian soul, whether on earth or in Purgatory, receives from Him love and compassion and help for the sake of its filial relation to the Church and to His most beloved Mother. In the present chapter we shall take occasion to dwell for a few moments on the last of these two relationships. Our Blessed Lady has a special interest in and power over the Holy Souls in Purgatory, and we can never treat adequately the subject of the means by which we may ourselves help them without taking this power into consideration, and reviving our own devotion to her as their Mother and Queen.

4. It would take many chapters to draw out at full length what can be gathered from Christian writers as to the particular interest with which our Blessed Lady regards the Holy Souls. It is probable that, as the saints, in Heaven or on earth, are higher and higher in their intelligence and love of God, in the same proportion do they "understand," as the Psalmist says, "concerning the needy and the poor," and so, in an especial manner concerning the neediest and poorest, in a certain sense, of God's children, the sufferers in Purgatory, who can do nothing for themselves. If this be so, then, as the knowledge of God and of our Lord, and of all that belongs to His glory, which our Blessed Lady possesses, is greater than that of all the saints and angels together, as her charity is, in the same way, alone more intense than that of all the rest of the dwellers in Heaven, so her desire to aid the Holy Souls would be in

proportion greater than that of all others. They may be considered, in one respect, as the choicest and dearest of her children, except the saints themselves, who need nothing and are deprived of nothing. She has been made in a particular manner their Mother by our Lord on the Cross, for in them the fruits of His Precious Blood are secured. Holy writers tell us also that she has received a special power and commission to move the mercy of God in their favour, according to the arrangements of His Kingdom, in which she fills a throne, only less lofty than that of her Son. This is altogether in accordance with the laws, if we may so speak, of the Kingdom of the Incarnation. Our Blessed Lady has a special compassion for the sufferings of the Holy Souls, on account of her own great sufferings on earth, in some respects very like those which are endured in Purgatory. She was conceived without original sin, and filled with all the graces from the first, her virtues and merits were ever increasing, she was confirmed in grace, she never committed sin, venial or any other. And yet she suffered most intensely, on account of the sins of the world which her Son had to bear, on account of the treatment with which He met, the very intensity of her knowledge and of her charity caused the intensity of her pain, while yet she was ever in perfect peace and union with the will of God, and she felt more than any other soul could feel the desire to be with God and with her Son, and so the pain of detention from Heaven. On all these accounts there is ground for saying that she feels, more tenderly than all the Saints, compassion for the Holy Souls. These and other considerations form the basis of the doctrine which attributes to our Blessed Lady a peculiar prerogative as well as a special care in regard of Purgatory and its prisoners.

5. In accordance with this doctrine, we find the lives of the saints, the chronicles of religious orders, and other such records, full of anecdotes and revelations which all tend to the same conclusion, that our Lady is constantly exercising her power in favour of these Holy Souls, and that, on the other hand, devotions that are practised in her especial honour are among the most efficacious means which the children of the Church on earth possess of helping those blessed sufferers. It will be enough here to speak of the universal devotion of the holy Rosary, with which all Catholics are familiar. Some writers tell us that this, after the holy Sacrifice of the Mass, is the most powerful weapon that can be used to obtain their deliverance. The holy Rosary stands, to the great mass of Christians, much in the same place as the Divine Office of the Church to those who are bound to recite it, or who have the custom of so doing. The Divine Office is the great public prayer of the Catholic Church, and it remains such even in the case of those who do not recite it in choir, but privately and singly. And it has great efficacy on that account, for in the Catholic Church there is a special power and blessing on united, universal

and, as it were, official prayer and praise, which cannot be altogether impaired even by the unworthiness of some who are the ministers of the Church for this purpose. The Holy Rosary is sometimes called the Psalter of the Blessed Virgin, and the universality of its use renders it, in a sense, the prayer of the whole Church, though not in the same degree as the Divine Office. Intrinsically, moreover, it has an immense impetratory power with God, because it is in fact the pleading before Him of the merits of our Lord and of our Blessed Lady in all the mysteries which it commemorates, and which embrace the whole range of the scheme of our Redemption as accomplished by Him. Then, again, it pleads all these merits, as it were, through the heart and through the lips of Mary herself, and so it adds to the power of the mysteries in themselves that of her perfect prayer and intercession, and the affections and intensity of charity which glow in her bosom. Again, it uses with all its marvellous power the words of our Blessed Lord in the *Pater noster*, and of the Archangel, St. Elisabeth, and the Church, in the *Ave Maria;* being also, at the same time, a chain of most excellent acts of faith, hope, charity, and other supernatural virtues, which are exercised in the consideration of the mysteries.

6. It would be almost impossible to exaggerate the importance which holy writers attach to the practice of this devotion, whether as a means of intercession for the Holy Souls, or for our own benefit, and, as a matter of history, it is of our

Lady, as honoured by this devotion, that the words
of the Church seem so particularly true, *Cunctas
hæreses sola interemisti in universo mundo.* The
devotion of the holy Rosary was first propagated
by St. Dominic with the express intention of freeing
large Catholic populations from the contagion of a
frightful heresy, and down to the present day it
seems to have this effect. We are speaking of it,
in this chapter, as a most powerful means of
impetration of mercy for the souls in Purgatory.
But in this, as in many other cases, the charity
which we practise towards them flows back in
abundant streams to the benefit of ourselves in
this world and in the next. The various forms
which devotion to our Blessed Lady may take are
almost innumerable, and we have in this chapter
spoken only of this principal and universal devotion
of the Holy Rosary. Masses in her honour, Masses
offered for the souls devout to her, or to whom she
may wish to apply them, alms given, or works of
mercy practised with the same intention, or again,
the recital of her Office, the visiting her statues,
honouring her pictures, and the like, may all be
used for the benefit of the Holy Souls as well as
our own. One act of devotion may be specially
mentioned here, as having to some extent revived
in our days, although there has never been a time
in the Church's history when it has been extinct,
and although it is not limited in its object to our
Blessed Lady. This act of devotion is the making
pilgrimages to shrines, whether ancient or new.
The facilities of travelling have indeed made

K

pilgrimages less difficult in our own time, and it may be thought by some that they are now more of a pleasant excitement than, as of old, a laborious work of penance and even of danger.   But, in the first place, a pilgrimage need not be made to a distant shrine, and a shrine of our Lady—let it be only her picture or statue in some neighbouring church—may be visited on foot, while a truer pilgrimage, costing toil and time, may be made to a greater distance.   If, even in a country like ours, shrines of our Blessed Lady were frequently visited in this manner, we cannot doubt that the devotion of the faithful would soon unlock the treasury of her marvellous favours.   In the second place, pilgrimages to the more celebrated shrines of modern times, places like Lourdes or La Salette, where our Lady has appeared in our own day to persons, still living, or to the spots more anciently connected with her name, as Loreto and the like, are protestations of Catholic faith very valuable in an age like ours, they cost more in human respect than of old, though less in bodily fatigue, and are therefore very acceptable to her who is essentially "the Faithful Virgin."

CHAPTER XV.

Our Lord's Mission to Purgatory.

(THE MIRACLES WROUGHT BEFORE THE DISCIPLES
OF ST. JOHN THE BAPTIST.)

St. Matt. xi. 2—6 ; St. Luke vii. 17—23.

1. St. Matthew and St. Luke tell us of an incident
in our Lord's preaching which seems at first sight
somewhat difficult to understand. It appears that
when our Lord's marvellous miracles came to be
spread about by report over the whole country, and
soon after the miracle of the raising of the widow's
son to life, the fame of these great manifestations
of power and mercy reached the little company of
the disciples of St. John who were still attendant
on their master in his prison at a distance. The
disciples told St. John of our Lord's miracles.
The Blessed Baptist took the occasion of doing
what, more than anything else, might prepare them
for the acceptance of our Lord as the Messias.
He himself, as we are told by St. John the Evangelist, had worked no miracles at all,* and now our
Lord was doing what were commonly understood
to be "the works of the Christ"—that is, the
marvels of healing and power which it belonged to

---

* St. John x. 41, 42.

the promised Messias, in particular, to perform. The Baptist, therefore, sent two of his disciples to our Lord with the formal question: "Art Thou He that art to come, or look we for another?" St. Luke tells us that our Lord answered the question in two ways—in deed and in word—"In that same hour He cured many of their diseases, and hurts, and evil spirits, and to many that were blind He gave sight. And answering He said to them, Go and relate to John what you have heard and seen. The blind see, the lame walk, the lepers are made clean, the deaf hear, the dead rise again, to the poor the Gospel is preached, and blessed is he whosoever shall not be scandalized in Me."

2. These words of our Lord may be considered as conveying a double proof of His Mission from His Father. In the first place, they were a reference to, almost indeed a quotation from, the Prophet Isaias, in a passage in which it is clear that he was describing the signs of mercy which should wait upon the Messias when He came, and also in another passage which had already been applied by our Lord to Himself in His discourse in the synagogue at Nazareth at the very opening of His preaching in Galilee.* These passages must have been well known to the disciples of St. John, and thus our Lord's answer amounted to an appeal to the fact that in Him the prophecies concerning the Messias were fulfilled. In the second place, putting aside for the moment the

* Isaias xxxv. 5, lxi. 1.

prediction of these things concerning Him by a
Prophet whom all acknowledged as inspired by
God, the things themselves were proofs that He
was "He that was to come, and that they did not
look for another," because they were the works of
healing and mercy, both in body and soul, which
might naturally be expected in the Deliverer of the
human race. The Jews, who knew the prophecies,
could understand both these arguments, but if they
had not had the prophecies, they would have been
able to take in the second. The perfect Christian
demonstration, as we know, embraces both these
heads of proof, and is made up of the combination
of both. For miracles that have been foretold
by prophets sent by God are a more secure and
infallible proof than miracles alone, even when, as
in the case of our Lord's miracles, their character
of mercy and love, and the manner in which they
present themselves, as relieving all the ills of our
human condition, give them an authentication as
Divine, which simple signs of power, such as the
Jews required of our Lord, could never have.
This, then, seems to be an explanation sufficient
for our present purpose of the incident here
recorded. It enables us to see that our Lord's
acts and words furnished St. John with the opportunity of bearing witness to his own disciples as
to the Divine Mission of our Lord, by pointing
out that the latter had now received the Divinely
appointed evidence from God that He was the
Redeemer of the world. This evidence consisted
in the works of power and mercy which marked

His footsteps through the world. These works amounted to a witness from God the Father, as our Lord said more than once, that He was indeed He that was to come.

3. We must now leave the disciples of St. John Baptist and turn to a company of sufferers, of whom those whom our Lord now healed were the images and representatives. The passage of Isaias, to which reference has been made, seems to speak almost as directly of the prisoners of Purgatory as of the various forms of earthly wretchedness. Taken as a whole, it describes even more truly, in all its particulars, the visit of our Lord to the lower parts of the earth, when He set so many souls free from Purgatory, than even His sojourn among men on earth. "The land that was desolate and impassable shall be glad, and the wilderness shall rejoice, and flourish like the lily. It shall bud forth and blossom, and shall rejoice with joy and praise. The glory of Libanus is given to it, the beauty of Carmel and Saron, they shall see the glory of the Lord and the beauty of our God." Such language paints even more truly the deliverance of the Holy Souls, and their admission to the Beatific Vision, than the earthly miracles of our Lord. "Strengthen ye the feeble hands, and confirm the weak knees. Say to the fainthearted, Take courage and fear not, and behold your God will bring the revenge of recompense, God Himself will come and save you." These words again describe the state of the Souls in Purgatory, accurately, as well as those which

follow. "Then shall the eyes of the blind be opened, and the ears of the deaf shall be unstopped. Then shall the lame man leap as a hart, and the tongue of the dumb shall be free, for waters are broken out in the desert, and streams in the wilderness, and that which was dry land shall become a pool, and the thirsty land springs of water. By the dens where dragons dwelt before, shall rise up the verdure of the reed and the bulrush. And a path and a way shall be there, and it shall be called the holy way : the unclean shall not pass over it, and this shall be unto you a straight way, so that fools shall not err therein. No lion shall be there, nor shall any mischievous beast go up by it, nor be found there, but they shall walk there that shall be delivered. And the redeemed of the Lord shall return, and shall come into Sion with praise, and everlasting joy shall be upon their heads, they shall obtain joy and gladness, and sorrow and mourning shall flee away."* It is not necessary here to do more than indicate the many points in which this passage illustrates the redemption of the Holy Souls from their state of infirmity and bondage, and their passage into the light and joy of Heaven. But even if this be not included in the literal sense of the words of the Prophet, still our faith teaches us that the deliverance of the prisoners of Purgatory was a part of our Lord's work, a part which He began to execute when He went down into the lower world after His Passion, and that this work has been going on ever since,

* Isaias xxxv.

having been committed by Him to His Church on earth, which would fail to carry out the whole of her appointed task and office, if she were to neglect it. And so it may be said of our Lord, in His own Person and in His Church—which is to carry on to the end of time that which He has begun—that we know Him to be He that was to come, and that we do not look for another, as much by His constant beneficence and mercy and the healing and consolation which He brings to the suffering souls, as by the corporal miracles which He wrought while in the flesh upon earth. For "He that was to come" was to be the Redeemer and Consoler and Saviour of our poor human nature in all phases and forms of its misery and need, and if He had left any form of wretchedness and suffering unprovided for, especially that keenest and most intense suffering of all which is in Purgatory, then it might be a question whether we should not look for another. As a matter of fact, the deliverance which our Lord wrought for the Holy Souls when He descended into the abode of spirits after His Passion, belongs, according to Catholic belief, to that article of the Creed in which we profess our belief in that descent.

4. Moreover, it may be considered certain that the devotion to the Holy Souls, which consists in endeavouring to assist them under their sufferings in every manner open to us, is a part of that original religion of mankind which was given to our first parents to hand on to their children, and

which was made the foundation on which the
written Law, and, afterwards, the Gospel itself
was founded. It is certain that the Jews offered
prayers, mortifications, and sacrifices for the dead,
and it is probable that, could we trace accurately
the distorted and disfigured principles of true
religion which are, as it were, embedded in the
false systems of the heathen world, we should be
able to see how the idea of applying to the departed
the satisfactory power of good works and acts of
religion, offered to God in the faith of the coming
Redeemer of the world, lies underneath the whole
system of funeral rites and observances which
prevailed among the ancients outside the pale
of Judaism. There is no positive precept as to
prayers or sacrifices for the dead, either in the
Mosaic or the Christian Law, and this is enough
to prove, when taken in conjunction with the
universal Jewish and Christian practice from the
beginning, that that practice was in existence and
honour before Moses and before Christianity.
Thus we must look upon it as having either sprung
up of itself from the natural instincts of the human
heart, or as having, like sacrifice, been a part of
the original revelation and teaching of mankind by
God. The latter is the more probable supposition,
especially as it does not altogether exclude the
other. In either case we may consider that our
Lord's great work in the relief of Purgatory was
foreshadowed in the universal belief and practice
of the religious part of mankind, and that in this
way also, when He came to fulfil it and to hand it

on to the Church, He showed that He was He that was to come, of Whom the prophets spoke, and for Whom the whole world yearned.

5. This enables us to understand how the neglect and disuse of prayers for the dead, and the practical or positive denial of their value or efficacy, is a certain mark, in any religious community, that it has fallen away from the Church of Jesus Christ. These things involve a mutilation, so to speak, of the mission of our Lord, a halving of His beneficent work as the Saviour of mankind, a curtailing of the effects of the merciful counsel of God in bringing about the great work of the Incarnation. It is very significant indeed that the practical dying out of charity for the dead, as of all intercourse by way of invocation with the other great parts of our Lord's family in Heaven and on earth, the saints and angels, has come about, in Protestant societies like the English Establishment, much more by a sort of mournful instinct and consciousness of separation, than by any actual legislation prohibiting these beautiful exercises of charity. Protestants feels that they cannot help the dead, that they have nothing to do with them, as if they almost in their hearts acknowledged the truth of the Catholic reasons why it is so—that they are themselves cut off from the Body of Jesus Christ, and cannot, in consequence, have any right to carry on the work of mercy which is the application, through the Church, of the merits of His satisfaction for the members of that Body. It is hardly too much to say, that just as we know a

man to be dead to all spiritual grace who does not, according to his opportunities, practise the law of charity to his neighbours, and just as we should know a religion to be un-Christian which forbade the exercise of charity, so we may be certain, without further proof, that a religious communion is cut off from our Lord which proscribes prayers for the dead, or even in which that charity is not practised. Such a communion has found another Lord, and not He that was to come, and in Whom the prophecies and the natural anticipations of mankind were to be fulfilled.

6. But our thoughts must not rest on those religious communities alone in which the doctrine of Purgatory is practically denied. We must think of ourselves, the children of the Catholic Church, and learn from this miracle, looked upon in the light in which it has here been set, that we must consider the work of the ransoming and deliverance of these holy captives as one which our Lord expects us to carry on as a commission from Himself, as a legacy which He has left us, as a proof of the truth of His Mission. The Catholic Church is the Spouse and Heir of Him that was to come, and she is known and proved as such by her universal charity, which embraces alike earth and Heaven and Purgatory. The world is always asking whether she is what she claims to be, and her answer is the same as that of our Lord to the disciples of St. John Baptist. But the truth of her answer is proved by the charity and self-devotion of her children as well as by her formal teaching,

and it rests upon us to make this proof so con-
spicuous and so convincing that no one can gainsay it.

———

CHAPTER XVI.

The Desire of the Holy Souls for the Society of Heaven.

(THE CURE OF THE DUMB AND BLIND DEMONIAC.)

St. Matt. xii. 22, 23 (see St. Mark iii. 22, seq.).

1. OUR Lord on several occasions delivered from
the power of the devils, who had possessed them,
persons who were afflicted by the loss of one or
more of their senses, as of sight, hearing, or speech.
In these cases the recovery of the use of the senses
in question followed on the casting out of the
devils, and this circumstance appears to have produced a great effect on the witnesses of the miracles.
Thus we find, both in the account in St. Matthew
of the miracle of which we are now about to
speak, and in that of a similar, though not identical,
cure, mentioned later on in the history by St. Luke,
that the people cried out in the one case, " Is not
this the Son of David ? " and in the other, that
" the crowd marvelled ; " while in a third, also
mentioned by St. Matthew, the people said, " It
was never so seen in Israel."* On all these three
occasions the splendour of the miracle not only
moved the admiration of the crowd, but also excited in an unusual degree the malice of our Lord's

* Cf. St. Matt. ix. 32, 33 ; St. Luke xi. 14.

enemies, who took occasion from these cures to propagate and repeat their calumny that He cast out devils in consequence of a league with the prince of the devils. We are now to speak of the first instance, in point of time, of a miracle of this class.

2. "Then was offered to Him one that was possessed with a devil, blind and dumb; and He healed him, so that he spake and saw. And all the multitude were amazed, and said: Is not this the Son of David? But the Pharisees, hearing it, said, This Man casteth not out devils but by Beelzebub, the prince of the devils." St. Mark tells us that the Pharisees, or, as he calls them, the Scribes, who uttered this calumny, had come down from Jerusalem. It is clear that the authorities had by this time determined to thwart and persecute our Lord to the utmost of their power, and that they had sent persons of learning and character from Jerusalem into Galilee in order to watch Him and take every opportunity of finding fault with Him and opposing Him.

3. We need not pause to dwell further on their great perversity and malice, nor on the singular pain which this accusation, so often repeated in the subsequent months of our Lord's public teaching, gave to His Sacred Heart. If we were meditating on sin, we might find some useful thoughts in the comparison which the state of this poor sufferer whom our Lord healed suggests between the diseases of the body and the evils of the soul. But as we are considering all these miracles in relation to

the Holy Souls of Purgatory, we may be satisfied with the image which is here presented to us of what must be a great part of their suffering. They are not, indeed, like the person before us, under the dominion of the devil. We have seen that they have been rescued from him, that they are full of gratitude on that account, and that they have been made aware how very near they have been to the danger of becoming his slaves for ever. We have also seen that in Purgatory it need not be supposed to be an ordinary suffering even to see or to be taunted by the devils. But though the Holy Souls are delivered from that kind of bondage to Satan which is involved in a state of sin, or even in exposure to mockery and insult from the devils, they are still, as we saw in the case of the paralytic, deprived of the use of many of their spiritual faculties or capacities for the functions of the blessed life of immortality and joy to which they are destined. The two senses of which this poor man was deprived for a time, while he was under possession by the devil, are those by which we communicate with the world around us, and especially with our fellow-men. If to the loss of speech and sight, the loss of hearing is added—as in the case with many who are dumb—then we become cut off almost entirely from intercourse with men like ourselves. The ingenious charity of Christians has, indeed, found a way of giving a kind of social life and enjoyment of intercourse even to those who are afflicted with the loss of all the three senses here mentioned; but the loss even

of one, much more of two of them, is a very
serious privation indeed. If those whom Providence allows to be placed in this unhappy condition are left to themselves, they are certainly
almost altogether cut off from all society, and from
the enjoyment and the love, as well as from the
cultivation of mind and intelligence, which is to
be found, in creatures like ourselves, chiefly in
society.

4. The sufferers in Purgatory are not only cut
off from the Beatific Vision of God, and from all
that it implies in regard to their knowledge and
love of Him as possessed by them, but also from
that intense happiness which consists in the mutual
love and converse of the saints and angels in
Heaven. God has made men for this wonderful
happiness; their minds and hearts are formed to
know and love one another, and to communicate
their thoughts and affections by means of speech.
The enjoyment of which we are thus capable is
higher and deeper in proportion to our own intellectual and moral perfection, to the degree of the
same perfection which those with whom we can
converse have attained, and to the mutual goodwill
and confidence which exist between us. To know
intimately and love tenderly only one very good
person who returns our love, opens to us a whole
world of delight and profit. Here on earth any
employment of this kind must be very limited
indeed. It is limited by our own very imperfect
knowledge of the hearts even of those who are
nearest to us, by the moral defects or imperfections

which prevent us from being entirely lovable or entirely unselfish in our love. It is almost the greatest blessing of which we are capable in this respect to have known one or two very holy persons. The great delight which we find in conversation with such persons is a faint reflection of what the joys of Heaven must be in this respect. Every one there is in the highest state of perfection, every one full of knowledge and love, every one able to communicate himself and to understand others in the most intimate manner, every one glowing with the most intense happiness and joy. We are often inclined, on account of the narrowness and pettiness of our conceptions concerning the things of God, to make difficulties to ourselves concerning the happiness of Heaven in this respect —how far we shall know one another, and be able to continue and make perfect the holy intercourse of love which has bound us on earth to those to whom we have been united by God's providence, and the like. We are actually sometimes inclined to think of transplanting the jealousies and selfishness of earthly affection into that abode of peace and charity, as if the love and joy that we could have there could be affected by any such childish imperfections. All these foolish fears and fancies vanish before a few simple meditations on the immense blessings which God has prepared for us, not only in the possession of Himself, but in that also of all those who are to share with us in the joy of possessing Him, our Blessed Lady, the saints and angels, our own companions and friends, and the whole innumerable society of Heaven. There indeed is true society, converse, love, and there alone, except in so far as, by the grace of God, we know what is true Christian friendship and affection on earth, and in so far as by our devotion to and childlike confidence in the saints and angels, especially those to whom God has in some particular manner committed us, we are able to anticipate here the blessings of this kind which await us.

5. It would be far from the truth to say that the Holy Souls in Purgatory have no share in the peace and love which must bind all the children of God together, to whatever realm of His Church they may belong. They are confirmed in grace, and full of charity, and so they must love very intensely indeed all that belongs to God, the saints and angels, their companions in Purgatory, and those who are still upon earth. Nor is it doubtful that they are visited and consoled, at least by the angels, and that they can have comfort by being allowed to know how the Saints love them and pray for them, and the affection which is borne them and the efforts which are made for them by those whom they have left behind here. It may also be considered that they may have some kind of holy converse among themselves, and that their mutual love is a source of peace to them. But still their state is essentially one of pain, and also one of banishment and privation, and on this account it must also be a state of intense longing for the more perfect love and communion which

L

await them with those who are to be their companions in the sight of God for ever. Their hearts are full, but they are bound to be mute—their tongues are tied by the justice of God, as the tongue of this demoniac was tied by the possession of the devil.

6. They may have seen, moreover, in the light of the Particular Judgment, that their banishment from the society of Heaven and from that free communion with the saints and angels for which they so much long, is partly a punishment for some inordinate or blameworthy use of that poor kind of intercourse with others which the gift of speech enabled them to enjoy while on earth. Without speaking here of the innumerable sins of the tongue which may have to be expiated in Purgatory, it may be enough to think of the faults which may infect social intercourse as such, the inordinate affections, the jealousies and rivalries, the small practice of charity, the neglect to resist human respect, the coldness to those whom we might have consoled or assisted, the numberless acts of self-seeking and vanity which may arise in the daily intercourse of life. There may be "silence from good words," and breaches of silence from bad words, which may be punished by the enforced silence of Purgatory. This is a very large subject for thought, and it is enough here simply to indicate it. Our Lord now, in Heaven, as on this occasion when on earth, is very desirous and ready to relieve this muteness, and to loosen the tongues which are now held back from the praises of God,

the exercise of charity, the expression of their joy and thankfulness. We have it in our power to hasten on this deliverance, and by doing this we may perhaps obtain the grace so to use our own gift of speech and our own conversation with our neighbour, as to escape the mournful self-reproach of seeing hereafter that we have prepared ourselves thereby, rather for the prison of Purgatory, than for the happy conversation of the children of God in Heaven.

———

CHAPTER XVII.

Peace of the Holy Souls.

(STILLING THE TEMPEST.)

St. Matt. viii. 23—27 ; St. Mark iv. 36—40 ; St. Luke viii. 22—25.

1. THE most striking of our Lord's miracles to those who witnessed them must perhaps have been those in which He displayed His power over the forces of nature, which are usually so far above all human control. For diseases are to a certain extent, and in certain cases, within the reach of science and experience, at least as to some allevia-tion of their evils ; and even when He gave sight to the blind or speech to the dumb, the organs of sight or speech were there in the first instance to make their miraculous use less startling when it, was bestowed. In the case even of the demoniacs

there was obviously present a personal power at work, different from that of the possessed themselves, which power was quelled and reduced to obedience by the command of our Lord. In the case of which we are about to speak there was nothing of this kind. For the powers of nature, as we call them, seem to us so entirely subject to the unchangeable laws which govern them, as to admit of no interference—at least any interference with them seems to appal and even alarm us, as if the most stable and certain things in all the world in which we live were being shaken. Thus it seems to be predicted by our Lord that, in His good Providence, some most marvellous alterations in the aspect and condition of the physical universe will be given by God as the last signs to arouse the wicked world from its sleep before the Day of Judgment. Again, there is nothing in all our experience before which we feel so utterly helpless and prostrate as some of the more violent demonstrations of physical power in the elements, which seem sometimes to unchain themselves, as if for the purpose of showing man how weak and insignificant he is, as in great storms, earthquakes, hurricanes, the eruption of volcanoes, and the like. What must be the power that can tame them? Thus it seems to have been like a new revelation of our Lord's Divine authority, when the disciples and others could say to themselves, "Who is this, that even the winds and the sea obey Him?"

2. The miracle is related by the three historical Evangelists, and the circumstances are placed by

them all in the same order, except in one particular. Our Lord is asleep in the stern of the ship,
when a violent storm falls on the lake, and there
appears to be imminent danger for His boat and
the others which were in company with it. The
disciples come in haste and alarm to wake Him up,
and, as St. Mark tells us, with a kind of complaint,
as if His sleeping at such a time was a sign of
some carelessness as to their fate : "Master, doth
it not matter to Thee that we are perishing?"
Our Lord in the first place rises up and rebukes
the waves and the winds, bidding them be still.
Then a great calm comes on as suddenly as the
storm which had preceded it, and our Lord turns
to the disciples and asks them why they were
afraid, calls them men of little faith, and the like.
Then follows the exclamation of the whole company, "Who is this, that even the winds and sea
obey Him?"

3. The circumstance in this miracle on which
we may fasten in our meditations concerning
Purgatory, is that of the great calm which came
over the lake after our Lord had spoken. This
calm was more than natural, because after so great
a commotion it is not usual for the sea to become
smooth and tranquil all at once. The sudden
change seems to have struck the witnesses, as it is
specially recorded by the Evangelists. But we may
certainly say, without fear of exaggeration, that no
sudden calm that ever fell on sea or lake, even
when the storm had been most violent and the
change most instantaneous, could compare with

the wonderful change to peace and perfect tranquillity which takes place at the moment of death
in the case of those who die in the grace of God.
This calm and peace is not, in the case of the Holy
Souls, a passing, but a permanent state, it lasts as
long as they remain in the holy prison of Purgatory ;
in some respects it becomes more intense as their
period of purification draws towards its close, and
then it merges itself in the ineffable repose of the
Beatific Vision.   This peace of the holy state of
Purgatory is as true and real an element in the
condition of those souls of whom we are thinking
in these chapters, as is the pain which they suffer
and the length of time for which it may last.   It
should be our endeavour to gain a complete view,
as far as may be, of their condition, and for this
purpose, it is necessary to dwell as much on one
side of it, so to speak, as on the other.   We may
therefore devote this chapter to some consideration
which may serve to illustrate the peace and calm of
which the tranquillity of the Lake of Galilee, after
our Lord had stilled the tempest, may be taken as
an image.

4. In the first place, then, it is certain that at
the moment of death those who die in the grace of
God are confirmed in that grace.   Here at once is
something stable and fixed, free from disturbance
and fluctuation, as when the ever-restless waves of
a lake are formed by the action of freezing into
solid ice, over which the winds, which have before
lashed them at will into perpetual sleepless motion
and agitation, sweep without the least power to

disturb their repose. Nothing on earth so nearly approaches the peace of Heaven as a soul which is practically and morally, if not literally and actually, confirmed in grace, as we believe the soul of our Blessed Lady, and the souls of the Apostles after the Day of Pentecost to have been. Again, the Holy Souls are not simply confirmed in grace, but they love God intensely, according to the degree of that love which He intends them to have throughout all eternity, and here again is another element in their state which enables us to understand how it is a state of the greatest peace. They love God according to their knowledge of Him and of His attributes and character, and among other things in Him which they know and love, is the infinite justice and holiness which places them where they are in His Kingdom—that is, in a condition of suffering, which is due to His justice and to their deserts. The love of God is the true peace of the soul, and in proportion as the fire of Purgatory does away with the impediments which their imperfections have placed in the way of His perfect reign in their hearts, so does their love of God grow and become more intense, because it is no longer kept out of the soul by those impediments. We know how the love of God has preserved the saints in tranquillity and peace amidst all the greatest troubles and anxieties and persecutions of this world, the most violent sufferings of mind and body, and thus we are able to understand that the same love of God may be the source of ineffable peace to the

departed, even amid the severe sufferings which
are inflicted in Purgatory.

5. Again, the Psalmist says, *Pax multa diligentibus
legem tuam*—"There is great peace to those who
love Thy law." And the Holy Souls are altogether
in love with the law of God, and would not have it
violated one atom in their own case, even if it
were to lead to their own immediate deliverance
from their punishments. And as to that special
law of God which is His will in every particular
matter, they are most perfectly and absolutely con-
formed to it, and would rather suffer for ever as
they do according to His will than be raised at once
to the highest glories and enjoyments in Heaven
against or without His will. In this again we see
how deep their peace must be. No one, moreover,
can be said to be without peace, who is perfectly
content with his lot and extremely thankful for it,
but the holy sufferers in Purgatory know that their
present condition is the very one condition which
suits them best, and is most for their good. They
know that God has used towards them infinite
mercy in not exacting from them a far greater
amount of suffering, that they have deserved far
more, and even Hell itself, and on this account
they are overflowing with gratitude that their case
is not harder than it is.

6. Besides these elements of peace in the Holy
Souls there are others which consist in or result
from their condition in itself. We all know what
are the dangers to peace in this life—dangers so
many and so great that it seems almost impossible

to be at perfect peace as long as we are what we are. What a blessing we should account it to be free from all external temptation, from all molestation of the evil one, from all provocations to sin from objects external to ourselves, whether they attack us on the side of the irascible part of our nature, or whether their seductions are addressed to our concupiscence! But in the case of the Holy Souls there are no disturbances to their peace from the things which cause us pain or pleasure, which appeal to ambition, or pride, or anger, or envy, or jealousy. All the beauty in the world cannot be a danger to them, all the riches or honours of the world cannot even seem to them desirable, much less be the occasion of serious temptation. But there is a more interior cause of unrest in us in our present condition, without which the external allurement to sin would not have any power to molest us. This is the interior division in ourselves, the struggle of the spirit against the flesh, of reason and conscience against passion and concupiscence, of the lower part of our nature, as we call it, against the higher, the struggle which makes us feel that we have traitors in our own camp, and produces a sense of insecurity which is destructive of all perfect peace. It is in this internal conflict and division that our great danger to sin consists, and so our great cause for perpetual anxiety and watchfulness. But all this is at an end for the Holy Souls. They have no external temptation and no interior conflict, and their state may well be compared to that of the calm lake, which was, as it were, charmed into preternatural repose and absolute tranquillity by the words of our Lord when He commanded the winds and the waves, and they obeyed Him.

7. And again, once more, even if we are tranquil and without fear for our present condition, still, as long as we are in the flesh, we have a very uncertain future before us, and yet a future on which our whole happiness depends. We cannot tell whether we are in the favour of God or not, we cannot know whether our sins have been forgiven or not, we cannot be certain as to our perseverance, as to the circumstances under which death will find us, or how it will find us disposed towards God. And as long as this is uncertain, our look to the future must be one of anxiety, not, indeed, untempered by hope and confidence, and even by a kind of moral certainty that if we have been trying all our life to serve God, or if we have turned to Him in good earnest, and if He has allowed us to work for Him, to become familiar guests at His table, and well acquainted with His means of grace and the practice of the virtues by which He delights to be honoured, He will not let our hope fail at the last. But still, as long as the future is uncertain, we cannot be free from trembling anticipations as to what we have deserved and what God may do to us. But after death all this also is changed; for those who are in God's displeasure then, there can be no more hope, and for those who are in His favour then, there can be no more fear. Even those who have the heaviest and the

longest debt to pay in Purgatory are absolutely
certain of their salvation, and they know that the
time is fixed in the decrees of Him Who is all
powerful, when they shall become fellow-citizens of
the saints and angels in Heaven; or rather, that
they are already their fellow-citizens, and shall
infallibly, at God's appointed time, enter on the
full possession of their inheritance. Thus their
state may be, as it is, a state of intense pain; it
may be a state the sufferings of which surpass all
that can be suffered in this world; it may be a
state in which every moment seems a long course
of years, and which may thus seem to them to
pass away with incredible slowness. But still it
must be a state of peace, because doubt and un-
certainty and anxiety as to the future can have no
place there, any more than they can have place in
Heaven itself, the very abode and home of that
peace which surpasseth all thought, and excludes
even the slightest ruffle of disturbance or disquiet.

CHAPTER XVIII.

Contrast between Purgatory and Hell.

(THE CASTING OUT OF THE LEGION OF DEVILS.)

St. Matt. viii. 28—34, ix. 1 ; St. Mark v. 1—21 ; St. Luke viii.
26—40.

1. THE consideration of the tranquillity and peace
which reign in Purgatory may help to show us
how, in a certain sense, the period of their detention there is to the Holy Souls a sort of foretaste
of Heaven, and a time when they feel with intense
gratitude their deliverance from the stormy and
unsettled existence which they have led during
their life on earth. The next in order of our
Lord's miracles gives us an opportunity of comparing the state of Purgatory with that of the other
place of punishment which the justice of God has
established. That other place is Hell, prepared,
as our Lord says in His last parable, for the devil
and his angels, but which is also to serve for the
eternal abode of men such as we are, if they die
in mortal sin, and where they will suffer in due
proportion to the sins of which they have been
guilty.

2. The miracle of which we are about to speak
is one of the most remarkable of all those which
our Lord wrought. It is so, partly on account of

the large number of evil spirits who had been allowed to take possession of the soul of the poor sufferer who was delivered, partly on account of the manner in which the circumstances of the story seem to lift the veil which hides from us the unseen world, at least as to certain conditions of the present existence of the evil spirits, and to show us at once their misery, their malice, and their power. We shall have to leave aside a great many thoughts which will occur to us as to these points, in order to dwell more exclusively on that which is to be the subject of this chapter. The miracle is carefully related by the three historical Evangelists, and its circumstances are familiar to us all. After the stilling of the tempest, of which we had to speak in the last chapter, our Lord lands on the coast of the Sea of Galilee opposite to Capharnaum. It was a wild tract, inhabited, as it seems, by a mixed population, in which there was a large proportion of Gentiles. In certain respects it resembled the countries, of which there are still so many in the world, in which the Church has hardly set her foot, and in which, in consequence of her absence, the evil spirits are allowed greater licence. Our Lord was met on His landing by two demoniacs, one of whom appears to have been in a worse case than the other, but they were both of them dwelling in the tombs among the rocks, and were so violent and savage that no one could pass along the road which led from the shore to the tombs. St. Mark, speaking of the chief of the two, says that it had often been attempted to bind him with chains, but all had failed, he had broken them all, and that no one could tame him, and he was always in the tombs among the mountains, day and night, crying out and cutting himself with stones. He was possessed, in truth, by a whole "legion" of devils, who forced him to go and throw himself at our Lord's feet, begging Him not to torment them, and then they revealed their numbers at our Lord's command, and also begged Him, first not to drive them out of the country, and then not to cast them out "into the abyss," that is, as it seems, to bid them leave this world altogether. Lastly, they besought Him to allow them to enter into a large herd of swine that were feeding near the place, and when our Lord permitted this, the whole herd was seen to run down the steep side of a hill above the sea, and throw itself over the cliff into the water. The keepers of the swine went into the town, and related what had happened, on which the people of the place came out to beg our Lord to depart from their country. The poor man from whom the devils had been cast out entreated our Lord, on the other hand, to allow him to follow Him and remain under His protection and guidance, but our Lord would not allow this, bidding him instead go home to his family, and tell them of the wonderful deliverance which God had wrought for him.

3. This narrative certainly sets before us, in striking colours, the sufferings which the evil spirits are allowed to inflict, and their own inveterate malice. Their abject fear at the presence of our

Lord contrasts with the extreme violence to which they had been able to urge the man who was at last delivered from them. We see their hatred to the human race in their desire not to be forbidden any longer to haunt the earth, which is the home of man. We see their malice and desire to injure any creatures of God which they are allowed to infest, in their craving leave to enter into the swine, and the immediate destruction of the whole herd, which ensued when that leave was granted. Power, malice, restlessness, hatred of God and of what belongs to Him, hatred of man for His sake— such are some of the features of the picture of the devils as drawn in the history of this miracle. We seem to see how they carry their hell with them wherever they go, and it is on this account that we may use this miracle as shedding light on the contrast on which we are engaged. We have a picture which may in some respects remind us of Purgatory, in the poor man who had been delivered from the devils, sitting down at our Lord's feet, clothed, in his right mind, and desirous to be admitted to the blessed company who now followed our Lord whithersoever He went. The difference between this man as he was after his deliverance and as he was before, is not so great as that which we are thinking of—the difference between the sojourners in Purgatory and the miserable dwellers in Hell; but few pictures of the kind in our Lord's life seem to set before us so vividly as this the fierce torments to which those last-named dwellers are subjected.

4. The sufferings which are to be endured in Hell may be divided thus : (1) The pain of loss ; (2) the pain of sense, under which head we may include the internal pains of the souls there imprisoned ; (3) the place and company ; (4) the eternity and consequent hopelessness of all relief; (5) the entire aversion of the will from God, for Whom man was created. This last is, in truth, a part of those pains which are included under the former heads, but for our purpose it may be better to consider it separately. Taking this division as embracing, more or less, all that can be affirmed as to the various pains of Hell, we shall not find it difficult to understand the difference which separates Purgatory from Hell. As to the pain of loss, that is in one sense the same in both cases, and in another sense very different. The souls who are suffering in Hell have lost God for ever, and the souls in Purgatory are banished from the sight of God for a time. In both cases they are debarred from the Beatific Vision, for which they were intended, and which became, as it were, their birthright when they were admitted to the blessings of the Christian Covenant in Holy Baptism. The sense of the eternity and utter irremediableness of this separation must add an immense and inconceivable weight of pain to the loss of the souls in Hell. And the Holy Souls in Purgatory are not separated from our Lord as to grace and charity, though there are certain features in their case which resemble those of the lost souls. For the souls in Purgatory have lost, in many cases, degrees of

grace and of glory in Heaven which can never be regained. When their time of purification is over, they will be rewarded eternally in the possession of God, according to what their merits have been, and not according to what those merits might have been if they had been more faithful. If therefore there were degrees of the knowledge and love of God which they have failed to gain when they might have gained them, that is a loss which cannot be in itself repaired, although the perfect union of their wills with that of God and their perfect charity and contentment will prevent any sense of loss in that regard when they are admitted to Heaven. We may find it well to make this part of the pain of loss the subject of a separate chapter hereafter.

5. If, continuing our comparison, we consider, in the second place, the pain of sense, we shall find that it is possible that some souls in Purgatory may suffer pain of that kind for a time to a greater extent and in a greater intensity than some of the lost souls may suffer it for ever. For the pain in each case is in proportion to the sin, and there may be souls who die in the grace of God, who have committed more sins for which punishment is due than others who die out of the grace of God, and who may have had far shorter lives and far fewer or less powerful temptations. This will hold good of the pains of sense in the strictest meaning of the term. If we go on to include under those words the sufferings which the lost souls have to endure from the torments which afflict their interior faculties, the memory, the fancy, the imagination,

M

the appetites on which the passions work, and the like, it may be said that the difference is immense. In the case of the lost soul, there is the greatest interior disorder and misery, the memory is full of the opportunities of grace lost and the emptiness of the pleasures for which they have been lost, the reason is distorted, the will is perverted, the imagination is haunted by the foulest and most hateful shapes, the whole mind and heart is at war with itself, with its past, with its future, with all around it, and with God. In the case of the Holy Souls, there must have been bitter self-reproval, confusion, and consequently pain and sorrow, when the whole of their lives was presented to them in the light of truth at the moment of their judgment by our Lord. And we cannot doubt that the misuse or disordinate indulgence of any one of the interior faculties of the soul will have its pain corresponding to it. But their present state is one of order, tranquillity, and peace, as we have already seen—they are in their "right mind," like the man in the miracle before us, after he had been set free from the devils, and the only pain that they can suffer is that which is required for the satisfaction due to the justice of God, not that which arises from any present interior imperfection or discord in them.

6. It is hardly necessary to dwell on the obvious difference, as to the next two heads, between Purgatory and Hell. It is true that many writers have placed Purgatory, locally, close to Hell, and have held that there is in each the same kind of fire. This need not be called in question, but if it be

not permitted, as we have seen above, that in
ordinary cases the devils should be the tormentors
of the Holy Souls, the actual juxtaposition öf place
would still leave a great difference between the two
classes of sufferers with whose state we are concerned. As to the company in each, the difference
is hardly less than that between Hell and Heaven
itself. All the suffering souls in Purgatory love
God and love one another, and although they are
not allowed that fulness of intercourse and mutual
consolation which is the lot of the Blessed in Heaven,
still their wills and hearts are all one, the union of
peace between them reflecting the internal peace of
each soul, as the discord and savage tumult of
Hell reflect the internal miseries of the souls there,
preying upon themselves, and as it were tearing
themselves to pieces. And then, in the next place,
we must add to whatever differences we have
already considered the circumstance which multi-
plies the weight of misery in Hell so infinitely—the
circumstance of the eternal duration of the pains
which are there to be suffered. One single ray of
hope that a change or an end might come after an
all but endless series of ages would go far towards
changing Hell into Purgatory. But that one ray of
hope can never shine. And, on the other hand, let
the pains of Purgatory be far more intense than
they are usually conceived to be, still they would
be endurable as long as the certain hope—not less
a hope because it is a certainty—remains, that the
end will come, and that it can be hastened on
indefinitely by the mercy of God and the prayers

of the Church. And when this hope, or rather knowledge, falls like a stream of light upon souls whose condition is already one of peace and resignation under their heavy sufferings, it gives an ineffable and heavenly firmness and strength to all the happier elements of their condition in other respects.

7. But that which, after all, is the true essence of the difference which we are considering, lies not so much in any external circumstances of place, or pain, or companionship, or even of duration, as in the radical truth that the souls of those who suffer in Purgatory are united to God and turned to Him with the whole force of nature and of choice, while the poor prisoners in Hell are altogether averse from Him, their only end, and have thus, by their own deliberate and now irreversible choice, rejected the end for which they were made. This aversion from God of the soul which has died in mortal sin, and which, according to the law of its creation, must remain for ever in the state in which it was when the time of its probation closed, is that which makes Hell what it is. This is so true, that the sufferings of Hell, the pain of sense, the pain of banishment from God, the pain of evil companionship, and the like, might conceivably be suffered eternally by a soul that had the love of God and underwent them by His will, and yet that soul could not find Hell in them. The will of God would make all things sweet to such a soul. And, in the same way, if it were possible for a soul which was averse from God, as are the souls of the lost, to be in the midst of Heaven itself, it could not

find Heaven there. The mere aversion from God would make Heaven itself a place of torment. This aversion from God is the root and principle of all the other interior torments of the soul of which we have been speaking—its hatred of itself and all other creatures, the discord and indescribable misery which convulse it for ever. But, when we cast our eyes on Purgatory, we see nothing of this aversion there, but rather the most entire conformity to God's will and the most perfect love of Him, which is the root of all else in the condition of the souls there, which is so happy and peaceful.

8. The comparison between Purgatory and Hell is one of those considerations connected with our general subject which may be used with the greatest possible profit to help us to avoid most carefully even the shadow of deliberate mortal sin. Every such sin, in truth, bridges the abyss between Purgatory and Hell. We all carry about with us, as it were, the seeds of Hell in our souls, because we all bear in our hearts the evil passions and propensities which, if allowed to grow to full maturity, issue in mortal sin. And in our wills, which may consent to the indulgence of such passions or turn away from them, we have the issue of life or death. Indeed, whenever mortal sin has been consented to, the hell of the soul, the essence of all that can be suffered throughout all eternity, has been already kindled, and its flames can never be extinguished but by a turning again of the soul to God by the assistance of His grace, an assistance denied to no one, but made most easy for the children of the

Church by means of the life-giving sacraments.
Again, the same consideration brings out into fuller
light the truth that the love of God and the union
of the will with Him, is the essence of Heaven, and
of all happiness elsewhere that is the forerunner of
Heaven. Through all their intense sufferings, the
love of God keeps the Holy Souls happy and
content, as it would keep the souls in Hell, if it
could penetrate there, happy and content. This is
a lesson of much practical power in every way, and
in none more so than in helping us to bear joyously
whatever sufferings and inflictions God may send
us, far inferior as they must be to those which are
so patiently borne in Purgatory. In truth, we
might have little satisfaction to pay hereafter, if we
bore well here the Purgatory which God sends us
in the course of His providence.

CHAPTER XIX.

The Sense of Shame in Purgatory.

(THE HEALING OF THE WOMAN WITH AN ISSUE
OF BLOOD.)

St. Matt. ix. 19—22 ; St. Mark v. 24—34 ; St. Luke viii. 42—48.

1. IT happens that we have a fuller narrative than
usual of our Lord's movements between the time
of His stilling the tempest on the lake and the last
of the miracles of which we shall have to speak in
the few following chapters. If we may judge from
the manner in which marvellous miracles are
crowded into these two or three days, we may
fairly suppose that such displays of power and
mercy were almost unintermittent with Him, and
that the only reason why we do not know of
hundreds more than are recorded by the Evangelists is that they were forced to make a not
very large selection from the multitude before
them. The three Evangelists tell us that on our
Lord's return from the farther side of the lake He
found the people thronging to meet Him, and that
He was very soon interrupted in His teaching by
the appearance of Jairus, the ruler of the synagogue, who came to beg Him to come and heal his
daughter, who was at the point of death. Our
Lord at once went with him, and on His way to

his house the miracle of which we are now to speak took place. A woman who had suffered for twelve years from an issue of blood, and had "bestowed all her substance on physicians, and could not be healed by any, came behind Him and touched the hem of His garment. For she said, If I shall touch but His garment I shall be whole. And forthwith the fountain of her blood was dried up, and she felt in herself that she was healed of the evil." Our Lord used so very commonly to charge persons on whom His miraculous cures were wrought not to divulge or publish them, that we might have expected that on this occasion He would have allowed the mercy which He had shown this woman to remain a secret between Himself and her. But for many reasons which have been assigned by holy writers, it did not accord with the counsels of His Providence that it should be so. "And immediately Jesus knowing in Himself the virtue which had proceeded from Him, turning to the multitude, said, Who hath touched My garments? And His disciples said to Him, Thou seest the multitude thronging Thee, and sayest Thou, Who hath touched Me? And He looked about to see her who had done this. But the woman fearing and trembling, knowing what was done in her," or as St. Luke puts it, "The woman, seeing that she was not hid, came trembling, and fell down before His feet, and declared before all the people for what cause she had touched Him, and how she was immediately healed. And He said to her, Daughter, thy faith hath made thee whole; go thy way in peace."

2. We must select only one of the lessons which are suggested by this miracle, and which might illustrate more than one point in the doctrine concerning Purgatory. The characteristic which distinguishes this woman among those who were the object of our Lord's compassionate power is the mixture which we see in her strong faith and natural shamefacedness. Her strong faith led her to the venturesome step of touching the hem of our Lord's garment, after she had so long tried in vain all the resources of human skill and knowledge. On the other hand, she was too much ashamed of herself and of her disease to come to Him openly when others would know for what she came. So she chose a moment when, as she thought, she could obtain her boon unseen and unknown. No one would notice it if she touched the hem of His garment when He was in the midst of a crowd passing through the street, so she would place herself in His path, win her cure, and go away undetected. But our Lord, for certain wise purposes, would not allow this. It is commonly thought that He forced her to confess what had passed, in order to strengthen the faith of Jairus, who was with Him, and who was just at that moment to receive the message from his home, telling him not to trouble any further, because his child, whom he had left dying, was now dead. But we may well suppose that even if there had not been this reason for the revelation of the

miracle, our Lord would not have allowed the woman who had been healed to go away without some acknowledgment of what had passed in her. There are false shames as well as true shames; there is a reserve in declaring our own miseries and the mercies of God towards us, which is wholesome and wise, and there is also a reserve as to the same which is not so laudable, or which at all events, on certain occasions, must be overcome. So this woman, who appears from her circumstances, not to have been of the poorest class, was obliged by our Lord to confess before all the multitude, both her own infirmity and the mercy which had been wrought upon her.

3. The feeling of shame which had kept her back may have been twofold in character. She may have shrunk from divulging her own malady from a sense of its foulness, and she may also have shrunk back, as St. Peter did, after the miraculous draught of fishes, out of a sense of her own unworthiness to be made the object of so extraordinary a mercy. If we turn to the Holy Souls of Purgatory, we may find in them examples of both these kinds of shame. We have often spoken of the new light which is cast at the moment of their judgment upon the whole of their lives, all their actions and words and thoughts, all their opportunities of grace and the like, the whole of God's dealing with them, and of their treatment of God. The great predominant affection which this revelation must cause in them is one of the most intense contrition, but akin to this, and

indeed a part of it—for it is founded on the recognition of their unfaithfulness and disloyalty to the ineffable majesty and goodness of God—will be the feeling of shame. This is one of the fruits which we are taught by St. Ignatius to draw from the consideration of sin, which leads us naturally to reflect on the miserable use which we have made of so much grace, our shameful ingratitude, the petty, shabby, niggardly return which we have made to so much tenderness and generosity, the silly way in which we have managed our lives, the disgraceful and discreditable motives of self-love on which we have often acted, and the like. Again, a great part of that for which, under this head, the souls which stand before the judgment-seat of our Lord will have to feel such intense shame, will be the indulgence of shame itself as a motive of action, which may so often have induced them to be afraid of men, to yield to human respect, to fear not only those who can kill the body, but those who could laugh at them, or make them unpopular, or put them to slight inconveniences, or the company in which they found themselves, rather than bear witness to the law or the truth of God in word or in action. Then, again, there are a number of reticences which are the result of self-love as well as of human respect, as when persons have made a mistake and do not like to acknowledge it, or are ignorant of what they have been supposed to know and will not say so, or have done some one wrong or been guilty of some rudeness and will not apologize, or have had credit given them which they do not deserve, and will not disclaim it. This is another class of the pettinesses which are the result of a false shame. Much more dangerous are those which prevent us from being perfectly open in confession, in cases where there may not be an absolute necessity for it, but when it would be much more ingenuous, and gain us much more light and grace from God, to speak, as in the confession of deliberate small sins to which we have an attachment, or again, when to acknowledge the truth about ourselves, our persons, our antecedents, our families, and the like, will bring on us some humiliation in the eyes of men. These are but instances of a very large class of defects and faults which may be represented as in an image by the natural shyness and reluctance of this woman to let people know what had happened to her. Our Lord, Who could have nothing in Himself which was not worthy of the highest honour and of the adoration of all Heaven and earth, hid all that was in Himself which might attract admiration, made Himself the most abject and despised of men as to His outward condition, and courted every kind of external shame and reproach, which He could not deserve, as men court the highest honours. The saints have learnt from Him the love of reproach and shame, and would be willing to make themselves ridiculous in public, in order to indulge their passion for humiliation, if such conduct were consistent with their devotion to the glory of God and the good of souls. The Holy Souls of Purgatory have learnt to look on these things with the eye of our Lord and of His Saints, and have seen how much loss they have to regret of opportunities of humiliation out of timidity as to human respect and the subtle power of self-love. And now, if they could choose, they would have all their faults and failings proclaimed to all the world on the housetops, in order that they might gain the merit of due humiliation, and that God might have the glory which belongs to Him for having borne with them and forgiven them.

4. This sense of the shamefulness of their faults and ingratitude towards God will have been one of the afflictions of the Holy Souls at the time of their judgment. It will also blend with that other shame for their own present unfitness for Heaven and the sight of God, of which we have already spoken in the chapter on the Centurion's Servant. Both will melt away, as causes of any pain or confusion, under the influence of their burning love of God and of the removal of all that has to be cancelled by satisfaction. It is not in accordance with the laws of God's Providence, nor, indeed, would it be well that all these causes of shame should become known to the world. But when the great day of account comes, at which time, among other things bearing on this subject, it will be true to say that no harm can possibly be done to any single soul by the publication of the faults of each and all, however shameful in themselves, then the whole story of each soul will

be known to the glory of God, as David says in his penitential Psalm, "that Thou mayest be justified in Thy words, and overcome when Thou art judged."* Our Lord will then "bring to light the hidden things of darkness, and make manifest the counsels of the hearts."† This will not be to the shame and sorrow of the redeemed children of God, because it will be to His glory, and because also their debt will have been entirely paid, and every lingering stain removed from their souls, so that they will be trophies of His victorious grace and ineffable mercy in regard to every single act which might otherwise cause them shame. But the truth that this is to be so may help to strengthen us against the foolish shame which would hide our sins from the eyes of others, and even, if we could, from those of God, and teach us the immense benefit and treasure that is stored up for us in openness to every defect, and in any humiliation to which that openness may lead.

5. The practice of this simplicity and humility will certainly bring great blessings on our souls, and enable us to advance rapidly in grace. But we must not part from the subject without adding that it may, in more ways than one, enable us also to help the Holy Souls. It may make our prayers for them more powerful, and it will give us the opportunity of offering to God a considerable number of acts of interior mortification, and sometimes even of exterior humiliation, by way of satisfaction for them, which may be accepted by Him

* Psalm l. 6.   † 1 Cor. iv. 5.

as expiation for the reserve and reticence which He may have been obliged by His justice to punish in the prison of Purgatory.

———

CHAPTER XX.

The Pain of Sense in Purgatory.

(THE RAISING TO LIFE OF THE DAUGHTER OF JAIRUS.)

St. Matt. ix. 18—26 ; St. Mark v. 22—43 ; St. Luke viii. 41—56.

1. WHEN our Lord healed the woman with the issue of blood, He was, as has been said, on His way to the house of Jairus, the ruler of the synagogue at Capharnaum, whose daughter had been left by her father at the point of death when, on hearing of our Lord's return from the other side of the lake, he had hurried off to beg Him to come and heal her. The incident of the cure of the woman with the issue of blood, our Lord's pausing on His way, and obliging her to come forth and declare before all what had taken place, must have caused a few moments of delay which were trying to the father. Just as our Lord was sending the woman away with His blessing, some messengers came from the house of Jairus, telling him that all was over and that he need not "trouble the master" any more. Our Lord turned at once to him, and bade him fear nothing, " only

believe, and she shall be saved." They went on together, followed by the multitude, and by the time when they reached the house, the customary mourning had already begun. They found musicians, and a number of people lamenting and weeping, and a confused crowd of weeping friends. Our Lord bade them all cease. "The maiden is not dead but sleepeth." He used these words in His own Divine meaning, for the girl was asleep in the sense in which sleep alone, and not death, admits of an awakening again in this life. They all ridiculed Him, for they knew well enough that, in the common sense of the words, she was truly dead. Then, as the Evangelists tell us, our Lord made them all leave the room, into which He went with the father and mother of the dead girl, and three of His disciples, St. Peter, St. James, and St. John. He took her by the hand as she lay, and said to her, "Damsel, arise! She arose at once and walked." She was about twelve years old, St. Mark tells us, of an age, therefore, at which, in those climates, girls are in the full bloom of youth, and approaching womanhood. Then our Lord earnestly bade the father and mother tell no one what had happened, and also ordered that the girl should take some food.

2. The Evangelists tell us nothing of the character or disposition, or of the after-life, of this girl whom our Lord raised from the dead. The mention of the office of her father as the ruler of the synagogue suggests that he was well known to our Lord, a friend of the centurion

whose servant had lately been healed, and also
of the nobleman whose son had been cured by
our Lord's word spoken at a distance. Our Lord
was now about to leave Capharnaum almost
entirely, probably on account of the unbelief of
most of its inhabitants and of the persecution
which the emissaries of the priests at Jerusalem
were raising against Him; but we find Him once
more in the synagogue, where He delivered His
great dogmatic discourse about the Holy Eucharist
which is related in the sixth chapter of St. John's
Gospel, after the first miracle of the multiplication
of the loaves. We may conjecture that one reason
for the marvellous miracle of which we are speaking in this chapter may have been the kindness of
Jairus in admitting our Lord to teach so often in
the synagogue. If we turn to the girl herself, it is
natural to think rather of the effect which this
mercy granted to her may have had on the rest
of her life, than of any special reason which may
have led our Lord to select her as the subject of
that mercy. She was, as has been said, just on
the threshold of full womanly life, when all that is
naturally enjoyable and delightful was opening to
her, the pleasures of the senses, the intoxication
of affection, the world, society, position, all that
can fascinate the soul and entangle the heart of
the thoughtless and the gay. She entered on her
new life with the gift of health and strength—for
we must suppose that our Lord never worked His
cures or His restorations, as we say, by halves—
the idol of her parents, dearer than she had been

N

ever before, and, like some of the children who
are now and then favoured with visions of our
Blessed Lady or made the instruments by means
of which a new devotion or a new shrine is set up
in the Church, the object of general interest and
curiosity, and even of a kind of veneration. We
may well ask how this world appeared to her after
she had come back to it with her short experience
of the next, and what were the thoughts which
she brought with her as to the dependence of the
future on the present and the relative importance
of the goods and evils here and the goods and
evils there.

3. All these things are hidden from us by the
short narrative of the Evangelists, who concern
themselves only with what more immediately
relates to our Lord Himself.   But the history
of the Church contains instances of persons who
have in like manner come back, as it were, from
the world beyond the grave, who have spoken of
its terrors or consolations, and the remainder of
whose years has been altogether coloured by the
impression made upon them.   The daughter of
Jairus may have been dead some little time when
our Lord arrived at his house, for there must have
been some notice required to bring the crowd of
mourners and musicians there.   But a very few
moments indeed after death are enough for the
instantaneous judgment which then takes place,
and for the assignment of the soul which has
left the body still warm, to its place in Heaven,
in Purgatory, or in the place of punishment.   It

may have been that in this case the judgment and
the sentence may have been delayed by our Lord's ·
intention to raise the maiden to life, but she may
nevertheless have been allowed to see the state of
things into which she would naturally have been
introduced, the peace of the saints in Limbus, the
sufferings of the souls in Purgatory or in Hell.
Such has been the case with others. That which
would strike her most in what she saw would be
that part of the sufferings of Purgatory which fhe
senses can most easily grasp. The pain of loss
might be made intelligble in many ways, to a
visitant who was allowed to stand on the brink
of Purgatory, but the pain of sense is that part
of the punishment of the Holy Souls which could
not by any possibility escape her notice. There
are many beautiful things in the writings of the
Saints about the pain of loss ; but the relations of
those who have seen what Purgatory is in some
preternatural manner have dwelt mainly on the
pain of sense. This, therefore, we may suppose
to have been one great indelible impression made
on the mind of the girl of whom we speak, which
may have saved her in many a temptation, and
urged her on to great efforts in the service of God,
even to heroic self-sacrifice, to a life of immense
mortification, and also of great and laborious
charity for the relief of the Holy Souls. We
may use her case, therefore, as the foundation of
our considerations on this point.

4. The manner in which the pain of sense
affects souls which are separated from their

bodies, and how, in particular, the fire of which our Lord speaks when He alludes to Hell acts upon such souls, belong to the class of subjects as to which schoolmen and theologians are full of difficulties and conjectures. All discussion of such questions would be out of place in a volume like the present, and therefore we need only say that it is clear from the language of Scripture, from reason, and from the sense of the Church, which is in full harmony with the general tone of the revelations contained in the lives of the Saints, that the pain of sense in Purgatory is something so severe and intense that we can form of it no adequate conception in this life. The revelations in question are not in themselves authoritative. If they are considered simply as expressing the thoughts familiar to the holy persons to whom they are said to have been made, which is the very lowest rank to which they can be reduced, then at least we have in them, and especially in their uniform tenour, an indication of the mind of the faithful children of the Church as to this matter. If they are considered as generally, or in many cases, representing preternatural communications which have been vouchsafed by God, then their authority rises higher than in the other case. But even then they do not stand by themselves. Reason itself seems to point to the conclusion that the sufferings of souls separated from the body must be very intense indeed, especially when these are inflicted by the special and particular justice of God as the exaction of the satisfaction due

for a great number of sins, both venial and
mortal. Purgatory has been created to be the
place of punishment for those who are not to
suffer for ever in Hell. It is not to be thought
that God would create a place of this kind but
for some strong necessity, or that when it is
created it would not fulfil its purpose in the
strictest sense. Whatever may be its characteristics, it is certain that they must witness to the
wisdom, the mercy, the power, and the justice
of God, to His ineffable holiness, and to the
manner in which He looks upon sin. "Whatever
a man soweth, that also he shall reap," the Apostle
tells us. But it is certain that the number of sins
which are committed in and through the body is
almost infinite, that their guilt is very great, and
that very little of sufficient penance is done for
them here. If we were to follow the opinion,
which can hardly approve itself to a Catholic
mind, that the fire of which Holy Scripture
speaks is metaphorical, even then we should
be obliged to admit that Holy Scripture had
used, as an image to represent the sufferings of
Purgatory, that one figure of all others which
suggests the most excruciating and intolerable of
all the pains which can be suffered, and a pain
which no one is able to endure for a few moments
together, while it is certain that the punishments of
Purgatory are continuous, and that, in many cases,
their duration is extremely long.

5. It must be remembered that this teaching
about the extreme severity of the pain of sense

in Purgatory, is found in the writers who have
dwelt the most on the happiness which the souls
there enjoy, as well as in those who have set
before us the more fearful pictures of their condition. St. Catharine of Genoa, who is the Saint
to whom the doctrine of the happiness of the
Holy Souls may be said to have been intrusted,
says, "The soul, understanding that Purgatory has
been instituted for the expiation and wiping off
of imperfections, willingly enters there in sub-
mission to the arrangement of God, and con-
siders itself to be very mercifully dealt with;
and yet the bitterness of Purgatory surpasses all
human understanding. But the soul, burning with
love, thinks its imperfections of more importance
than the pain of Purgatory, although that pain is
so extremely terrible, that all that in this life we
can know, or describe, or experience, or believe,
appears to me a falsehood when compared to it.
So that although I am obliged to say this, yet I
am confounded at the greatness of the matter,
which I have explained so much less adequately
than I wished." This is very much the same kind
of language as that of the Blessed Veronica, of
whom the author of her Life writes, after relating
some of her visions: "After she returned from
that vision to the use of her body and her senses,
she gave signs of vehement sadness, terrified
sorrow, and great feelings of horror, striking her
hands together, shaking her head, and speaking
in a woful voice, and saying, 'Alas, alas! what
pains and what kinds of torments have I seen

to-day, inflicted by those same tormentors who
are in Hell, and by the same fire which is there ! '
And saying this, she fell on the ground, and a
violent fever seized her, and her whole body was
marked with marks as it were shining with fire, of
the size of the palm of a hand." Very much the
same is the testimony of the famous St. Christina,
who was called back to this world after having
seen the sufferings of the next, and who spent
the rest of her life in the most severe penances
for the relief of the Holy Souls. She stated that
immediately on her soul leaving her body, she
was taken by the angels to a dark and horrible
place, full of the souls of men; the torments
which she there witnessed were so terrible that
no tongue could express them, she saw there the
souls of many whom she had known in this life,
and was moved to intense compassion for them.
She asked what the place was, thinking it must be
Hell, but she was told that it was Purgatory, and
that the souls whose sufferings moved her compassion so much had been sinners who had
repented of their sins, but not done sufficient
penance for them. But, in truth, there is but
one tone about all these revelations—they uniformly
represent the torments of Purgatory as severe in
the very utmost degree.

6. Many persons are in the habit of adopting a
tone of complaint, and even of indignation, at the
manner of speaking of the pains of Purgatory
which is, in the main, founded on such revelations
as those to which we have been referring. They

object, further, to the representations of those pains which are sometimes to be found abroad, pictures of the souls, or rather bodies, representing the souls of Purgatory in burning flames, under excruciating tortures, which are sometimes administered by demons as the executioners of the justice of God. Such pictures are frequently used in missions to the people, or are to be found in popular books of devotion about Purgatory. The objection to such representations is not confined to those which depict the pains of Purgatory alone, but extends itself to those in which the sufferings of Hell are the subject which it is sought to bring home to the mind. It may be worth while to say a few words on the subject in general. In the first place, then, we need hardly ask whether any Catholic doubts that the truth which it is thus desired to represent be a truth indeed, or whether it is a truth which it is highly expedient and charitable to enforce in all lawful ways. It is no doubt a great shock to modern notions of the dignity of man and his independence of God, to speak or write as if there were any future torments at all, or as if these torments were very severe. In the same way, there are societies in which it is very improper to mention or even allude to death, or to anything else which interferes with the unruffled tenour of sensual enjoyments in which so large a part of what is called civilized society would so gladly spend, not only its short span of life here, but an eternity if it could command it. It is certain, then, that no Catholic can see anything to complain of in the constant teaching about the punishments of sin which has so much authority in the words of our Lord Himself. These things are undoubtedly true, and the only question can be as to the manner of representing them to the people. In the second place, it may be said that a vision is of necessity addressed to the eye of the mind, and the language which it uses must of necessity be that of sensible objects. If the pain of sense is to be put before the soul at all, except by word of mouth, it must be by images which represent the several senses as suffering torments which are intelligible to the mind through the eye. What is true of a vision is true of a picture. There is no difference in this respect between representations of the saints or angels, of our Blessed Lord or His sacred Mother, and the representations of Hell or Purgatory. In each case the thing to be set before the mind must be set before it by means of a picture, rude, it may be, and altogether inadequate to be the full image of celestial beauty or of intense suffering, but still cognate in kind to the thing or person which it has to represent. This is the simple account of so many descriptions of what people have seen of Purgatory, or have endeavoured to depict of Hell. Those who find these things of use, as so many do, had better use them. Those who can represent to themselves the sufferings of our Lord without a crucifix need not use one, and those who can imagine the pains of Purgatory for themselves, may leave the representations of which we speak to others. But it is unreasonable to blame those who use them, or propose them for the use of others, on the ground of the horrible character of any particular picture or sculpture, unless we are prepared to say that the doctrine as to Purgatory or Hell which is there embodied, in the only way in which it can be embodied so as to strike the senses, is exaggerated or untrue.

7. It is here, perhaps, that the real difficulty lies. People are only too glad to persuade themselves that they may forget the severe truths of our faith as to the retributions for sin, whether temporal or eternal, and they turn with anger on whatever reminds them of these truths, rudely and palpably. If these truths themselves are once mastered by the soul, it is not likely that objections will be made to the manner in which the memory of them is refreshed. It will be better hereafter to have quailed in terror before some picture of Purgatory in which the most fearful torments have been depicted in the grossest way, in which the souls are represented as writhing on spits in the midst of flames, torn to pieces by devils, screaming in agony and afflicted by some special visible weapon of torture in every limb and every sense, than to have persuaded ourselves that these sufferings of which the Saints of God think so much are light and short, and that it can be no such very terrible a thing to fall into the hands of the living God in the day of His judgment.   And if we are to return for a moment to the consideration of the case of the Holy Souls themselves, and their claims on our charity, it can be no kind thing to them, any more

than to ourselves, to listen to the teaching or the instincts of self-love and sensuality, as to the supposed exaggerations which the most pious children of the Church may have believed to be truths, with regard to the intensity of sufferings such as theirs.

CHAPTER XXI.

The Eternal Losses of the Holy Souls.

(THE LAST CURES IN CAPHARNAUM.)

St. Matt. ix. 27—34.

1. ONE of the circumstances connected with the miracle of the raising of the daughter of Jairus from the dead, although in itself a common feature in many such incidents in our Lord's life, is still in itself and in its connection very remarkable. This circumstance is the strict injunction to secrecy which our Lord laid on those who witnessed that miracle. It could hardly, under any circumstances, remain long unknown. But it appears to be the case that our Lord was at this time especially anxious to escape observation in Capharnaum. The probable reason to be assigned for this anxiety is the persecution to which He was now exposed, and in a particular way the calumny about His league with Satan, which was one of the features of that persecution. A study of our Lord's life reveals the fact that He was now taking leave, as it

were, of Capharnaum. The three miracles which St. Matthew subjoins in the passage cited above were evidently connected in point of time with the miracle on the daughter of Jairus, and the Evangelist is careful to notice this connection between them. They were, as it were, forced upon our Lord, and were not worked in public. The last of them, however, gave occasion to a renewed outburst of the calumny already mentioned.

2. The history of these miracles is very simple. As our Lord passed away from the house of Jairus, two blind men followed him. They must have been led to the place by those who had the charge of them, or they may have been sitting in some public place or street, and heard of His passing. They kept crying out to Him, by the popular name of the "Son of David," to have mercy on them. But He did not heal them in public. He went to the house where He usually abode, and they were brought in to Him. Then He asked them whether they believed that He could do for them what they wanted, and on their saying yes, He said, "According to your faith be it done unto you." They were at once healed, and though our Lord severely charged them to be silent about their cure, they went at once and spread it abroad over all the country. Then, after they had gone out, another poor sufferer was brought to Him, whose case was very like one of which we have already heard. He was dumb, and had a devil. Our Lord cast the devil out, and then the dumb man spoke. The multitude, who appear either to have followed our

Lord to the house, or to have been collected by
the cure of the blind men who had received their
sight, "wondered, saying, Never was the like seen
in Israel. But the Pharisees said, By the prince of
devils He casteth out devils." Thus our Lord's
precautions against the danger of occasioning a
revival of the calumny were rendered vain. He
left Capharnaum, and was seldom there after this
time.

3. The circumstances in these miracles to which
our thoughts may be directed, in order to gather
from them some illustration of the doctrine concerning Purgatory, may be that which has already
been mentioned, that these were the last miraculous
cures which are recorded by the Evangelists as
having been worked in Capharnaum by our Lord.
The time was come when He was forced to withdraw
more and more from the city which He had made
His own, and in which so many of His dearest
friends lived—for this city was the home of some
of the first Apostles, of St. Matthew, of the centurion, and the nobleman whose son He had healed,
of Jairus, and perhaps of St. Mary Magdalene.
Nevertheless, the inhabitants as a community had
turned a deaf ear to His teaching—at all events
the teachers and priests had turned away from Him
themselves, and had led others to reject Him. It
may not be certain at what precise time of His
Ministry we are to place His famous denunciations
of this city, along with others, in which so many
mighty works had been done. These denunciations
may have been repeated more than once. "Wo

to thee, Corozain, wo to thee, Bethsaida; for if in Tyre and Sidon had been wrought the miracles that have been wrought in you, they would long ago have done penance in sackcloth and ashes. But I say to you, it shall be more tolerable for Tyre and Sidon in the Day of Judgment, than for you. And thou, Capharnaum, shalt thou be exalted up to Heaven? Thou shalt go down even unto Hell. For if in Sodom had been wrought the miracles which have been wrought in thee, perhaps it would have remained unto this day. But I say unto you, it shall be more tolerable for the land of Sodom in the Day of Judgment, than for thee."* These words, and the departure of our Lord from His usual haunts at Capharnaum, suggest to us the thought of the immense loss which is incurred by the neglect of the opportunities of grace with which our life is filled by the good providence of God. Loss of this kind is not incurred by those alone from whom grace is altogether withdrawn, and who have in consequence to suffer eternally in Hell. Such loss is also incurred in various measures and degrees by all who do not faithfully co-operate with grace, and who thus forfeit higher graces which they might have received, and fall into faults or defects which they might have escaped. We have already mentioned the sorrow which the Holy Souls in Purgatory must have felt when the amount of their own negligences as to grace was made clear to them in the light of their Particular

* St. Matt. xi. 21—24.

Judgment. We shall make the fuller consideration of this loss the subject of the remainder of this chapter.

4. It is certain that a great number of Christians go out of this world in a state of grace, indeed, and so with the blessed destiny of eternal glory awaiting them, but still, after having lost a great part of the opportunities which were offered them in God's providence of "laying up treasure in Heaven" by good works, and multiplying the graces vouchsafed to them. The consequence of this is that they have forfeited for ever an immense number of degrees of glory, each of which degree, as being eternal, is of infinite value, both from the honour which might have accrued from it to God, and also from the blessings which it would have brought to the soul which has forfeited it. St. Paul*
tells us that "star differeth from star in glory," and, as there are very great distances indeed between the glory of one saint and the glory of another, so also may there be immense differences between the height in Heaven and the nearness to God to which men do attain, and the height and the nearness to which they might have attained. Now the loss which the Holy Souls have thus incurred, and which has been made known to them, we cannot doubt, at their judgment, is a loss which is in itself irreparable. Purgatory can do away with the stains that remain on the soul, cancel the debt of satisfaction which they owe to the Divine justice, but it does not restore to them the time or the

* 1 Cor. xv. 41.

graces or the opportunities which have been squandered and have become unfruitful for eternity. This, in truth, amounts to a change, if we may so speak, in the counsels of God towards the souls which are to be eternally glorified in His Presence. According to His first counsel, as we may say, He had intended to give them a certain, it may be a very high, place in His Kingdom, to which they were to rise by their correspondence to the great chain of graces which He was prepared to bestow upon them. But their own unfaithfulness has made the fulfilment of this counsel impossible according to the law of His justice. In consequence of this unfaithfulness, God has adopted another counsel in their regard : that is, He has determined that they shall gain another, but a far lower, grade of glory, and of all that is involved in that glory. He has withdrawn Himself from them to a certain extent, they have forfeited to a certain extent the fulfilment of the designs of His love, and as to that which they have forfeited, He has turned away from them as our Lord turned away from the cities in which His mighty works were done, and in which, after a time, He would work no more. This loss, as has been said, is eternal. It is made known to the Holy Souls, and a terrible sorrow is inflicted on them in consequence which is one of their most severe punishments. " I think," says Suarez, " that their sorrow, considered as a punishment laid upon them for their purgation, is rather on account of the grades of blessedness which they have lost for ever, or which they have

not gained through sloth and venial sins, than on
account of the simple deferring of that blessedness
which they are, after a time, to gain.   In this way,
therefore, the souls that are more imperfect, and
which have the greater amount of guilt, have to
suffer greater sorrow."

5. It seems certainly a hard thing to say, that
the sorrow of the Holy Souls for the glory which
they have eternally lost, is greater than that which
they feel because they are shut out for a time from
that which they are destined to enjoy.   For this
last-named sorrow must be extremely intense, as
we may come to see when we consider it separately.
Still, what the great theologian above cited has
said seems nothing more than what is strictly
reasonable and natural.   All their love of God, all
their knowledge of His beauty, all that they know
about the bliss of Heaven, the splendour of grace,
the value of time, the power of the sacraments, the
all but omnipotence of prayer, the treasures to be
accumulated by good works, or penances, or almsdeeds, or satisfaction—everything of this kind
must add to the self-reproach which they must
entertain, when they consider how ungrateful, how
unfaithful, how foolish they have been in their use of
the opportunities and aids which God has given to
them.   It seems, indeed, wonderful that this pain
can ever pass away.   But it must be remembered
that it is inflicted as a punishment only, and therefore only for what has been wilful in the way of
neglect.   As a punishment, it must come to an end,
and then the soul is left with nothing to impede its

o

love of God from rushing forward to its full fruition. The saints who have been most faithful to the graces which God has given them have no regret for other higher graces which have not been offered them, though those other and higher graces would have secured them a higher glory, and so a closer knowledge and a more intense love of God. And so, when the punishment has been exhausted which He has inflicted on the imperfect souls who have been so far less faithful than the saints, they remain absolutely contented with their lot, because they have paid to His justice for the forfeiture of the glory which they might have reached. It is one of the marvels of the wisdom and love of God that a pain like this can be felt in Purgatory, that the cause of it can remain for ever in its effects, and yet that the pain itself can be entirely assuaged.

6. This consideration is of immense value to us, though it relates to a part of the pains of Purgatory which are connected with an eternal and irreparable loss. It may be said generally that the class of souls on which these pains will fall most heavily, must be the great number of those called to a certain closeness and intimate service of God who do not aim at the perfection to which God calls them. If we once admit, as the practical though unavowed rule of our life, that it is enough for us to aim at avoiding mortal sin, and so escaping Hell, then we may be quite certain that, if we do by the mercy of God die in His grace, we shall have a very large share in the forfeiture of glory which is the cause of the pains of which we have

been speaking. It seems impossible but that such souls should miss daily a thousand opportunities of advancing in grace and so gaining higher glory. On the other hand, if we are earnestly and sincerely bent on making the best of our time and of our grace, on abounding in good works in whatever way is open to us, in making the service of God the one great aim of our life, and on using the means of grace in the most perfect manner, then we may have reason to hope that we shall so live and so die as not to have incurred a very severe punishment for very many graces of eternal happiness which we have lost.

7. We know by our faith that the creation and sanctification of a single human soul is a greater and nobler work of God, than the creation and conservation of the whole physical universe. It is a simple truth, that intellectual and spiritual gifts are more beautiful than all the beauties of earth and sea, sky and mountain, trees and flowers and animals, and the whole starry firmament. In both these orders of His magnificence, intellectual and spiritual on the one hand, and the physical and visible on the other hand, God may create kingdom upon kingdom, grander and more splendid than any that He has as yet created. But what if by our own act we had been able to stay His hand, and strike out all that is most glorious and majestic, all that reflects in the highest actual degree His wisdom and beauty and power, and forced Him, as it were, to content Himself with a poorer world, a narrower display of His marvels, something far less

honourable and glorious to Him than what we see around us? What if we had been able to stint the profuse multitude of the stars which fill the heavens, to forbid Him to endow the sun with more than a mere millionth part of that light and heat which it now possesses, to limit Him to the peopling of dreary and unfruitful regions with a few puny forms of life, such as perhaps the tricks of Egyptian magicians aided by evil angels may have been able to seem to make to live and move? Yet this is but a faint picture of the losses of glory to God which have been caused by the unfaithfulness of His children. The life of each soul is dearer to Him than a thousand worlds, and He has agreed to adorn every moment of it with magnificent gifts, which He wooes His creatures to accept, in order that they may issue, by the working of His grace, in marvellous fruits of glory which are to last for ever. What a thing it is for Him to suffer at the hands of His friends, this sterility of His grace, this niggardly return from the soil which He has watered with His Blood? We may look upon the life of each Christian as intended by God to raise to His honour a stately temple, spacious, lofty, rich in all that can enhance the costliness of its fabric and its adornments with all the beauty that the highest art can bring out of the resources of nature and mind. It has to be finished and made complete in every part within a short space of time, and every day of every year has something to contribute of its own if the pile is to be accomplished. He places in our hands

an abundance of materials, He labours Himself
with us, He takes care that all that happens to us
may work for us, and that all His friends in
Heaven and on earth shall stand by to aid us and
cheer us on. And the glorious temple which we
are to raise for Him to dwell in is our own soul,
which is to enjoy the fruit of its labour through all
eternity. Alas ! in how many cases is the fabric
not begun at all ! in how many more does it halt
at its very outset, so that the time of judgment
comes when hardly the foundations have been
laid ! Such are the thoughts which rise in the
mind when we consider what we have done for
God, and compare it with what our work for Him
might and ought to have been.

CHAPTER XXII.

Purgatory and Natural Piety.

(THE MIRACLES WROUGHT AT NAZARETH.)

St. Matt. xiii. 54—58 ; St. Mark vi. 1—6.

1. IT has already been said that the last cures wrought by our Lord at Capharnaum were shrouded by Him in as much secrecy as was possible under the circumstances, probably in order not to provoke the calumnies of His enemies. These calumnies, however, as we have seen, broke out afresh. St. Mark tells us that He now passed from Capharnaum to Nazareth, to pay to that once blessed town what was to be, as it seems, His last visit. He took refuge, as it were, from Capharnaum in Nazareth, as He had before taken refuge from Nazareth in Capharnaum. The two accounts in St. Matthew and St. Mark, referred to above, evidently relate to the same visit. Our Lord, then, went to Nazareth, and began to teach in the synagogue on the Sabbath. The Evangelists tell us three things concerning this preaching. The first is that the people "were in admiration at His doctrine, saying, How came this Man by all these things ? and what wisdom is this which is given to Him, and such mighty works as are wrought by His hands ?"—referring, as it seems, to the great

miracles with which the whole country was ringing, rather than to any which He had wrought at Nazareth itself. In the second place, they went on to speak of our Lord as of one in Whom nothing great could be expected. "Is not this the carpenter?" or "the son of the carpenter? The son of Mary, the brother of James and Joseph and Jude and Simon? are not also His sisters here with us? And they were scandalized in regard of Him." They tell us also of our Lord's famous answer, in which He referred to what He had said in the same synagogue at the very outset of His Public Ministry. Then He had said, "No prophet is accepted in his own country." * Now He adds, that He is accepted elsewhere. "Jesus said to them, A prophet is not without honour, but in his own country, and in his own house, and among his own kindred." Then we come to the few miracles which may furnish us with the subject of the present chapter. St. Matthew tells us, "He wrought not many miracles there, because of their unbelief." St. Mark puts it more strongly : "He could not do any miracles there, only that He cured a few that were sick, laying His hands upon them. And He wondered, because of their unbelief."

2. There are many thoughts which rise to the mind at the mention of these few miracles wrought by our Lord in the home of His boyhood and early manhood, the town in which He dwelt by far the greater part of His earthly life, whose streets were more often pressed by His sacred Feet than

* St. Luke iv. 24.

those of any other place in the world. The incident seems to typify the reception of our Lord by mankind, the race which He chose out of all creation with which to unite Himself, when " He came unto His own, and His own received Him not." It seems to represent most forcibly the truth that so few of those who do receive Him allow Him to work in their souls what He desires to work, and that other general truth, of the extent to which the work of God in the world at large is impeded, so that it almost seems as if the fruits of the Incarnation were scanty indeed. But we shall use this motive which may have had some weight with our Lord in bringing about this visit as the ground of our considerations in this chapter. We seem to see that He was led by a holy piety to the place which was so long His home, to His old acquaintances and kinsfolk, in the loving hope that He might do them some little good. Thus we come to a subject which divides itself into two heads. In the first place, it is well to consider the love which, out of natural piety, the Holy Souls may bear to those whom they have left behind them, their own kith and kin, or others with whose lives their own lives have been bound up. In the second place, we may reflect on the duty which presses on us of relieving, to the utmost of our power, those among the souls in Purgatory between whom and us this sacred bond exists. These considerations will be quite enough to occupy us for the present.

3. As to the first point, no one familiar with

Catholic doctrine, or with Catholic modes of feeling, can suppose that the love of God with which the Holy Souls are so inflamed can, in their case, any more than in that of the Saints and Blessed in Heaven, dull the lawful and natural love which they bear to those who remain behind them on earth, or to those who may be with them in Purgatory, or who have gone before them to Heaven. All natural and human love is transformed and ennobled and purified, but it is also intensified and strengthened, by the surpassing charity which reigns beyond the grave among the children of God. This is the only reasonable conclusion to which we can come on the grounds of Christian theology, although, perhaps, we feel so much the imperfection and the want of spirituality and unselfishness of our human affections, that we are tempted to think that there can be nothing of the kind in the next world. There can be nothing sensual or selfish or imperfect in kind, but that is all. It would almost seem as if our Lord had vouchsafed to give us a hint as to this in His teaching concerning the Rich Glutton, whether that narrative be considered as a parable or not. We see that even in that poor soul there were the remains of natural piety and affection, for he desired that Lazarus might be sent to warn his brethren on earth lest they also should come to the same place of punishment with himself. Some writers have thought from this that the soul of the Rich Glutton was placed in Purgatory, as if it were impossible for the souls in Hell to feel any such affection as that which is manifested by His prayer. It may seem that this is an improbable opinion, because it need not be supposed that all natural affection is extinguished in the poor lost souls ; and, again, it may be thought that the prayer of the Rich Glutton,* which was for something which it was contrary to the disposition of God's Providence to grant, and which was, in fact, not granted, was not the sort of prayer which the Holy Souls of Purgatory would make.   But if we suppose the soul of whom we are speaking to have been in Hell, it can only increase the evidence which the case affords, for it is most certain that if there can still be anything like love for those on earth in Hell, there must be immensely greater love for the same persons in Purgatory.

4. We may well, therefore, suppose with what tender a love the Holy Souls will yearn for all that is good to those whom they have left on earth : parents for children, or children for parents, husbands and wives, brothers and sisters, friends and spiritual guides or those whom they have guided, one for the other.   The love of the Holy Souls must be intense in its purity, and most enlightened as to the true welfare of those for whom they are interested.   There seems to be no doubt that they can pray, and their prayer must be very efficacious (though not for themselves), because it has all the conditions which belong to prayer which God will hear.   There may be some doubt as to the amount of knowledge

* St. Luke xvi. 27.

which is imparted to them as to the state of the
living, but a perfect knowledge as to this is not an
element so necessary as to make its absence imply
that they cannot pray for us—for those who belong
to them most nearly, for their benefactors, those in
particular who are helping them towards their
perfect deliverance, those whom they may have
imperilled by their example or otherwise, and the
like. And it is certainly a matter of very frequent
experience among those who give themselves to the
devotion to Purgatory, or who even occasionally
offer spiritual alms to the Holy Souls for the obtaining of some blessing, to find themselves helped in
return in some very wonderful manner. But for
one favour which is thus consciously obtained by
means of the prayers of the holy dead, we may
safely assume that there are a hundred others of
which we are not conscious. And we may think of
Purgatory as a prison indeed, and as a place of
banishment, exile, and intense suffering, and yet,
because those who are there detained are princes of
the Kingdom of Heaven and on fire with divine
charity, it is also a place from which God derives
continual glory and men perpetual and innumerable
benefits by means of the prayers which proceed
therefrom.

5. As to the second point, a good deal has
already been said which need not be repeated here,
both concerning the general duty of piety to the
dead and as to the special duty which lies on us
with regard to our own near relatives and friends.
It has been said in a former chapter, that the

abandonment of prayer for the dead may be said to
be a mark that a community calling itself Christian
has become separated from our Lord. We may
also apply here the words of St. Paul, that "if a
man have not care of his own, and especially
of those of his house, he hath denied the faith, and
is worse than an infidel." It is most sad to see
the practice of good and kind-hearted people outside the Church, full of natural affection, and
conscientious in the discharge of all their known
duties, in this matter. No pains are too great, no
sacrifices too severe, no attentions too laborious for
them in the nursing and tending the sick, and the
grief with which they mourn when death at last
comes is most intense. And yet, while everything
is done for the memory of those whom they have
lost, while their pain remains for months and years
unassuaged, so that they are said never to forget
the dead, or to recover their loss, there is no
thought whatever of praying for them or helping
them. On the other hand, it is most touching to
see the large space which the holy departed fill in
the religion of a simple Catholic peasantry, as well
as among other classes, in countries which have
preserved the faith. The Masses and Communions
and almsdeeds and prayers and pilgrimages which
are directed to their aid are almost endless.
Catholics in a Protestant country may sometimes
.be chilled by the atmosphere in which they are
forced to live with what would seem indifference
to their departed when compared to the fervour
which is seen elsewhere, and it is therefore well

that we should revive our devotion in this respect by considerations such as those which are suggested by the miracle before us. The reflections contained in the next and in some following chapters will help us as to the means by which this devotion may become more fruitful, both to the Holy Souls and to ourselves.

———

CHAPTER XXIII.

The Holy Souls and the Sacrifice of the Altar.

(THE FEEDING OF THE FIVE THOUSAND.)

St. Matt. xiv. 13—21 ; St. Mark vi. 30—44 ; St. Luke ix. 10—17 ;
St. John vi. 1—13.

1. THE next of our Lord's miracles in order of time is that wonderful display of His power in multiplying the five loaves and two fishes so as to furnish food enough and more for the multitude which had followed Him into a desert place, which consisted of five thousand men besides women and children. This splendid miracle, on account of its great magnificence, and also on account of its great doctrinal importance, is related by all the four Evangelists, and it is the only miracle which is so related. The circumstances are so well known to us that it is hardly necessary to repeat them here. The miracle was wrought at a spot on the shores of the Lake of Galilee, to which our Lord had retired with His Apostles for the sake

of recollection. But they were followed by the multitude, and our Lord had compassion on them, as St. Mark tells us, "for they were as sheep not having a shepherd, and He began to teach them many things, and healed their sick." When the evening came on, the disciples suggested that He should send them away, but He bade them themselves give them to eat. They objected the impossibility of buying food for such a multitude, and then He inquired how much they had with them, and St. Andrew answered that there was a lad with five loaves and two fishes, " but what are they among so many?" Then our Lord made the multitude sit down on the green grass in order, by hundreds and fifties, and "looking up to Heaven, blessed them, and brake, and gave to His disciples, and the disciples gave them to the multitude, and the two fishes He divided unto all. And they all did eat, and had their fill, and they took up the leavings, twelve full baskets of fragments, and of the fishes."

2. The clear relation which this miracle bears to the Blessed Sacrament of the Altar is enough to suggest to us to consider in this chapter the importance of the Adorable Sacrifice as a means of relief to the Holy Souls of Purgatory. The doctrine concerning that Blessed Sacrament is naturally divided into two heads, considering it both as a Sacrifice and as a Sacrament in the strict sense of the term. As this miracle was repeated by our Lord on another occasion soon after this, we may leave the latter part of this doctrine till

we come to the second multiplication of loaves, and attend at present to the Sacrifice of the Altar alone. Very few words will be enough to remind us of the efficacy of this Sacrifice for the relief of the Holy Souls. All Catholics know that in that Sacrifice the merits of the Sacrifice of the Cross are offered to the Eternal Father, and that it thus presents to Him a satisfaction in itself infinitely greater than any debt which those souls can owe to His Divine justice. These Holy Souls are a part of the Church, and when her priests are ordained, they receive the power of offering the Sacrifice for the living and the dead. St. Anthony of Padua in his sermon, *In Cœna Domini*, tells us that the division of the Sacred Host into three parts, which is made by the priest before his Communion, signifies the three parts of the Church, the blessed in Heaven, the living on earth, and the dead; and St. Thomas* adds that the Mass has a threefold effect, forgiving sins in this world, alleviating pain in Purgatory, and increasing glory in Heaven. Many texts and figures in Holy Scripture are applied in this meaning by the Fathers and Saints. Theologians tell us that the temporal punishment due to sin is directly remitted by the Holy Sacrifice, and that this is the tradition of the Apostles. They tell us that this Sacrifice is the most powerful means of all that we possess for satisfaction, as the Council of Trent lays down that the souls in Purgatory are helped by the suffrages of the faithful, "but chiefly by the accept-

* *Opusc. de Sacramento Altaris* (21 or 58), cap. xxv.

able Sacrifice of the Altar." Indeed, the chief fruit of the Holy Sacrifice is said to be that of satisfaction : "for, as sacrifice, especially that of the Cross, has the power given to it of satisfying for the punishment due to our sins, so this unbloody Sacrifice, which is a living image of that Bloody Sacrifice, is properly and directly instituted for the application to us *ex opere operato* of the fruit of satisfaction, so that, as they say in the schools, what is done in that first Sacrifice by way of sufficiency, is wrought in this other by way of efficiency."* Again, some great theologians hold that the application of the satisfaction which is derived from this Sacrifice benefits the holy dead *ex opere operato*, and by a law of justice, while other things, such as Indulgences, and the application of our good works, benefit them by way of suffrage, that is, out of the mercy and liberality of God Who accepts them for that purpose. An argument for this opinion is based on the words of ordination above mentioned, and on the statements of Councils and Fathers, that the Adorable Sacrifice is to be offered for the dead in the same way as for the living.

3. The lives of the Saints are very full of anecdotes which illustrate the efficacy of the Sacrifice of the Altar for the relief of the Holy Souls, but we are obliged in these considerations to omit matter of that kind on account of the great space which it would occupy. But it may be

* Hautin, *Patrocinium Defunctorum*, lib. iii. col. 2, § 1. (n. 934).

useful to add here some of the reasons which are found in various writers for the Christian custom of celebrating Mass on certain special days for those who are departed. Five Masses may be said to be almost prescribed by that custom, when there is nothing to prevent them, that is, on the day of burial, on the third, seventh, and thirtieth days after death, and on the anniversary. In many parts of the Church it has been the rule never to let any Christian be buried without the celebration of Mass. The Mass of the third day is mentioned in the Clementine Constitutions,* and it is said to represent the Resurrection of our Lord on the third day, or the restoration in the soul of the image of the Ever-Blessed Trinity, or the threefold purification of thoughts, words, and deeds. The Mass of the seventh day is also significant of the eternal Sabbath or rest of the holy dead. We find a connection between seven days and the length of mourning in the Old Testament, as in the case of Joseph mourning for Jacob.† The thirtieth day is said to be chosen, as that was the number of days during which the Israelites mourned for Moses, or for the mystical reason that our Lord was thirty when He was baptized, or that thirty is the full-grown age of man, in which, it is said, we are all to rise again. The institution of anniversaries is traced by some up to the time of the Apostles, and it is so natural and universal as to need no explanation.

* Lib. viii. c. 48.
† Gen. l. 10 ; see Ecclus. xxii. 13.

P

4. There are many questions which have arisen as to Masses for the dead, on account of the great frequency of such Masses, and the various circumstances which may attend their celebration. Thus although a solemn Mass, with all its ceremonies and accompaniments, is in itself of no greater intrinsic value than a simple Low Mass, still the Church encourages the practice of celebrating the former, which may cause greater devotion, and so greater benefit to the soul for which it is offered.   Again, it is clear that a Mass of Requiem, in which all the prayers have a distinct reference to the relief of the dead, on that account profits them more than another Mass, although the intrinsic value of the Sacrifice is the same in each case.   Again, it must be clear that a Mass celebrated at a privileged altar is more directly and powerfully beneficial to a soul in Purgatory than another, and that, if the words of the concession of the privilege require that it should be a Mass of Requiem, such a Mass alone will gain the Indulgence.   The thirty continuous Masses which are recommended by St. Gregory the Great to the Abbot of his monastery of St. Andrew in Rome for the soul of one of his monks, seems to have become the foundation of the custom of celebrating thirty Masses for the dead on thirty continuous days, though of course it would not always be possible that such Masses would be of Requiem.   At one time there was a custom, according to which these thirty Masses were necessarily votive Masses of certain fixed

'kinds, but this custom appears to have died away since a decree of the Congregation of Rites in 1628. The custom of the thirty Masses still remains, and it would be well if this holy devotion were revived amongst us, as far as is possible, at least as to the number of Masses which those who are able should procure for their own relatives and friends. Some writers would prefer that they should be said at once, and not one by one for thirty days. A kindred question to this would be another, whether it is better to found anniversary Masses for the dead for perpetuity, or to procure a great number of Masses to be said at once. As to this it must be remembered that, although there can be no doubt that many souls in Purgatory are best benefited by procuring them the relief of the Adorable Sacrifice as soon and as plentifully as possible, there are still many circumstances about pious foundations which make them great acts of devotion and charity, by contributing to enhance the splendour of the Church by supporting her ministers, and the like. If the souls for whom such Masses are sung or said are already in Heaven, they may still profit by them in the way of fresh joy or accidental glory. In the last place, it is well that we should remember the custom which prevails among the faithful in many countries, of having Masses celebrated or celebrating them for their own souls, the satisfaction of which Masses is to be applied to their deliverance when they come to Purgatory. In some respects this also is a great act of devotion, inasmuch as it costs us much more to do this now, than to arrange that it shall be done after our death by those who represent us.

5. It may also be well to remember that to hear Mass for the holy dead is an act of religion and devotion which is certain to benefit them very much. This is a great incentive to the hearing of as many Masses as possible, and with the special intention of hearing them for the Holy Souls. In this way those who are not priests may in some sort share their power as to helping those in Purgatory, and those who are too poor to be able to procure Masses for them may be able to supply the effect of their poverty by hearing many Masses for them. It is certain that to hear Mass is a very high act of religion, next to that of saying Mass; and that those who hear Mass do in truth offer it, according to their power, to the Eternal Father, which is the most excellent act of worship that can be performed. The priest in the Mass, when he turns to the people at the *Orate, fratres,* calls it "my and your Sacrifice," and the hearers therefore honour God by offering that Holy Sacrifice as well as the priest. Suarez says that as the oblation of this Sacrifice is fruitful in the way of satisfaction and impetration *ex opere operato,* all those who offer it, and therefore those who hear it, receive its benefits in the same way, and not only in proportion to their own devotion. This is not certain, because, as other theologians say, the satisfactory fruit of the Adorable Sacrifice *ex opere operato* is received by the priest alone, who alone

offers it in the name of Christ. But at all events the fruit of impetration, as it is called, belongs to the hearers also *ex opere operato*, inasmuch as the priest, in the name of Christ, offers the Sacrifice for all, and more especially for those who are present. This fruit may be applied by them for the benefit of the Holy Souls for whom they may hear Mass. These are more or less theological considerations, on which Christian piety may feed itself, and which may be made the solid foundation of a great amount of practical devotion. A Mass heard every day for the special intention of relieving the Holy Souls may be in many cases, not only a daily alms of immense value to these sufferers who are so dear to our Lord, but also the source of immense benefits and great protection to ourselves, not only from its own intrinsic efficacy, but also on account of the numberless prayers which we may thus win from those for whom we perform this most blessed act of religion.

CHAPTER XXIV.

Pre-eminence of Charity to the Holy Souls.

(OUR LORD WALKING ON THE WATERS.)

St. Matt. xiv. 22—36 ; St. Mark vi. 45—56 ; St. John vi. 14—21.

1. THE Evangelists tell us that immediately after the miracle of the multiplication of the five loaves, our Lord made His disciples embark in the boat in which they had crossed the lake, and pass over to Capharnaum. He Himself remained alone on the spot where the miracle had been wrought, and went up into the mountain to pray. The disciples, fresh from the fatigue of ministering to so many people at the end of a long day of teaching, now found themselves without their Master in the midst of the sea, with the wind and waves against them. They laboured at the oars till it was past midnight, when a strong wind arose against them, and their progress became more difficult than before. Our Lord's eye was still upon them, as St. Mark tells us, and seeing them toiling, about the fourth watch of the night, as it was near the dawn, He came to them, walking on the waters, and made as if He would pass them by. " But they seeing Him walking upon the sea, thought it was an apparition, and they cried out. For they all saw Him and were troubled. And immediately He spoke with

them and said to them, Have a good heart, it is I,
fear ye not. And Peter made answer, and said,
Lord, if it be Thou, bid me come unto Thee upon
the waters. And He said, Come. And Peter
going down out of the boat, walked upon the
water to come to Jesus. But seeing the wind was
strong, he was afraid, and when he began to sink,
he cried out, Lord, save me! And immediately
Jesus stretching forth His hand, took hold of him,
and said, O thou of little faith, why didst thou
doubt? And when they were come up into the
boat, the wind ceased. And presently," adds
St. John, "the ship was at the land to which they
were going."

2. The contrast must have been very great to
the disciples, between the magnificent display of
power in the miracle of the multiplication of the
loaves, and their condition so soon afterwards,
toiling by night, without the presence of our Lord
to cheer and protect them, over a tossing sea and
with an adverse wind, to a shore which seemed
hardly nearer to them after many hours of labour.
They had had their share, not indeed in the
miracle of the loaves itself, but in the distribution
of the bread, which seemed to grow in their hands.
They had been made the instruments of bringing
home to the hungry people the fruits of our Lord's
power and mercy, and they had no doubt shared
in that holy enthusiasm and exultation with which
the multitudes must have been filled. Perhaps
they almost took part in the intoxication of the
people, who wished to take our Lord and make

Him a king.   And then, so soon afterwards, they
found themselves in the pitiful condition which the
Evangelists describe.   The miracle which followed,
when our Lord walked on the waters, seems to
have been wrought out of compassion for them, or
certainly, if this was not the only reason for it, it
was at least one of the reasons.   We may consider
them, in many respects, as representing the condition of the Holy Souls in Purgatory, who are
without the consolation of our Lord's presence,
and in a state of darkness, solitude, misery, and
pain.   They are not indeed labouring, for their
state is one of reposeful and tranquil, though most
intense, suffering.   But they are kept back by the
justice of God from the shore which they are
yearning to reach, and in some respects they are
worse off than if they could labour.   A part of
their suffering is that they cannot do anything that
is meritorious or satisfactory for themselves.   Thus,
putting these two great miracles side by side, we
may consider that they afford us an opportunity of
making the contrast that has been insisted upon by
many writers on this subject—who have made a
comparison between works of mercy which are
done for the relief of the living, and the similar
works which may be done for the dead.   This,
therefore, may be the subject of the present
chapter.

3. The case of the Holy Souls, however, is so
clear and their needs so urgent, that it is enough
to state positively the good which we have it in
our power to do by aiding them, instead of draw-

ing out a strict comparison between this and any
other work of spiritual mercy; all the more, as the
works of mercy by which we relieve the living,
may be applied by a holy intention, as works of
satisfaction for the dead. It is well known that
the spiritual works of mercy are more excellent
than the corporal works, on account of the greater
dignity of the soul, which is benefited by them,
of the greater good which is conferred, and the
higher excellence of the acts of virtue which are
exercised, in these spiritual works. In the same
way we may find many reasons for esteeming very
highly indeed the opportunity which our Lord
allows to us of conferring immense spiritual benefits upon souls very high in dignity and in their
nearness to Him, when we distribute our spiritual
alms to the sufferers in Purgatory. It is not
difficult to draw out in meditation a parallel
between the works of mercy, as they are ordinarily
enumerated, and this work of spiritual mercy—
for it is easy to see an image of the wants of the
Holy Souls in the hunger and thirst, the naked-
ness, the homelessness, the state of confinement
and of sickness or languor, which call so loudly
upon our compassion in the ordinary subjects of
such corporal works. Indeed, no hunger or thirst
can be equal to that yearning for God and the
delights of Heaven which consume them. They
are naked of that heavenly clothing of which
St. Paul speaks in the Second Epistle to the Corinthians, they are without shelter and detained from
their home, they are sick and almost plague-

stricken, until the effects of their sins are done away, and they are the prisoners of the justice of the King Who is great in all that He does, and thus great also in His punishments. In this way, comparing any earthly miseries with their spiritual sufferings, it is easy to soften our hearts with compassion towards them as afflicted in a degree which has no true parallel upon earth. As has been said, their dignity also surpasses all earthly dignity, and the goods from which they are kept out surpass in excellence any that we can procure for those who are in need upon earth. The work of charity to them is thus in every way most excellent.

4. Thoughts such as these have been the foundation, in many pious persons, of a form of devotion to the Holy Souls which goes far beyond the common bounds of charity. For in charity we are not ordinarily led to give away that which is of the utmost importance and necessity to ourselves. Such charity is considered heroic, especially when that which is given to others is our own life, or something that is hardly less precious to us. Nevertheless, the impulse of charity which is aroused by the consideration of the very great affliction in which the Holy Souls lie, and of the immense goods which are awaiting them in Heaven, their possession of which may be hastened on by our self-sacrifice, has urged many devout persons to the practice of giving to them all their own satisfactions and Indulgences, reserving nothing at all to themselves. This holy practice was at one time questioned, as being inconsistent with the charity

we are bound to have to our own souls; but the mind of the Church has been quite sufficiently declared in its favour by the sanction which it has received and the encouragement which has been afforded to it by the special Indulgences which have been granted to those who adopt it. This is not the place for any lengthened argument on the subject. It is sufficient to say that the charity which gives away to the Holy Souls all the satisfactions which we gain, or which are applied to us in any way, may at the utmost involve to ourselves what is no doubt a very great and momentous loss —that is, that, when it comes to be our turn to take our places in the holy prison of Purgatory, we shall be detained there far longer than we might otherwise have been detained, in consequence of our want of these satisfactions. We may, therefore, in strictness, make ourselves liable to a great deal of suffering and a very long detention in Purgatory, if we spend, as it were, our satisfactions on others, instead of applying them to ourselves. We may be in the case in which the prudent virgins in our Lord's parable would have been, if they had given away their oil to the others, instead of refusing, "Lest perchance there be not enough for us and for you." * If this parallel were certainly apt and true in all particulars, then we might perhaps think that we had even our Lord's special warning against any such practice as that of which we are speaking. But it is certain that our Lord in that parable is not speaking of a temporary exclusion from the

* St. Matt. xxv. 9.

Marriage Supper of the Lamb, but of an eternal banishment from His presence, while, on the other hand, the result of the practice of which we are speaking cannot be more than a temporary delay in our own entrance into Heaven. At the utmost then, it would be like the charity of St. Paul or of Moses, who were ready, as it appears, to be excluded from the enjoyment of God, though not, of course, from His grace or His love, for the sake of their brethren, and it would be like the charity which is mentioned in the case of St. Martin, who was willing to remain on earth and labour longer in order to be more useful to the Church. The same thing is related of St. Ignatius of Loyola, and of other Saints. And if such are the actions of Saints who are set before us as examples which we are to imitate, there can be no question as to the excellence of charity of this kind.

5. But it must be added that it cannot be certain that a soul which, while on earth, has made over to others, in the way here mentioned, all the satisfactions which it may have gained and all the suffrages which may be made for it after its decease, will in truth be allowed by God to lose anything by that act of charity. For, in the first place, it is certain that it will gain great merit in the sight of God by such an act, and that therefore, if it comes to be delayed longer in Purgatory than might otherwise have been the case, it will at least enter Heaven with greater merit, and therefore will enjoy greater glory for all eternity. In the second place, the increase of merit would be accompanied by an

increase of grace, by means of which such a soul would become dearer to God and more able to advance rapidly in perfection, and thus have less need of satisfaction when it came to Purgatory, as well as a greater accumulation of virtuous actions. In the third place, it would, in a certain sense, throw itself, not only on the justice of God, but on His special love, and—inasmuch as the application of numberless suffrages which are made in general for the Holy Souls depends upon His will, and is made according to the desires and choices of His Sacred Heart, or of our Lady, or of the Saints— it is very likely that those who have thus exposed themselves to the danger of a very long detention in Purgatory for the sake of others, will share very largely in our Lord's distribution of these general suffrages, and so reach Heaven even sooner than they might if they had retained their satisfactions for their own benefit. Certainly such a soul will have a great number of special friends, both in Purgatory and in Heaven, who will exert themselves both out of justice and out of charity to make its period of purification as short as possible.

6. We may well imagine that our Lord has given us an example which may be used to spur us on to this or any other signal act of charity for the benefit of the Holy Souls, when instead of resting for the night on the mountain, or even of continuing His blessed communion with His Father in prayer, He walked over the water to cheer and relieve the Apostles in their trouble on the lake. His coming into the ship had the double effect of

making the wind cease and bringing the boat, without further effort, to the land. Those who forego the relief which they might enjoy themselves for the sake of helping others to reach the eternal shore more quickly, may hereafter find that they themselves also reach it almost immediately by virtue of that act of charity. But it must be remembered that it may be otherwise, and that an act of this kind, which is by nature heroic, is not to be made without forethought and consultation. People who think very little of venial sins, who do not carefully guard their consciences from stain, who do no penance and take no pains about Indulgences, are hardly persons to give away their satisfactions to the Holy Souls. Such an act should be, as it were, the crown of other less perfect kinds of charity, of prayers, of almsdeeds, of mortifications, of Communions, Masses, and the like, offered for the relief of the Holy Souls. If Esau had given away his birthright knowing its value, and at a great cost to himself, it would have been a signal act of charity which God would have rewarded. He gave it away thoughtlessly for a mess of pottage, and he lost the favour of God thereby as well as his birthright. The act of which we are speaking, therefore, should not be lightly done, as if we did not care about our satisfactions and had little fear of Purgatory. The more we know about Purgatory, the more we shall fear it, and the more store we shall set by anything that can deliver us from its pains. The more we fear it, and the more precious we consider our satisfactions, and the suffrages to be made for us to be, the most precious in the sight of God will be the charity that makes them all over to others, and leaves ourselves exposed to the utmost rigour of His justice.

———

CHAPTER XXV.

Privileges of the Children of God.

(THE HEALING OF THE DAUGHTER OF THE SYROPHŒNICIAN WOMAN.)

St. Matt. xv. 21—28 ; St. Mark vii. 24—30.

1. IT appears that after our Lord's return to Capharnaum from the place where He had worked the great miracle of the feeding of the five thousand, He did not remain long in that city. The time which He spent there seems to have been chiefly given, as far as the narratives of the Evangelists inform us, to discussions with the Jews in the synagogue and elsewhere on the subject of His teaching or the necessity of the eating and drinking of His Body and Blood, and on the non-observance of certain traditions with which the Pharisees from Jerusalem charged His disciples. Our Lord was, as before, desirous to avoid publicity, which, in the present temper of His enemies, involved persecution and the blackest calumny. So He left the city without, as it seems, working a single miracle, and went into the country of the Gentiles, the

parts of Tyre and Sidon. "Entering into a house," says St. Mark, "He would that no man should know it, and He could not be hid. For a woman, as soon as she heard of Him, whose daughter had an unclean spirit, came in and fell down at His feet. For the woman was a Gentile, a Syrophœnician born. And she besought Him that He would cast forth the devil out of her daughter. Who said to her, Suffer first the children to be filled, for it is not good to take the bread of the children, and to cast it to the dogs." St. Matthew mentions one or two circumstances as to this application and our Lord's answer which add to the fulness of the picture. He tells us that the poor woman first applied to our Lord using the name by which, it seems, He was popularly called, "Have mercy on me, O Lord, Thou Son of David, my daughter is grievously troubled by a devil. Who answered her not a word." But she continued her importunities, and "His disciples came and besought Him, saying, Send her away, for she crieth after us. And He answering said, I am not sent but to the sheep that are lost of the house of Israel." Then, it seems, she obtained admittance, or forced her way into the house. "But she came and addressed Him, saying, Lord, help me!" Then our Lord gave her the answer related by St. Mark as well as by St. Matthew, about the bread of the children. "But she said, Yea, Lord, for the whelps also eat of the crumbs which fall from the table of their masters." Such faith could not go unrewarded.

"Then Jesus answering her said, O woman, great is thy faith! be it done unto thee as thou wilt. For this saying, go thy way, the devil is gone out of thy daughter. And when she was come into her house, she found the girl lying on the bed, and that the devil was gone out."

2. It is clear that our Lord was highly pleased with the faith of the Gentile woman, as before He had been moved to commend so strongly the faith of the centurion at Capharnaum, but that, as His special mission was to the Jews, and as the Church was not formally to open its gates to the Gentiles until after the day of Pentecost and by the ministry of St. Peter, the distinction between Jew and Gentile had not as yet been put away, and thus the Syrophœnician woman and her daughter were, strictly speaking, outside the "covenant of Israel" and the range of those to whom our Lord's special and personal mission applied. But it is clear also that the mercies of God, as well as the tender compassion of the Sacred Heart of our Lord, are ever ready to leap beyond the bounds of the covenant which has been made with men, and that, in particular, our Lord's Heart rejoiced over this woman as over the centurion, because each represented to Him the multitude of the Gentiles who were so soon to be brought within the fold of the Church. Thus we have two principles, as it were, set before us in this incident, and in the words of our Lord to the woman. The first is, that of the exclusiveness of the covenanted mercies of God to man—which means little more

Q

than that God exacts certain easy conditions for the reception of His favours, and that if these conditions be not complied with, those favours must not be reckoned on. The second is, that any conditions, which God may lay down as necessary for the special favours which He may promise or impart, do not tie His hands so strictly as that when their exact fulfilment has not taken place without deliberate fault, He is bound not to give His bounties as He may choose, in consideration of the faith or charity of those on whom He would not otherwise bestow them. God is always free to distribute His graces as He chooses, and as a matter of fact He may give them wherever a true faith can exist, as in the case of this woman, who was not, in the strict sense, a child of the house of Israel, but who was, after all, a child of a still earlier covenant than that which was made with Abraham, because she had faith, without which it is impossible to please God. Thus her case shows us that there may be some outside the visible limits of the Body with which God has now made His covenant, who yet, as the Father speaks, belong to the Soul of the Church. It may be well, therefore, to take this miracle as a text which suggests to us to consider the application of these principles to the holy realm of Purgatory, and to remind ourselves who those are who may be admitted into it, and who are therefore the rightful objects of our compassion and charity, and who are those who are excluded from it by the laws of the Kingdom of God.

3. It is clear that, as Purgatory is an intermediate and temporary state, in which those souls are detained who are destined to be in Heaven throughout all eternity, it cannot be the place of sojourn either for those who enter Heaven at once after their death, or for those who are never to enter Heaven at all. In the first class we must place the saints of God and all the blessed souls who die in the state of grace, either with no debt at all to the justice of God upon them, or having entirely and perfectly cancelled that debt by contrition, penance, and the like. In the same class must be placed the souls of baptized infants, who have been regenerated, and made members of Christ and heirs of Heaven, and who have after that incurred no debt whatever to God's justice because they have never attained the use of reason, and so the capacity of deliberate sin. The fundamental reason why these children, and, indeed, all others who enter Heaven, are able to do so, is that they are members of Jesus Christ, through Whom alone access to Heaven can be obtained, as the Church says, *Tu, devicto, mortis aculeo, aperuisti credentibus regna cœlorum.* And the word "believers" is used here in strict accordance with Christian theology, which teaches us that before the institution of Baptism, the removal of original sin, which is the great essential bar to the entrance of Heaven—inasmuch as no moral excellence whatever can enter there if original sin be not removed—was to be obtained by the exercise of faith, certain truths as to God, and, implicitly

at least, as to the Redemption of man, being always proposed to mankind as the subject-matter of faith, according to the character of the various successive dispensations under which men have been placed in the course of their history. We have only a few lines back referred to this prerogative of faith, and to St. Paul's words concerning it, "without faith it is impossible to please God. For he that cometh to God must believe that He is, and is a rewarder to them that seek Him."* These then form the class who cannot enter Purgatory because they are to pass to Heaven at once—all those who die with no actual sin to suffer for, and with the stain of original sin removed, the condition of that removal, under the present law of God, being Christian Baptism.

4. On the other hand, we must place as the class of men who cannot be admitted to Purgatory, because they can never pass to Heaven, all those who under any dispensation whatever, primitive, patriarchal, Mosaic, or Christian, have died out of God's grace in a state of mortal sin, which mortal sin cannot be committed by any soul except knowingly and wilfully. Even a single mortal sin unrepented of—in which case the soul departs out of this life in a state of sin—is enough in the justice of God to render that soul guilty of the eternal punishment of Hell. And we must add to this class all those, infants and others, who have died, indeed, without mortal sin on their souls, but who have never in any way been made partakers of

* Heb. xi. 6.

the inheritance of the children of God by the removal of original sin. Thus we see who can and who cannot be admitted to Purgatory. All those can, who belong to the body of Jesus Christ, and who have had the guilt of original sin removed by the application of His merits. All these can be, but not all these are, admitted to Purgatory, because the birthright which is conferred on them when original sin is cancelled may be lost by their own wilful unrepented sin. On the other hand, no one can be admitted to Purgatory in whom original sin remains unremoved, or who is destined to the eternal punishment of Hell on account of his own deliberate sin, that is, by his own unrecalled choice.

5. These statements, it may be said, leave a large part of the human race practically unallotted, and, as it were, unprovided for. That is, it may be said, there may be multitudes of human souls in whom the guilt of original sin has never been removed, and who are therefore incapable of Heaven, and yet they may not have died in the guilt of a deliberate mortal sin, either because they have never had the opportunity, on account of an early death, or because they have been shielded from temptation, or have followed their conscience and what they have known of the law of God faithfully, or because they have had the grace to be truly sorry for sin. These souls, it may be said, belong neither to Hell, nor to Heaven, nor to Purgatory, and yet they make up, as has been said, a very large portion of the human race. For, to

speak only of one class among those mentioned, as it is probable that of those who attain Heaven a very large proportion will be composed of children who have had the stain of original sin removed through Jesus Christ, without living long enough to attain the age of reason, so it is even more probable that of those in whom the stain of that sin is not removed, a very large proportion is composed of those who have never lived long enough to be guilty of actual sin. For a great part of the human race dies in infancy, and out of this large portion of the children of Adam there are certainly more unbaptized than baptized. For more infants survive in Christian than in heathen countries, in which it is often the custom to expose them to death, or otherwise ill-treat them. It may also be said that the considerations suggested above open many questions as to Purgatory itself. For they suggest that original sin may perhaps have been removed in many cases outside the chosen people of God, by the faith which was the condition from the first, which may also, in the case of many adults, have "worked by love," and have been acceptable to God. They suggest that the earlier conditions of participation in the redemption of Jesus Christ may have remained in force in parts of the world in which the Church has never been set up, long after the first preaching of the Christian religion, and that on this account the entrance to Purgatory may have been open to some who were not Christians. They suggest also that a great number of baptized persons, who have been born outside the fold of the Catholic Church, and who have died in their infancy, or without any deliberate mortal sin upon their soul uncancelled, may find a place hereafter in Heaven, and some of them in Purgatory. The tendency of all these suggestions, if true, is to enlarge very much the range, so to speak, of admittance into this blessed prison—a prison indeed, a place of intense suffering, and yet the necessary ante-chamber, so to speak, of Heaven, to a very large number of the adults who are to find entrance at last into the presence of God.

6. It would be foreign to our purpose here to enter fully into all these questions. But a few remarks may be in place, chiefly in order to guard against any wildness of conjecture, and also to stimulate our exertions for the Holy Souls. For it would be a great stimulus to our charity and our exertions for the sufferers of Purgatory, to know that, in the mercy of God, they are far more numerous, and, so to speak, heterogeneous than we had perhaps imagined. But it is well to remember that two of these suggestions must be carefully combined with one another. That is, it is true to say that no one can be doomed to Hell except for deliberate sin, and also that there may be a great many baptized persons outside the Catholic Church who may reach Purgatory on their way to Heaven. But it is equally true, though not always so carefully remembered, that to remain wilfully outside the pale of the Catholic Church is in itself a mortal sin of schism, against charity, and that wilfully to reject any portion whatever of the Catholic Creed

is a mortal sin of heresy, against faith. There are positive precepts of God which, when known, are as binding as the precepts which belong to the natural law. Man is as much responsible to God for what he believes as for what he does. And the probation of many a man may be chiefly intellectual —the use which he makes of his will in the acceptance or rejection of truth, as well as in the obedience or disobedience which he shows to the moral law. It is also evident, that this kind of probation is very common indeed in the present day, when education is so common, when matters of controversy are made so much matters of discussion everywhere, when every one has the evidence as to the true Church so very much more within his reach than in former generations.

7. But, after due allowance has been made for this and kindred truths, it may still remain probable that the world beyond the grave is very different from our common thoughts concerning it, and that there may be large classes of souls for which we do not ordinarily make provision. Scripture is the record of revelation, of God's dealings with man, and principally and directly of the great Economy of the Incarnation. The Catholic Creed states the great series of truths which sum up this Economy. Both Scripture and the Creed intimate to us that there are large dispositions of God in His Mercy and Justice, of which we have but the slightest glimpses at present. When the divinely inspired historian of the Creation added to his account of the formation of the sun and moon the simple

words, "and the stars also," he passed lightly
indeed, in comparison to the magnificence of the
work of which he spoke, over the creation of the
whole sidereal universe, so far more beautiful and
wonderful than the earth with its greater and lesser
lights. In the same way the mind is lost in
thinking of the countless millions of human souls
with whom the Providence of the Father of all has
to deal with perfect justice, or rather with justice
tempered by immense mercy, in arranging for their
eternity according to the manner in which they
have met their probation here. It is enough to
know that no one is eternally lost in Hell without
his own fault, and that the grace of God is never
wanting to any human soul which truly does what
it can to make its peace with its Creator and Judge.

8. In our present considerations, however, we
have only to deal directly with the subject of
Purgatory, and, with the limitation already made,
there is every reason why we should continually
remind ourselves of the multitudes of souls who
may be there, who have been Christians indeed, by
virtue of their baptism, but who, for no fault of
their own, have lived and died outside the pale of
the visible Church. It is no part of our duty to
limit the range or power of good faith in excusing
men even from inquiring after the Church, as long
as they are not obliged to such investigations
under the pain of serious sin. Wherever the case
of excusable ignorance and good faith exists, there
is a soul which has peculiar claims on our compassion. For it has been a child of God deprived of

its birthright on earth, stolen away from its home, brought up in ignorance of so much which would have stirred its heart to love and helped it to the practice of noble and heroic virtues of which it may never have heard. There is a soul which may have learnt the elementary truths of religion, the "beginnings of Christ," of which St. Paul speaks to the Hebrews,* but which has been kept in bondage under a hard system, deprived of the food of the children, and knowing little of the Divine charity of which the Catholic Church is the earthly home. It has never been taught to love our Lord in His Sacramental Life, or to know the true sweetness of confession or of communion, or to bask in the smile of Mary, or to exercise its brotherly rights with Saints and Angels. The blessings which it has missed are untold, and it may have forfeited great glories in Heaven on account of the cold atmosphere in which it has languished upon earth. In it the counsel of Satan has been defeated to the glory of God, but the glory of God has suffered much loss from the counsel of Satan. As has been already said, such a soul has few to pray for it on earth of those on whom that duty would naturally fall. It is in any case under the bar of a terrible penalty in its almost certain destitution of the aid of prayer and suffrage, and sacrifice after its death. All the more has it special claims on the charity of the faithful. In one of the revelations of St. Gertrude, our Lord is said to have spoken to the Saint of the manner in which He delighted to impart to souls

* Heb. vi. 1.

which were dear to Him the suffrages which her community made for those for whom they were under special obligations to pray. Some of the souls of whom we are speaking may be of the class who are so dear to our Lord ; those who " do what they can," though it is but little ; those "who are faithful in small things ; " those who have had little to give, like the widow in the Gospel, but who have given it all. The Prophet Malachias* speaks of those who remain faithful to God in the midst of generations who turn from Him, and his words may apply to the souls of which we speak, " A book of remembrance was written before Him for them that fear the Lord, and think upon His Name. And they shall be My special possession, saith the Lord of hosts, in the day that I do judgment."

* Malachias iii. 17.

CHAPTER XXVI.

Particular Punishments in Purgatory.

(CURE OF THE DEAF AND DUMB IN DECAPOLIS.)

St. Mark vii. 31—37.

1. THE miraculous deliverance of the daughter of the Syrophœnician woman was almost immediately followed by another miracle, which is carefully related to us by St. Mark. Our Lord again changed His place of abode, for He returned from the sea coast of the Mediterranean to the remote country at the north-eastern side of the Sea of Galilee, a tract which was known by the name of Decapolis. Here again He was solicited to show mercy to the poor sufferers from disease. "They bring unto Him one deaf and dumb, and they besought Him that He would lay His hand upon him." There seems to have been a multitude present, and our Lord may have been teaching them, but He would not work this miracle in their presence. "And taking him from the multitude apart, He put His fingers into His ears, and spitting, He touched his tongue, and looking up to Heaven, He groaned, and said to him, Ephpheta, which is, Be thou opened, and immediately his ears were opened, and the string of his tongue was loosed, and he spoke right."

Our Lord tried in vain to keep the miracle a secret. "And He charged them that they should tell no man. But the more He charged them, so much the more a great deal did they publish it, and so much the more did they wonder, saying, He hath done all things well, He hath made both the deaf to hear, and the dumb to speak."

2. The circumstances of this miracle, all of which were ordered with the utmost care by the providence of our Lord, are in some respects peculiar, and it is some of these features which we may fasten on as furnishing us with the special subject of this chapter. There is no mention of any devil possessing the poor sufferer. Our Lord did something by way of application of His own Sacred Humanity to each of the senses which were afflicted, putting His fingers into the ears of the man, and touching His tongue with His spittle. The looking up to Heaven, the groaning, and the use of the word Ephpheta, are also remarkable, as well as the comment of the multitude, that He had done all things well, and made both the deaf to hear and the dumb to speak. Each affliction, therefore, of the poor man had its special remedy. Our Lord did not simply bless him, or touch him, or lay His hands upon him, but healed each sense separately by contact with Himself. This action of our Lord may serve to remind us of the particularity of the pains of Purgatory. In Purgatory, as in Hell itself, each sin has its own punishment, and each sense is afflicted in a marvellous manner for the sins which have been

committed through it.   As there are sins committed through the eyes, or the ears, or the
tongue, or the touch, or the smelling, so there
are special afflictions which correspond to each
one of these senses, no sin and no class of sin
being left without its chastisement in kind.   It is
the soul which has sinned through each of these
senses, and the presence of which in the body has
enabled them to perform their functions, to receive
the unlawful pleasure, and so minister to the sin.
It is the soul, detached from the body, which has
to suffer the punishment of each several sin in
Purgatory, or, as it may be, in Hell.   Penance
must be done for each here, or Purgatory must
be suffered in each hereafter, and the satisfactory
power of penance or of the suffering in Purgatory
comes from the stores of healing which are laid up
for us in the Sacred Humanity of our Lord.

3. This truth is of great value to us in our
considerations concerning Purgatory, whether we
apply them to the subject of the pains of the Holy
Souls and of our power in relieving them, or to
that of the careful avoidance of sin in ourselves.
It is a natural complement to, or even a part of,
the doctrine of the pain of sense on which we had
to reflect in a former chapter.   In that chapter we
dwelt more especially on the intensity of the sufferings which are inflicted in Purgatory, and in this
we have to consider especially their particularity.
Without this last point, we might be inclined to be
vague and indefinite in our ideas of the sufferings
for sin.   Those sufferings are not general, the

chastisement of a general unfaithfulness to God in the use of our senses, but most carefully measured and adapted to each several sin of each kind. We had occasion to refer, in that former chapter, to the narratives of the visions which are to be found in the lives of the Saints in illustration of Purgatory, and to the pictorial and sensible representations or descriptions by which it is so often sought to bring home to the minds of the faithful the severity of the sufferings there. Now, it is this very circumstance of the particularity of these descriptions which is so uncomfortable and painful to many who may be unfamiliar to the truth which it is thus attempted to represent. Any account of the suffering of the soul must of necessity be conveyed in language which uses the image of bodily suffering to convey what is intended. But any image of bodily suffering must be particular — it must represent the torment of this sense or that sense, this or that part of the body, and the like. Here again, we may say, let those who can bring home to themselves the truth of which we are speaking without the aid of such representations do so by all means, but let them not find fault with others, who find it useful to aid themselves or those to whom they speak or write by the material means of which we are speaking. The one thing of importance is the truth, and not the manner in which the truth is represented or brought home.

4. The use which we make of our bodily senses is a great trust committed to us, for which, as we

see by the truths now suggested to us, we shall
have to give in each case a separate account.
That is, it is not simply our body for which we
are responsible, but for each sense of our body in
particular. Each one of these senses opens to us
a separate world. The loss of any one shuts us
out from a separate world. Each one is a great
gift of God, meant to be used for His service and
for our delight, or rather, not in all cases for our
delight, in the ordinary sense of the word, for the
service of God often requires that we should
mortify them instead of gratifying them. But
each one opens to us a separate field for the
practice of virtue, a field in which we may gather
day after day fruits which will remain to us for
ever among the rewards of Heaven. As to each
we have the example of our Blessed Lord to study
and to imitate. That is, He has in a true sense
touched each one of our senses, and blessed their
use, and taught us what that use may be, in order
that they may be to us indeed the source of infinite
joy hereafter. When we receive Him in Holy Communion, we receive the Body Whose senses were
used in so perfect a way to the glory of His
Father, and if we are faithful and diligent in our
imitation of Him in the use of these senses,
our contact with His Sacred Humanity in Holy
Communion will give us both light and power for
the purpose here spoken of. His presence will
not only calm and enlighten the mind, and fill
the soul with graces and gifts, but it will in
particular soothe down the rebellion of the

senses, give strength to the ruling power within us which has to control and regulate their use. To get the full fruit of this benefit, we must study to use them modestly and reverently, like precious gifts which may be injured and ruined by carelessness and sensuality, giving thanks for them, keeping them in order as parents keep their children, examining ourselves regarding them, and subjecting them to discipline in order that they may not lead us astray, and to chastisement if they have done so.

5. This would be enough reason of itself for constant watchfulness, and continual self-restraint as to each one of our senses. But it may be added, as is so well known to those who study the spiritual life, that the conquest of the senses is an essential means to the gaining of the spirit of prayer, and of the other immense blessings to which prayer introduces us. This, however, is a large subject, on which it is not necessary now to enter. And, as we shall soon have to speak of the various means of mortification which can be used for the help of the Holy Souls, it may be enough in the present chapter to say in general, that we shall have greater power to satisfy for them, by way of prayer and other methods of impetration, if we unite to these some special mortification of the senses; and that such mortification will in itself be a most acceptable satisfaction, which can be directly applied to the relief of the particular sufferings which the Holy Souls may have to endure in the manner here considered.

R

CHAPTER XXVII.

The Holy Souls relieved by Holy Communion.

(THE FEEDING OF THE FOUR THOUSAND.)

St. Matt. xv. 29—39 ; St. Mark viii. 1—19.

1. THE circumstances under which our Lord
wrought the second miracle of the multiplication
of the loaves are in many respects similar to those
of the first. The people in the neighbourhood of
the Lake of Galilee, from which He was now
absenting Himself from time to time, and which
He was soon to leave altogether, seem to have
been on the watch for Him when He returned and
to have flocked to Him with their sick, in hopes of
obtaining their cure from His unwearied mercy.
This was the case on the occasion of which we are
now to speak. St. Matthew tells us that He came
nigh the Sea of Galilee : "And going up into a
mountain, He sat there. And there came to Him
great multitudes, having with them the dumb,
the blind, the lame, the maimed, and many
others, and they cast them down at His feet, and
He healed them. So that the multitude marvelled,
seeing the dumb speak, the lame walk, the blind
see, and they glorified the God of Israel." This,
however, was only the beginning of the marvellous
mercy which He was now to show them. "And

Jesus called together His disciples and said, I have compassion on the multitudes, because they continue with Me now three days, and have not what to eat, and I will not send them away fasting, lest they faint in the way." It is not impossible that the Apostles remembered the former miracle, but did not venture openly to suggest its repetition. "And the disciples say to Him, Whence then shall we have so many loaves in the desert, as to fill so great a multitude? And Jesus said to them, How many loaves have you? But they said, Seven, and a few little fishes. And He commanded the multitude to sit down upon the ground. And taking the seven loaves and the fishes, and giving thanks, He broke and gave to His disciples, and the disciples gave to the people, and they did all eat and took their fill, and they took up seven baskets full of what remained of the fragments. And they that did eat were four thousand men besides children and women."

2. We have already said that it will be well to consider this miracle, which is the second in which our Lord foreshadowed the great marvel of love which He was to leave behind Him in the Church in the Adorable Sacrament of His precious Body and Blood, as suggesting to us the benefit which we may confer on the Holy Souls of Purgatory by means of Holy Communion—having already spoken of the blessing which remains for them, as well as for ourselves, in the Sacrifice of the Altar. It has been sometimes maintained that the satisfactory power of the act of Communion may be

made beneficial to the Holy Souls, like the satisfaction which is contained in the Holy Mass itself, as theologians speak, *ex opere operato*, and thus independently of the dispositions and devotion of the person who may receive Holy Communion. This, however, does not seem to be the truest doctrine on the matter. The Holy Communion is directly the food of the soul, and not the Sacrifice of our Lord. The office of food is to nourish, and not to satisfy—and it is even uncertain whether Holy Communion, simply and of itself, satisfies for the sins of the recipient, or whether this effect is to be attributed to the devotion and charity, and the like, with which It may be received.

3. Leaving this question to theologians, we may content ourselves with those more general considerations concerning Holy Communion, as an act of the virtue of religion, and as including so many acts of various virtues most dear to our Lord, which may enable us to understand that it may have a very great and almost unparalleled power in the way of obtaining pardon and relief for the blessed sufferers with whom we are concerned, by way of impetration, if not by that of direct satisfaction. No act of religion can be imagined more fruitful of benefit to the soul, or of delight and joy to our Lord, than the act of Holy Communion. It is the highest act of faith that we can perform, it expresses and embodies hope in its most perfect aspirations, it is the consummation and crown of charity, of personal devotion and

love of our Lord, and to all who belong to Him in
Heaven, on earth, and under the earth. The soul
who devoutly receives Him in Holy Communion,
and gives itself to Him, as it were, in that most
intimate act of love and union, rejoices Him as
Mary rejoiced Him when she received Him into
her pure womb, as Joseph delighted Him when
he carried Him in his arms, as St. John moved
His Heart to special love when he lay in His
bosom, as St. Martha when she received Him into
her house, as St. Magdalene when she anointed
Him and washed His feet with her tears, as the
holy women when they prepared to honour His
Body after it had been committed to the Holy
Sepulchre. The due reception of Holy Communion implies a thousand holy affections, acts of
sorrow for sin, of resolution of amendment, of thanksgiving, of self-oblation, of intercession, and the like.
The giving Himself to us in Holy Communion
is the last and extreme act of love in our Lord to
us, and the receiving Him in Holy Communion is
the act by which we show our love to and confidence in Him to the utmost, and by which we
take to ourselves in the fullest measure the
treasures of grace and the spiritual benefits which
are stored for us in His Sacred Humanity. In
Holy Communion, He becomes the source of that
abundant life to the soul of which He spoke to the
Apostles; He fills us with light, and opens to us
the sweetness and joy which are perfectly to be
imparted in Heaven itself, at the same time
strengthening the soul with the powers of immortal

life. In Holy Communion He wipes away the remains of sins, He forgives in large measure the pains that are due to former transgressions, He fortifies us against our spiritual enemies, and gives us the vigour and resolution which help us to rise again quickly, even if we fall. He increases in us all virtues, especially charity, He confirms all that is good in us already, He imparts to us the capacity of perseverance, a gift altogether foreign to our poor and frail nature, and secures for us the glory to which He destines us, and for the winning of which He has done all that He has done by becoming Man and dying for us on the Cross.

4. It cannot then be imagined, but that this act of Communion, so full of acts on our part which give pleasure to God, and so rich in the spiritual benefits which it brings home to the soul, must be an act which, if offered like any other act of religion, for the Holy Souls of Purgatory, must turn upon them very powerfully the streams of the Divine mercy and compassion. The histories of the Saints contain more than a few instances, in which the Holy Souls themselves have made it known that they are helped in a special manner by the devout Communions which are thus offered for them. It may be, that in many cases they are conscious that a part of their detention in the prison of God's justice is owing to their coldness in receiving Holy Communion, or to their neglect to receive It as often as they might. Those then who help them in this way may use this thought as an additional motive for great fervour in pre-

paration and devotion in reception, as well as for
the frequency of the act of Communion itself.

5. Again, we may remember that we have the
power of renewing in our own hearts as often as
we like the affections and holy acts which prepare
for, or accompany, or follow, the actual reception
of Communion, making at any time of the day or
night, and many times in each, those spiritual
communions of which the Saints have been so
fond. It cannot be doubted that our Lord, on
His part, is always ready to crown these tender
and secret acts of love with great graces, renewing
and confirming in us the effects of His own
Sacramental Presence. This is another method of
helping the Holy Souls most effectually, as well as
ourselves.

6. There is another circumstance about both
these great miracles, which we have considered as
having so special a reference to the Blessed
Sacrament, whether as a Sacrifice or as a Sacrament strictly so called, which it may be well to
dwell upon before we part altogether from the
subject. It was a sort of necessity for the
splendour of the miracle of the multiplication of
the loaves, that there should be a great multitude
of persons who should receive the benefits of our
Lord's mercy, although the miracle would not have
been less a miracle if He had fed only a few scores
of persons with the bread that was miraculously
increased. If He had fed a hundred persons, for
instance, with a single loaf, it would still have been
a very great miracle. But on each of these

occasions our Lord chose that the persons who were witnesses and recipients of His bounty should be numbered by thousands rather than by hundreds or scores, and we cannot doubt that besides the additional splendour of feeding of so large a body of men, women, and children, there was, in the circumstance of the great multitude itself, something which increased the devotion and kindled the enthusiasm of the disciples and of the crowd. At the same time both these miracles are remarkable also for a certain solemnity and holy order which our Lord insisted on, as in the making the multitude sit down in companies of fifties and hundreds, and in the distribution of the bread by the hands of the Apostles to these companies. The whole scene thus reminds us of some of the most solemn occasions in the Church when there are very large numbers of men present at the celebration of a single Mass, or, still more, of the general Communions which take place at the end of missions, or of the great festivals of the Christian year.

7. No acts of our religion are more naturally accompanied by this circumstance of the union of large numbers for the purpose of devotion than the celebration of Holy Mass and Holy Communion. The first is the celebration of the One Sacrifice offered on the Cross for the living and the dead. The second is the appointed symbol and testification of our union, through our Lord, with one another, the unity of heart and faith and visible government which is the mark of

the Catholic Church, the representation to the world of the charity which unites all the parts of that Church, in Heaven, on earth, and in Purgatory. It seems therefore very right and seemly that the Holy Souls, as well as the Angels and Saints, should have their share in these solemnities of charity and unity. Now we find that the Holy See has specially encouraged the devout practice of general Communions for the benefit of the holy departed, by granting Indulgences to such Communions, and in other ways. It is the custom in some Catholic countries or cities to celebrate these general Communions once a month for this special intention. It cannot be questioned that a great act of such devotion on the part of large numbers of people is in itself very pleasing and honourable to God, Who delights in seeing His children join together in worship and adoration, in prayer and praise and thanksgiving, that there is a special blessing in the Church on united ·prayer and public devotion, and that very great graces are often attached to such acts, greater than might have been obtained if each person had performed the same devotions privately. It is on this principle that it is customary to organize pilgrimages to shrines, and other such devotions, and it cannot be doubted that many persons are very much helped in the performance of them by the simple fact of having a great many companions, and that others are led by the popular character of the devotion to join in it, who would not perhaps have the piety or courage required for it if it were to be made by themselves singly.   At such times as those of which we speak there seems to be an outpouring of the spirit of prayer, devotion seems to be easier than at other times, and we may hope that the interior graces which correspond to the exterior manifestation of religion are great and large in proportion.   It would therefore be a devotion very much to the honour of God and to the consolation of the Holy Souls, as well to the promotion of piety among the faithful on earth, to revive some such holy practices as are here spoken of; as, for instance, if the monthly general Communion for the relief of the sufferers in Purgatory were to be made a common practice in all large churches in great towns and elsewhere.

CHAPTER XXVIII.

Degrees of Punishment in Purgatory.

(THE CURE OF THE BLIND MAN AT BETHSAIDA.)

St. Mark viii. 22—26.

1. THE miracle of the feeding of the four thousand was followed, like the other great miracle of the multiplication of the loaves, by our Lord's retirement from the spot in which it had been wrought. This time He bent His steps towards Bethsaida, as it seems, on His road to the extreme north of the Holy Land, under Mount Hermon. Here again He would fain have been unobserved, but He was pursued by those who desired the exercise of His miraculous powers in favour of the sick. "They came to Bethsaida, and they brought to Him a blind man, and they besought Him that He would touch him." Here again our Lord seems to have objected to performing the miraculous cure in public. "And taking the blind man by the hand, He led him out of the town, and spitting upon his eyes, laying His hands upon him, He asked him if He saw anything. And looking up, he said, I see men as it were trees walking. After that again He laid His hands on his eyes, and he began to see, and was restored, so that he saw all things clearly. And He sent him into his house,

saying, Go into thy house, and, if thou enter into the town, tell nobody."

2. The characteristic feature of this miracle is the gradual restoration of sight to the blind man. On ordinary occasions, a word or a touch from our Lord was sufficient to work the greatest cure instantaneously, whereas in this case there were stages in the restoration, as our Lord knew was to be the case, for He asked the man, after the first imposition of hands, whether he could yet see. Thus there seems to have been an unusual difficulty about this cure—a difficulty which could not, of course, have been the result of any failure of miraculous power in our Lord, and must therefore have been either a consequence of some slowness of faith on the part of the poor man himself, or caused by some intention of our Lord to set forth or symbolize some truth. With regard to Purgatory, it is not difficult to find a truth which may well be illustrated by this narrative. Just as we have seen that the punishments of Purgatory are particular, and are applied in exact measure and proportion to the various kinds of sin which have to be expiated there, so also is it true that there are some persons whose purgation is far longer and more gradual than that of others, or, what amounts to the same thing, there are some sins the punishment of which is longer and more difficult than that of others. This is a practical truth of great importance, the understanding of which is necessary to a complete intelligence of the Catholic doctrine concerning Purgatory

3. The truth seems to be that there are immense differences in the next world, between those who belong to the same great kingdoms, so to speak, of which we know anything at all—the kingdoms of Heaven, of Purgatory, and of Hell. The differences in glory and nearness to our Lord between one saint and another, one hierarchy of angels and another, may be so great as to be comparable to those which are known to exist between the various celestial bodies, all of which seem to us so much alike and so near each to the other. So it may also be between the sinners who have to suffer the eternal separation from God which is the punishment of Hell, and so it may be between the various sojourners in the prison of Purgatory—for the differences between the several classes of persons who die in the grace of God are very great indeed. Some are so innocent as on that account to have little punishment, although they may not have served God in any heroic degree of virtue. Some have laid up very great treasures in Heaven by good works of various kinds, and yet they may have a considerable debt to pay in Purgatory on account of the great things which God has intrusted to them as to which they have been unfaithful, or on account of serious faults of character, and the like. Others may have been away from God and His grace for a greater part of their lives, and have been brought home at the last, dying before they had time to do much penance, and saved, perhaps, by His sacramental grace at the last, which has made their sorrow

acceptable in God's sight. In a great many different ways these diversities may exist. Thus the purification of some souls may be almost instantaneous, others may remain but a short time in Purgatory, and then pass to thrones in Heaven less glorious than those which await others who have yet a greater debt to pay. Others may have to remain a longer time than the rest in Purgatory, and then may have to occupy some of the lower seats in the Blessed Kingdom of our Lord. Cases such as these may be considered as represented by the slowness with which the miracle on which we are now commenting was wrought.

4. One of the great passages in the New Testament which are used to illustrate the doctrine of Purgatory is to be found in the First Epistle of St. Paul to the Corinthians, where the Apostle is undoubtedly referring to the Purgatorial fire. He is speaking of the various kinds of ministerial work which may be raised by those who have or who assume the office of teachers in the Church. St. Paul says : " The fire (of God's judgment) shall try every man's work of what sort it be. If any man's work abide which he hath built thereupon, he shall receive a reward. If any man's work burn, he shall suffer loss, but he himself shall be saved as by fire." In the verse immediately preceding he gives various figures which represent the different kinds of work which are to be tried. The works are represented by gold, silver, precious stones, wood, hay, stubble. It is common with Christian writers to see in this enumeration an image of various

good works and various kinds of lighter sins, all of which are to be tested by the fire of judgment, and some to be consumed in the fire of Purgatory. The gold, silver, and costly stones are good works, of various degrees of value in the sight of God, and for these there can be no suffering in Purgatory, but only various degrees of reward in Heaven. The other three members of the enumeration are supposed to represent three various kinds of sins which have to undergo punishment before the soul can attain its perfect salvation, that is, its admission into the presence of God. The writers to whom we refer say that wood burns slowly, hay quickly, and stubble instantaneously. There are various kinds of venial sins which correspond to this classification; there are some venial sins which are in the same order as mortal sins, but they are saved from being mortal by want of full intention, advertence, and some other circumstances. Such sins, for instance, are evil or uncharitable thoughts not fully consented to, while full consent would have made them mortal. Other sins are lighter in substance, even though there be full consent, such as a deliberate lie or theft in a small matter. Others, again, are ignorances, omissions, distractions, and other defects which are hardly altogether sinful, because they are in great part the result of human frailty, and yet they might have been avoided if we had greater carefulness, more recollection of God's presence, more reverence in His service.

5. If we are to give ourselves a complete idea of

the various degrees of the punishments in Purgatory, we must add to this division of venial sins, founded on the words of St. Paul, the number of mortal sins for which many of the Holy Souls may have to suffer, the guilt of which has been forgiven, but the punishment of which is, as yet, unpaid. Indeed, it is the punishment due to the venial sins just now spoken of with which we have to do, and not with the guilt. Now, it must be very clear that the difference between the lighter and the heavier kinds of sin is in itself very great. It is also clear that the debt of punishment which may be due for mortal sins of which the guilt has been forgiven, may be very great indeed, when their number has been large, and the affection to them very deeply rooted in the soul. On the other hand, we cannot think that God's justice will not deal with, comparatively, a very light hand in the case of imperfections as to which there is some little wilfulness, frailties with which negligence and levity are mixed up, and the like. It is certain, then, that the gradations of punishment must be very many, and the intervals, so to speak, very considerable. The same may be said as to the cancelling of the debt of punishment which is practically common and easy in this life. It is not very easy to cancel the debt of punishment incurred by a number of mortal sins, which may have become in some cases almost habitual, while, on the other hand, there are a great many ways which Christians ordinarily practise, which have the effect of doing away with the punishment of lighter sins. There is, however, one serious condition for the application of the number-less easier satisfactions which the mercy of God has provided for us, and that condition is that where there has been an evil will in any degree—as in the case, mentioned above, of a deliberate falsehood in a light matter—then the sin must be retracted by sorrow before the satisfaction can be applied. The effect of this and the other truths which have now been mentioned is to enhance our ideas of the difficulty which many souls will find in obtaining deliverance from Purgatory, except after a long period of suffering, as also to move our charity towards those who may be in so much need of help. Well also will it be, if the same thoughts lead us to a more careful avoidance of all wilful sin, however light, a greater exactness in retracting any that we may have committed, and a greater value of, and diligence in, all works of satisfaction.

S

CHAPTER XXIX.

The Holy Souls helped by Prayer and Fasting.

(THE CURE OF THE LUNATIC BOY.)

St. Mark ix. 16—28.

1. WE are all familiar with the miracle of the cure of the lunatic boy, which took place on our Lord's descent with His three chosen disciples from the mountain of Transfiguration. We all have remarked the contrast which the two scenes present as they are pictured by some great Christian artists, between the heavenly and ecstatic joy of the three Apostles on the holy mountain, enjoying the vision of our Lord in His glory with His two great Saints of the Old Testament, and the struggle, perplexity, and weakness of their brethren below, with the crowd pressing around them, the father of the boy entreating them, and the evil spirit, as it were, mocking at them on account of their inability to cast him out. Then the Evangelists tell us in considerable minuteness of detail how our Lord was met by the crowd, who, as St. Mark tells us, were "astonished and struck with fear" when they saw Him, how the father told Him the pitiful circumstances of the case. "I have brought my son to Thee, having a dumb spirit, who, wheresoever he taketh him,

dasheth him, and he foameth, and gnasheth with the teeth and pineth away, and I spake to Thy disciples to cast him out, and they could not." Our Lord complained of the unbelief of the generation to which He was sent, and bade the father bring the boy to Him. He questioned the father about the facts of his case, and when with some little confidence the poor man begged Him to help them, " Have compassion on us if Thou canst do anything," our Lord answered, "If thou canst believe, all things are possible to him that believeth." In the end our Lord cast out the spirit, who left him, " crying out and greatly tearing him, and he became as dead, so that many said, He is dead. But Jesus taking him by the hand, lifted him up, and he arose."

2. The description of this possessed boy shows us that his case must have been one of those in which the enemy of God and man is allowed a very great power, and in which he sets up his dominion over the body of his poor victim very firmly. The nine disciples asked our Lord afterwards in private why they had been unable to cast out this devil. He told them, as St. Matthew informs us, that it was on account of their want of faith : but He added also, that that particular kind of evil spirit was only to be cast out by prayer and fasting, that is, that there are certain spiritual powers which are not ordinarily granted, even to the servants and ministers of our Lord in the Church, unless they accompany the exercise of their functions by prayer and fasting. We have

here, then, a truth which it is not difficult to apply
to our present subject. It may very well be the
case, that God, in His inscrutable wisdom and
justice, will not allow the deliverance of certain
souls from Purgatory, or the cancelling of the debt
due to certain sins, on any other condition than
that of the offering to Him of a considerable
amount of prayer accompanied by severe mortifications. We have seen in a former chapter that
there are some sins the punishment of which is
remitted with much greater difficulty than that of
others. But this is only one part of the subject
before us, because the words of our Lord suggest
to us quite as much the positive value of the great
spiritual weapons of prayer and fasting, as the
comparison between them and other less powerful
means. This, then, may be the subject to which
our considerations in the present chapter may be
addressed.

3. It cannot certainly be denied that the words
of our Lord as to prayer and fasting seem to place
them, in a certain sense, on a higher level, with
regard to the end in view, than other works unac-
companied by them. It seems as if He left us to
imply that prayer and fasting, without anything
else, might accomplish much, but that there were
many things beyond the power of other works to
effect without prayer and fasting. It is remarkable
that we should have so many instances in this
series of our Lord's miracles, in which the casting
out of a dumb devil was considered as a work of
unusual power, such as to call forth particular

enthusiasm on the part of the believing crowd, as well as the special opposition of calumny on the part of His enemies. This, then, was a difficult miracle to perform, beyond the power of an exorcist, even though commissioned by our Lord, unless aided by prayer and mortification. The power of these two great weapons as to the release of the Holy Souls is thus enhanced to us by the comparison suggested by the miracle. As to prayer, we know that it is in general the key to all good graces and favours, and certainly not less than in any other case, the key which opens the doors of His mercy to the sufferers in Purgatory. The power of prayer is reckoned by theologians as twofold—the power of impetration, and the power of satisfaction. Some great and holy writers seem to have hesitated as to the direct power of impetration in regard to the relief of the punishments in Purgatory—just as we have seen the same kind of hesitation with regard to the intercessions of the Saints. Thus they have allowed to Christian prayer, for the object of which we are speaking, the power to move the intercession of the Saints for the Holy Souls, to obtain from God that the satisfactions offered for those Holy Souls may be applied to them, to obtain the favour that a great number of persons may be inspired to pray for them, and to offer for them works of acceptable satisfaction. It has also been thought that prayer may win from the mercy of God the boon that the length of the pains which the Souls ought to suffer may be diminished, the intensity of those pains being proportionately increased. And yet they have stopped short of the assertion that prayer may obtain the direct remission of the pains of Purgatory, and this hesitation has been grounded on the reason that justice requires that the punishment of sins shall not remain unpaid.* Such teaching shows the very high sense which these holy writers have of the claims of the justice of God, but on the one hand, we have seen so many reasons in the course of these considerations for thinking that His mercy is ever ready to be moved in favour of these holy sufferers, and in the second place, for looking on the prayer of faith as almost omnipotent with Him, that we shall not very easily persuade ourselves that a very large part of the debt of punishment may not be remitted for faithful and constant prayer, even by way of impetration. For we began these reflections by dwelling on the thought that our Lord anticipated His otherwise appointed time for the beginning of His miracles at the prayer of our Blessed Lady. Now He would not have done this—that is, He would not have permitted our Blessed Lady to exert the sweet constraint of her intercession to overrule what was appointed, unless He had meant us to understand that that which we call overruling was, in this instance, and, in principle, in others, exactly that kind of interference which He most of all desired and delighted in. In the same way, in the case of the Syrophœnician woman, we have seen that He allowed Himself to be, as it were, forced to go

* Suarez, *De Purgatorio*, disp. 48, § 5.

beyond the letter of His commission from the Father, and we may be certain that this too was a case in which His Sacred Heart very much delighted, and that it would have been a disappointment to Him if that poor woman had gone away without further persistence after He had first rebuffed her. And, with regard to the point before us, we may gather the mind of the Church from the prayers which she suggests and puts into the mouths of her ministers. Now many of these ask directly for the remission of the pain which the Holy Souls have to suffer for the claims of God's justice against them. It is true that many of these prayers are offered in connection with the Adorable Sacrifice, which has the power of satisfaction as well as that of impetration. But then all our prayers are offered to the Eternal Father "through Jesus Christ our Lord," and so plead His merits, and the impetration which belongs to those merits.

4. In any case, however, prayer most certainly possesses a power of satisfaction besides that of impetration, and therefore on this ground there can be no doubt of its immense efficacy for the direct remission of the pains of Purgatory. The power of satisfaction is not necessarily, as it appears, limited to works of piety and devotion which are in themselves in some degree painful, as requiring either bodily suffering or fatigue, or mental strain and exertion. Both these latter qualities are to be found in prayer, which is always to some extent a strain on our poor feeble nature, especially if it be prolonged. This must be the answer to such as

complain of the tediousness of the long Offices
which the Church enjoins as to be said for the
departed. They are, indeed, full of beauty and
delight to the fervent. They contain the thoughts
which have fed the heart of the Church and her
saints in all ages. They are the forms of converse
with God, so to speak, which our Lord Himself
and His Blessed Mother used while on earth—but
still, if they tax the attention and fatigue the head,
it is not much that we should pay that amount of
mortification for the sake of relieving the souls of
our brethren from the torments of Purgatory. In
this connection we may remind ourselves of the
long "Psalters" recited, sometimes daily, sometimes more than once in the day, by the saints and
servants of God in old times, of which the history
of the Church is so full. It would be easy to fill
pages with the accounts that exist of the various
long prayers which have been enjoined by particular
Churches, or by particular Religious Orders, as
intercessions and satisfactions for the departed.
St. Peter Damian tells us that the hermits of Fonte
Avellino recited the Office of the Dead every day;
but that when one of their own number came to
die, the remainder were bound to assist him by
fasting seven days continuously, by taking seven
disciplines each of a thousand stripes, by chanting
the Psalter thirty times, by celebrating Mass for
his soul thirty days continuously, after which three
hundred Masses were said for him, besides seven
more by each priest. If any one died before he
had completed these suffrages for the dead, then

the remainder was fulfilled for him by the survivors
of the community.* This is but a single instance
of the active charity of Religious Orders for the
dead—a charity which shows the mind of the
Church as to their needs, and as to the power of
prayer to help them.

5. It must be added, that our Lord in the
passage upon which we are now commenting, does
not speak of prayer alone, but of prayer united to
fasting, under which head we may include mortifications of every kind. It would be natural, therefore, to go on in this chapter to the consideration
of the efficacy of fasting, and of mortifications in
general, in the relief of the sufferings of the Holy
Souls. But, in order not to make this chapter too
long, the subject of fasting must be put off for the
present. Meanwhile, it is well to remember that
our Lord is not here speaking of a work which is
principally a work of satisfaction, but of a work,
principally, of impetration. He is speaking of the
casting out of a particular class of devils, and He
tells us that prayer and fasting together are required
for that effect, according to the ordinary laws of
God's Kingdom. And it is a matter of common
experience, that a great many things which we
make the subjects of our petitions to God are not
granted to us when we simply pray, but are granted
to us when we unite fasting and other mortifications
to our prayers. Now if this is the case as to other
things, when what we desire to obtain is a matter

¹ See St. Peter Damian, *Opusc.* 14, quoted by Benedict XIII.
Triges ii. Serm. 7.

of impetration, it is much more likely to be the case when that which we ask for is mainly a matter of satisfaction, such as is the release of the Holy Souls from the pains of Purgatory. For fasting and mortification have, as has been said, a direct power as to satisfaction which does not always belong to prayer. This may serve to show that there is no case in which it may be more necessary to join mortifications to prayer, in order to obtain our requests, than the particular case to the consideration of which these chapters are devoted.

CHAPTER XXX.

Union between the Holy Souls and our Lord.

(OUR LORD PAYING THE DIDRACHMA.)

St. Matt. xvii. 23—26.

1. ST. MATTHEW relates an incident which occurred on the return of our Lord from Capharnaum, after an absence of several weeks, during which the miracles of which we have lately been speaking had taken place. This incident was the payment of the didrachma, an annual tax which every Jew was bound to furnish for the expenses of the Temple. It seems that the collectors of the tax came to St. Peter, and asked him whether his Master did not pay the tax. St. Peter replied that He did. On his entering the house in which our Lord was

—it may have been St. Peter's own—our Lord anticipated any question from him, by asking him whether earthly kings exacted taxes from their children or from others. Peter replied from strangers. "Jesus said to him, Then the children are free. But that we may not scandalize them, go to the sea, and cast in a hook, and that fish which shall first come up, take, and when thou hast opened its mouth, thou shalt find a stater, take that, and give it them for Me and thee."

2. There may have been some reason in the circumstances of the case, as, for instance, if our Lord were at that time the guest of St. Peter, and so his debtor for shelter and food, why He should have told that blessed Apostle that the coin which was to be found in the mouth of the fish was to be paid for both of them, and not for any other. But the whole incident is symbolical, as well as simply historical, and forms one link in the chain of acts and sayings of our Lord which set forth the privileges which He intended to bestow on the Prince of the Apostles. We may apply it in another symbolical sense, in order to gather from it a truth concerning the Holy Souls of Purgatory, which is independent of all symbol and figure, but which may be illustrated thereby. The tax which had to be paid for the maintenance of the service of God in the Temple may remind us of the penalties which are exacted from the Holy suffering Souls to fit them for admission into God's presence in Heaven, where they are to praise Him for ever. The poverty of our Lord and the Apostles, and the

recourse which He chose on this occasion to have to the Providence of His Father, may remind us of the inability of the Holy Souls to help themselves, and the extent to which God has placed their case in our hands for succour. And the tender affectionate tie, the existence of which is implied in our Lord's words, "for Me and for thee," may remind us of the union of these Holy Souls with our Lord, so that it is indeed true that what is done for them is done for Him also.

3. We may make this last point the subject of special consideration in the present chapter. For it is of great importance that in all that we do for the Holy Souls we should have our Lord before us as the Person Who is relieved in them, and that this motive for our exertion in their behalf, based upon our love for Him, should be constantly dwelt upon to enchance our zeal and urge us on even to sacrifices and sufferings for their sake. It has been already said, that all the various works of mercy, such as feeding the hungry, clothing the naked, and the like, may be practised towards the Holy Souls in a spiritual sense. When we perform any one of these acts of mercy, it is natural that we should remind ourselves of the words of our Lord concerning them in His description of the Day of Judgment, where He declares that, "I was hungry, and you gave Me to eat, I was thirsty, and you gave Me to drink, I was a stranger, and you took Me in, naked, and you clothed Me, sick, and you visited Me, I was in prison, and you came to Me." * And He

* St. Matt. xxv. 35, seq.

adds, that when the just ask Him, when have they
done all these things, He will reply, "Amen, I say
to you, as long as you did it to one of these My
least brethren, you did it to Me." In this sense,
then, it is certain that charity to the Holy Souls is
charity practised to our Lord Himself, for He has
no least brethren who are in greater hunger or
thirst, who feel so much their separation from their
home, who are so truly naked, and sick, and in
prison, as these Souls. Indeed, it may be said that
they are, in many respects, not the least, but the
nearest and dearest of His brethren.

4. Again, we know well that our Lord had a
special love for certain classes of persons, as
belonging to Himself in a particular way, representing Him bearing His Cross, reflecting His
character, and the like. He had a great love for
the poor, and He has left the poor behind Him in
Christian countries, instead of abolishing the holy
state of poverty, in order, among other reasons, that
they may represent Him to others, and give them
the opportunity of being merciful to Him in them.
He had a special love for children, because the
innocence and simplicity and humility, which are in
them only natural shadows, as it were, of great
Christian virtues, made them like Him, and in
some sort reflections of His character. He had a
great love for the afflicted in every way, body and
soul, because all such affliction is a certain figure
of His Cross, by which He came to heal the world,
and He chose to be among us as one whom God
had smitten and afflicted. All such affliction bears

witness at once to the misery of sin and to the hollowness of the world, and every instance of it which He came across gave Him an occasion, which was most delightful to Him, of mercy and compassion. The poor, the young, the sick, the afflicted in any way, are thus our Lord's own chosen representatives in the world, and it is the secret of perfect Christian charity, not only to relieve them for His sake when occasion offers, but to seek them out and fall on them, as it were, as on a long-sought prey or a most valued treasure, especially because of its love for Him. But in all the characteristics in which they resemble Him and bear His livery, it is not difficult to see that they are even surpassed by the Holy Souls—for they are poor as to spiritual treasures more necessary to them than what is required by the poor for the sustenance of life, the virtues in which they resemble our Lord are not merely natural images of true virtues, as in the case of children, but virtues seasoned by struggle and well worn by practice, and their afflictions are more like those which He endured on the Cross than any sufferings which strike the eye and the heart in this world. And again, their endurance of their sufferings is more like His ineffable patience, for they are perfect in their resignation, in their love of God, and in their union with His adorable will.

5. Again, although it be true that the Holy Souls are in this manner the most perfect images of our Lord on which we can exercise our compassion and charity, it is also true that they have another pre-eminence as to the point on which we are meditating,

because they are so perfectly and inseparably one with Him. The poor, the young, the afflicted, represent our Lord to us, and that representation is enough to justify His own Divine words, " As long as you did it to one of these My least brethren, you did it to Me." We are not to seek in them more than this representation of Jesus Christ, for it is not our business to inquire into the state of the souls of those whom we relieve, except in some particular cases, and then to a certain limited extent. It is enough that they are in the place of our Lord, and that our charity is directed to Him as its motive. But in the case of the Holy Souls there is far more than the representation of our Lord. There is in them perfect and indissoluble union with Him. Holy writers tell us that the pain which our Lord felt in the Garden at the thought of the loss of sinners who had belonged to Him, was far more intense than the agony which might have been caused, if such had been God's will, by the cutting off of limbs from His Body. But the Holy Souls are members of His Body over which He rejoices, because there is now no more any danger or possibility of their separation. In this sense they are more firmly united to Him than even the Saints while on earth; and this union is a source of intense delight and thankfulness to Him, greater in proportion to the degree of grace to which they have attained, and without anything to alloy or mar it, because there is no internal malice, no admixture of evil with good left in them, but only the debt of punishment to pay, which does not interfere with

their absolute love for Him. And their condition
of punishment is one which is dear to Him on
account of His love for the justice of His Father,
while it gives them a special claim on His tenderness, moving His Heart towards them, as the
sufferings of an invalid child draw on it all the
tenderest affections of a loving parent. Weak and
suffering as they are, they are His, they are one
with Him for ever, and the air of pain which hangs
over them recalls to Him all that He has suffered
for them Himself, through which alone their punishments have any healing power, as also the severity
of the conflict from which they have emerged.
Thus it may be said of their case and of our Lord's
care for them that both awaken in Him a special
feeling of love, not altogether unlike that joy of
which He spoke when He said that " there shall be
joy in Heaven upon one sinner that doth penance,
more than upon ninety and nine just who do not
need penance." *

6. Such are some of the thoughts which are
suggested by the truth of the union which exists
between our Lord and the Holy Souls. Of all
those whom we can pray for or benefit by our
almsdeeds or other good works, they are the most
closely one with Him, so that we may say that
what is offered to God for them is like the stater,
given for Him and for them at once. Our own
union with Him is the condition of our spiritual
life. That life is strong and penetrating in us in
proportion to the degree of that union. It seems

* St. Luke xv. 7.

almost impossible to be closely united with our Lord unless we have a most tender love and thoughtful care for all that are one with Him like ourselves, and of all such, the Holy Souls have the highest claim on those exercises of our love to Him which consist in charity and mercy. On the other hand, the exercise of those heavenly virtues is certain to intensify them in the soul, and thus, in this case, as in so many others, the good that we may try to do to others returns upon ourselves in abundant blessings.

———

CHAPTER XXXI.

The Pain of Loss. I. The Beatific Vision of God.

(THE CURE OF THE MAN BORN BLIND.)

St. John ix. 1—7.

1. ALTHOUGH the miracles wrought by our Lord in the city and neighbourhood of Jerusalem were very few in number, in comparison to those which made His preaching in Galilee and in the country parts of Judæa so famous, yet those which are mentioned are among the most remarkable of all, especially on account of the great effect which they produced on the minds of His enemies, who, in every recorded case, seem to have been driven to great fury against Him thereby. We have now to speak of one of these remarkable

T

miracles, which took place within a few months of
the Passion, and which provoked the ecclesiastical
rulers to such an extent as to make them excom-
municate the man on whom the miracle was
wrought.   Our Lord was at Jerusalem when
"passing by, He saw a man who was blind from
his birth.   And His disciples asked Him, Rabbi,
who hath sinned, this man or his parents, that he
should be born blind?   Jesus answered, Neither
hath this man sinned, nor his parents, but that
the works of God should be made manifest in
him."   That is, the reason why this man has been
born blind is not any sin of his own or of his
parents, but he has been afflicted in this way in
order that the works of God may be made manifest
in him by his cure.   "I must work the works of
Him that sent Me, whilst it is day; the night
cometh when no man can work.   As long as I
am in the world, I am the Light of the world."
Then He proceeded, as in the case of the man
whom He had cured at the Probatic Pool, to
work the miracle unasked in order that His
Father might be glorified by this great manifestation of the power of His Incarnate Son.
"When He had said these things, He spat on
the ground, and made clay of the spittle, and
spread the clay upon his eyes, and said to him,
Go, and wash in the pool of Siloe (which is
interprated Sent).   He went, therefore, and washed,
and he came seeing."

2. This miracle is related by St. John, as is his
wont, chiefly for the purpose of dwelling upon the

results to which it led. It was in itself a very remarkable instance of power, and the enemies of our Lord had no resource but to endeavour to intimidate the poor man to whom the wonderful world of sight was thus miraculously opened, and when they found they could not succeed in this, they excommunicated him. We need not dwell on these results, nor on the long conversations related by St. John as following on this miracle. But it enables us to consider that which is the chief among all the pains of Purgatory, and of which we have as yet hardly spoken. This is the pain of loss, which consists in the sufferings of the holy dead, because they are debarred from the Beatific Vision of God during their detention in Purgatory. This pain is also the chief pain which the poor sufferers in Hell have to endure, but it differs in them from that pain which the Holy Souls suffer, because in these it is only for a time, while the lost souls know in their case the loss is eternal. The Catholic doctrine on the subject amounts to this. The essence of beatitude consists in the vision and possession of God, the possession or fruition of God being inseparably connected with the vision and knowledge of Him. According to the great school of St. Thomas, this alone constitutes the essence of beatitude. According to the other school, the greatest name of which is that of the Seraphic Doctor, St. Bonaventure, the love and joy which result from the knowledge and possession of God also belong to the essence of beatitude. That is, the good of goods, which is God, is not perfectly and absolutely possessed unless it be, as it were, joyously embraced as well as seen and known, and unless the soul satisfy all its affections in this knowledge and love. This is the good of which the lost souls are deprived for ever, and of which they know that they are deprived by their own fault. This is the good of which the Holy Souls are deprived for a time, and of which they know that they are deprived by their own negligence. As it would be difficult to compress all that may be said on this great subject into a single chapter, we may treat at present of the knowledge and fruition of God alone.

3. We can imagine few surprises more great than that of this poor man, mentioned by St. John, when for the first time the beautiful world in which our lot is now cast was, as it were, revealed to him after he had spent so many years in darkness, without the slightest memory to aid him in picturing to his mind the scenes in the midst of which he was moving. We may be quite sure that if he had formed any conceptions of light and colour and form, of the sunshine, and of the various beauties of earth and sky, tree and flower, the human form and face, and the works of the mind and hand of man, such as the magnificent Temple at Jerusalem, and the like, those conceptions would have seemed to him as meagre and miserable indeed when compared with the sights now opened to him by the gift of his new sense. But no marvels of nature or of art can bear the slightest comparison with the beauty of

God as He is to be seen by the Blessed in Heaven,
nor can we now form of that beauty any conception at all, however poor and unequal to the
original, because the knowledge and possession of
God constitute a good altogether above our nature,
and are concerned with a range of being of which
He is Himself the one single instance. It follows
from this that we shall weary ourselves in vain, if
we endeavour to frame any description at all of
what it is that is known and possessed in God.
The fullest sight and knowledge of material things
does not make them ours, does not make them
present to us or enables us to enjoy them, but it is
otherwise with the spiritual sight of God which
is imparted in the Beatific Vision. To see God is
to possess His Eternity, Wisdom, Love, Mercy,
Power, Holiness, Truth, Sovereignty, Justice, and
Infinite Happiness. "So great," says Suarez, "is
the beauty and sweetness of this Eternal Light,
that even if it were not allowed us to remain
therein longer than a single day, yet, for this alone,
we might well and rightly despise innumerable
years of this present life, full of delights and abundance of all temporal goods. For that has not
been falsely or wrongly said, 'Better is one day in
Thy courts than a thousand years.'"* For what is
seen in God, even although He can only be fully
comprehended by Himself, is more truly beautiful
and noble than all that can be enjoyed in this
world, and it is seen and enjoyed in a truer
and more noble way. This sight of God is so

* Suarez, tom. i. *De Lib. Arbitrio*, lib. iii. chap. 23.

great a good, that its possession even for a moment would be an abundant and more than abundant reward for all the toils and sufferings of this life. If God were to exact that we should suffer all the torments of the martyrs, or the pains of sense in Hell itself for a time, as the condition of enjoying the sight of Himself, it would not be too much to pay as a price for such a blessing, even though it were to be enjoyed only for a time. Indeed, it is so great a good that nothing but the infinite merits of our Lord can earn such a prize— not even the most difficult works of heroic virtue, or the most terrible sufferings faithfully borne. St. John, speaking of this vision, says that it will make us like God : "We shall be like to Him, for we shall see Him as He is."*

4. The possession of God being so great, and, in a certain sense, infinite a good, it follows that to be deprived of it for any time is in itself a proportionate loss, a loss greater than can be calculated by the mind of man or angel. The eternal loss of God is, as has been said, the greatest of the pains of Hell, and the temporary loss of God the greatest of the pains of Purgatory. This loss is not less a loss to them for the time that it lasts, because that time is to come to an end. For it is not a simple loss, or rather, absence of possession, of a thing which they know nothing of and could not in any case gain. The want of the possession of God is thought by some theologians not to have been felt, at least as a great pain, by the Fathers in

* 1 St. John iii. 2.

Limbus, and it is commonly thought that it is no pain at all to children who have died without Baptism, and brings them no sorrow, because they never could have obtained it. For no wise person can afflict himself because he is not in possession of a good which he has not lost by his own fault, and which it was never in his power to gain. In order that there may be true sorrow in such a case, there must have been a power of enjoying the good which is absent, there must have been some fault which has been the cause why it has been lost, and there must be a longing desire for its possession. If we apply this to the case of the Holy Souls with regard to their privation of the Beatific Vision, we find all these elements of intense sorrow. They are capable of that Beatific Vision, they have lost it through their own fault, which bars against them, for a time at least, the gates of Heaven. There is no longer any low or bad affection in their will, or any error or ignorance in their mind. St. Thomas* tells us that the affection with which the Holy Souls desire the chief good after this life is most intense, because it is no longer hindered by the weight of the body, and because their time for enjoying that good would already have come if there had not been an impediment. The reason of this intense longing is simply their love for God and their inability to enjoy Him.

5. Their love of God is measured by their knowledge of Him ; a knowledge which may be greater or less in various souls, but which in all that die in

* St. Thomas *in Sent.* lib. iv. dist. 21, qu. 1, art. 1.

grace is very great. In the first place they have the gift of faith, and although nothing new in kind may be added to this on their entrance into the world beyond the grave, yet still the soul separated from the body is able to grasp far more firmly than before the truths of faith. It is no longer troubled by the clouds raised by fancy, imagination, evil affections, and the like, and so it can see what is before it, and especially God, far more clearly and in a purer light than before. Thus it understands and loves the Goodness, the Mercy, the Wisdom, the Truth, the Justice, the Holiness of God, and all His other attributes, which are natural causes of love and desire. There is nothing in the new state, in which the soul finds itself, to prevent it from reaching forward to such objects and working upon them with all the intensity of an unbroken energy. There is no langour, or interruption, or weariness, or feebleness about the operations of the soul in the next world, and thus the same faith, which has been, as it were, drowsy or half dead in this life, is there full of vigour and keenness, and gives birth to a love of God which is proportionate to the full intensity of its powers. Moreover, no thought can conceive the immense effect, on the soul which dies in grace, of that vision of our Lord as Judge in the Particular Judgment, which it takes so few words to speak of. That vision has opened to them an entirely new sense of the wisdom, the justice, the love of God, and we may say the same of the keen insight which is imparted to them at the same moment

as to the whole of their past life, with its bound-
less accompaniment of graces and blessings and
mercies, what God has been to them, and what
they have been to Him, and also as to their future,
the rewards which the faithfulness of God has in
store for them after their faults have been expiated
in Purgatory. All this, as we have said, is grasped
by the soul with the utmost firmness and understood with the utmost clearness, and it rivets the
attention and engrosses the affections without any
intermission or relaxation. They see the Truth
Itself, and they are drawn to its embrace by an
attraction absolutely irresistible, and urging them
with its whole force at every moment, the power
of which is but faintly pictured by any physical
attraction which the world knows. Their love,
like their faith, is set free from all impediment,
and is secured in one strong unchanging and most
intense act of desire to its true and only object.

6. These thoughts may enable us to understand
the intensity of the longing which the Holy Souls
feel for the assistance of the suffrages of the Church,
and the immense claims which they have upon our
charity. We may conclude this chapter by repeat-
ing the often-quoted image in which St. Catharine
of Genoa has endeavoured to express the longing
of the Holy Souls for God. "If there were in
the whole world but a single loaf of bread, the
mere sight of which was destined to appease the
hunger of all creatures, and if a man who had that
desire to eat which is natural to all of us in a
normal state of health, yet could not satisfy it,

and yet, though deprived of all food, could neither die nor fall sick, is it not clear that he would suffer a hunger that was always increasing? Suppose this man to know that the single loaf in question could alone, by his seeing it, satisfy him, and that, without it, he would remain in his hunger in a state of intolerable torture, is it not evident that the nearer he came to that loaf without being able to look upon it, the more would his hunger be provoked, and that his torments would be all the more cruel in proportion as his appetite yearned with greater force for the sight of this loaf, the single object of his desire? And again, if in the midst of this torture of hunger devouring him always more and more as time went on, this man were to acquire the dreadful certainty that he was never again to see that loaf, what would take place? He would at once feel the beginning of Hell within himself: he would from that moment be as are the souls of the damned who have lost all hope of seeing the Bread of Life, God, their Saviour. Well, then, the hunger which this man would feel is precisely that which the Souls of Purgatory experience, with the exception of the despair—for they have the hope that they shall one day see that loaf, and satisfy themselves with it as they will. But the hunger and martyrdom which they suffer are something which cannot be described, as long as it is not given them to fill themselves with the Bread of Life, which is Jesus Christ, the true God, our Saviour and our Love." *

* St. Catharine, *Treatise on Purgatory*, c. vi.

CHAPTER XXXII.

The Pain of Loss. II. Exercise of the Love of God.

(THE CURE OF THE MUTE DEMONIAC.)

St. Luke xi. 14—26.

1. THE miracle which comes next in order of time to that of the giving sight to the man who had been blind from birth, is the casting out of the dumb devil, mentioned by St. Luke in the place cited above. This miracle is very like a former miracle on which we have already commented,* except that in that case the demoniac was blind as well as dumb. That miracle was worked in Galilee, and this in the country of Judæa, and it is possible that each of them has been selected by the Evangelists—this by St. Luke alone—on account of the calumny to which it gave occasion from the malignant enemies of our Lord. For it seems, as has already been said, that the casting out of a devil who had the power of inflicting dumbness on his victim was considered a work of very singular power, and thus, whenever our Lord performed this work, His adversaries were driven, either to acknowledge His Divine mission, or to impute the power which He exercised to a league with Satan. When it was our business to speak of

* See chap. xvi.

the former miracle of this class, it was used as an occasion which suggested the consideration of the longing desire which the Holy Souls feel for the society to which they are destined in Heaven, and the enjoyment of that blessed communion and intercourse with the angels and saints which is to form so great a part of the blessedness there, from which they are, for the time, detained. We may use the present miracle in the same way, as illustrating that part of the pain of the loss in Purgatory which consists in the inability of the Holy Souls to converse, not with saints and angels alone, but with God Himself, in acts and exercises of love. It has been already said that the Beatitude of Heaven consists in the knowledge and possession of God, but that these cannot be separated from the exercises of love and joy which spring from them. Inasmuch as love on earth finds its chief vent in language, the gift of which enables us to communicate the feelings and thoughts of our hearts to each other, the restoration of the gift of speech to the poor man on whom the miracle was wrought may be used as an illustration of that admittance to the love of God which the Holy Souls are for the present forbidden to enjoy.

2. It must be remembered that the vision of God, which is the foundation of that love for Him which reigns in the hearts of the blessed dwellers in Heaven, shows Him to them in a manner which is far higher than that in which faith represents Him. The vision of faith is certain, but it is not clear and distinct—for now we see, as St. Paul

says, "through a glass in a dark manner, but then face to face." * Thus the intuitive vision of God represents Him to us, if we may so say, almost as a new God—as if we had never before known anything about His Goodness, His Wisdom, His Charity, His Justice, and the rest. And the novelty of the effect on the will is the same as that of the effect on the mind, and thus an entirely new kind of love is kindled, so that it seems as if they had neither known nor loved God at all before. The difference may be compared to that between the delight which is produced by exquisite and scientific music on persons who have no ear and no knowledge of the science, and that which the same music produces on persons who are by nature endowed with a marvellous perception of its beauties, and who are able to understand the skill and genius with which the whole of a great piece is arranged and combined. Or we may use the sense of sight to furnish us with a comparison, and say that the difference is that between the pleasure caused by a most beautiful landscape on a person whose eyes are so dim that he can only see the principal objects vaguely, and this while a mist hangs between him and it, and the rapture occasioned by the same landscape glowing in the rich sunshine, and flecked with the varieties of light and shade, on the eyes of men who are fully able to take in all that lies before them. Some writers speak more strongly than this, and say that our knowledge of God now is like that

* 1 Cor. xiii. 12.

which a blind man has of the sunshine. But it is probable that no difference of this sort that we can imagine can span the distance between the two kinds of knowledge and the two kinds of love respectively, while those which are here suggested are enough to let us see, at least, how immense that distance is.

3. That, however, which it is difficult for us to find images adequately to express, is clear and well known to the Holy Souls, or at least, if they do not yet know the Beatific Vision in itself and its effects on the heart, they know how immeasurably it surpasses the knowledge of God and the love of God which they now possess, and that it is their own fault which shuts them out from the experience of what they thus know. In their prison of Purgatory they love God most ardently, but as they are still limited to the darker perceptions of faith, and as they know how far more intense is the love of Heaven, with which they would now be burning if it were not for their own negligence, the comparative coldness of their present love is a source of regret and self-reproach. Their hope reaches forward to the possession of God, but all the love which they now have is absorbed in an intense longing for that more perfect love for which they are destined, the very least delay of which is the cause of a pain which is almost intolerable. We see something of this in the longing for death which has consumed so many of the saints, the cause of which has been their unquenchable desire to see God as He is, in order that they may love

Him with the love of the celestial home. In that immense longing of theirs we see some image of what is common in Purgatory.

4. The effects of the love of God, as they are described to us by spiritual writers, must not be passed over here, although it is difficult to speak of them and still more difficult to understand them where there has been no practical familiarity with them. But we are not at liberty to treat the experiences or the descriptions of the Saints as if they did not embody the most substantial and real of truths, merely because they are truths of which ordinary Christians have no practical perception. We read, for instance, in the lives of the Saints, of their frequent ecstasies, in which they are drawn so forcibly to God by their love that the powers of the body fail, and the usual operations of vitality appear to cease. This is the consequence of the great weakness of the body, and there can be no effect of this kind in the state of glory, and we do not find it in our Lord or in the greatest of His Saints. But, putting this accidental accompaniment of the state of ecstasy apart, the state itself, which consists in a most close and inseparable clinging of the soul to God, is one of the conditions of the state of glory, and one of the effects of the love with which the Blessed in Heaven are drawn to Him. This does not prevent their seeing and knowing and caring for all other things in Him, any more than its prevents their conscious and perfect adhesion to Him and to His will in everything, even when,

if so it be, those whom they have loved dearly on earth have to be separated from Him and them for ever. But this perfect rapture of the soul in God is not as yet the possession of the Holy Souls, and their love has not as yet mounted up to this high perfection. Another effect of the love of God on the Blessed in Heaven is that which spiritual writers speak of as union. The minds and hearts of the Blessed in Heaven cannot divert themselves from God. It is part of their immense happiness to be most perfectly united to Him Whom they so love, as a willing instrument to its mover and end, for all that belongs to His will or greater glory. It is the part of love to wish well to the person who is loved. The highest good that can be wished to God is His own glory, whether His intrinsic glory, which embraces all His Divine perfections, or His extrinsic glory, which consists in His being known and praised. This glory they desire to be rendered to Him by all, but they themselves give it to Him in the most excellent way, by knowing Him and loving Him most perfectly. All this is understood by the Holy Souls, and yet they know that they have shut themselves out for a time from the exercise of love, and the delay which is to be their punishment for this negligence is felt by them as a cause of the most intense pain.

5. Spiritual writers tell us of two other effects of the love of the Blessed for God, with which we may conclude this chapter. The first is a kind of absorption of the blessed soul in God, by means

of which it is said, as it were, to melt away and lose itself in Him. " He who does not intuitively see God," says Lessius,* "stands without, and is even far distant from Him, because God is to Him as One Who is far distant. But he who sees Him in clear vision is present to Him, and he does not remain as it were outside on the surface, but enters into Him, and plunges himself, as far as may be, into that great depth. For love desires to abide within the Beloved, for there is its place, and home, and rest, and security, and all. But each one penetrates more or less into that depth, and is more or less deeply merged therein, as he has more or less of the light of glory, or of charity." This is the "circle" of which St. Dionysius speaks —the Divine Light shedding forth the light of glory on the soul, love proceeding from that light, which in turn draws the mind to God and plunges into Him. The Blessed in Heaven see that they proceed from God as from a principle of the most marvellous fecundity, and they endeavour with all their might to return to Him wholly by contempla- tion and love. Again, the Holy Souls know all this, while they themselves, instead of plunging into that great abyss of the Deity, are detained in another abyss of misery, because, when on earth, they turned away from God, and spent themselves on created goods, which are not true goods, but only shadows of good, vanities of vanities. God is their home, and yet they are shut out from Him. " How lovely are Thy tabernacles, O Thou Lord

* *De Summo Bono*, ii. 12.

U

of hosts! my soul longeth and fainteth for the courts of the Lord, . . . for the sparrow hath found herself a house, and the turtle a nest for herself where she may lay her young ones, Thine altars, O Lord of hosts, my King and my God. Blessed are they that dwell in Thy house, O Lord, they shall praise Thee for ever and ever." *

6. These words lead us to the fourth effect of the love of God in the Blessed in Heaven, which is that they are for ever praising Him. "And all the Angels stood around about the throne, and the ancients, and the four living creatures, and they fell down before the throne on their faces, and adored God, saying, Amen, Benediction, and glory, and wisdom, and thanksgiving, honour, and power, and strength, to our God for ever and ever." † The Holy Souls in Purgatory do indeed sing the Divine praises. They break out into constant thanksgivings for the certainty of their salvation, and for the suffrages which are made for them. But they know that these praises of God are cold indeed, in comparison to the praise which they might be rendering to Him in Heaven. They know, if they do not hear, as some have thought, the curses and blasphemies which assail the majesty of God from Hell. They know that they themselves cannot make Him as yet the compensation of that praise which springs from beatific love. They cannot sing the Lord's song in a strange land. The loss of these great privileges and effects of the love of which we speak is to them a reality,

---

* Psalm lxxxiii. 1—5.   † Apoc. vii. 11, 12.

since it is from their own fault, tormenting them with a pain which no human words can describe. Their suffering is indeed a lesson to us to advance as far as possible in the love of God which is open to us while we are yet alive, and, by our suffrages for them, to set them free as soon as may be to love God for us with that beatific love of which we have been trying to speak.

CHAPTER XXXIII.

The Pain of Loss. III. The Loss of the Joy of Heaven.

(CURE OF THE WOMAN WITH A SPIRIT OF INFIRMITY.)

St. Luke xiii. 10—17.

1. THE holy writers whom we have been following on the subject of the pain of loss add a third element of the sorrow which that pain produces in the souls of the prisoners of Purgatory. This third element is the result of their forfeiture, though only for a time, of the ineffable joy which results from that knowledge and love of God which reign in Heaven. The present chapter, therefore, must be devoted to some thoughts on this subject, and we shall find that they may very well be connected with the next miracle of our Lord, as related by the Evangelist St. Luke. It is one of the miracles wrought on the Sabbath day by our Lord, in that

latter period of His preaching in Judæa of which
the third Evangelist has made himself specially the
historian. In its main circumstances it is very like
other miracles of the same sort wrought in Galilee.
That is, the miracle was wrought without any application first made to our Lord to work it, and it
aroused the indignation of our Lord's adversaries,
an indignation which found a mouthpiece in the
ruler of the synagogue. Our Lord answered His
enemies in the same way as in earlier instances in
which the same objection was made against works
of Divine mercy on the Sabbath. His adversaries
were silenced, and the people, on the other hand,
rejoiced.

2. St. Luke then tells us that our Lord "was
teaching in their synagogue on the Sabbath." It
is not the wont of this Evangelist, writing for
persons who did not know the Holy Land, to
specify the places in which such miracles were
wrought, but there need be no doubt that it was
in the country parts of Judæa that almost everything that is mentioned in this part of his Gospel
took place. "And behold, there was a woman
who had a spirit of infirmity eighteen years, and
she was bowed together, neither could she look
upwards at all." This woman may well represent
to us the state of the Holy Souls detained in many
cases from the vision of God for a term quite as
long as that here mentioned,—a state of joyless-
ness, their hearts bowed down with grief, on
account of the punishment of loss. "Whom when
Jesus saw, He called her unto Him, and said,

Woman, thou art delivered from thy infirmity. And He laid His hands upon her, and immediately she was made straight, and glorified God." We need not dwell at any length upon that part of the narrative which relates to the hostility which this miracle aroused. Our Lord answered the objection in His usual way. "Ye hypocrites, doth not every one of you on the Sabbath day loose his ox or his ass from the manger, and lead them to water? And ought not this daughter of Abraham, whom Satan hath bound, lo, these eighteen years, be loosed from this bond on the Sabbath day? And when He had said these things, all His adversaries were ashamed, and all the people rejoiced for all the things that were gloriously done by Him."

3. This rejoicing of the people at the glorious things which were done by our Lord may serve as a sort of image of the joy of the Blessed in Heaven, which, as we shall see, is founded on God and on His glorious works. Joy, we are told, is the necessary complement and filling up of beatitude : so that, if we can separate in idea the three elements of beatitude of which we have spoken, the knowledge of God, the love of God, and the joy which results from these two, it may be said that beatitude itself would be incomplete without the last of the three. Joy is the very quintessence and crown and flower of happiness. Innocent joy, even on earth, is the most beautiful thing that can be seen in this valley of tears, and the supernatural joy of the Blessed is, in like

manner, the most beautiful thing in their state in
Heaven.   Joy has three causes, each of which
must be present if it is to exist.   There must be
the possession of a great good, there must be the
apprehension of this good and of its possession by
a high and excellent faculty, and there must be
a great love for the thing which is thus possessed
and apprehended.   In the case of the joy of which
we are speaking, the good thing which is possessed
is nothing else than God Himself, the highest and
most ineffable of goods, the only True Good, the
good perfect in every degree of goodness and of
perfection.   The organ or faculty which, as it were,
appropriates this immense Good, containing infinite
beauty, sweetness, and perfection, is the beatified
mind, the noblest faculty of man, raised far above
its natural powers by the light of glory, and strengthened thereby for the participation and possession
of that supreme essence of the Divinity.   The
love with which the soul clings to its object is,
again, the most sublime and intense that can be
conceived.   These, then, are the causes of the
intense joy in which the Blessed in Heaven live
—a joy to which no delights of the senses can be
compared without degrading it, which rises as far
above even the joy in God of the Saints on earth,
St. Paul, St. Francis, and others, as the light of
the sun above that of a poor candle.   All the joys
that can be felt on earth, even of the highest kind,
if they were gathered into one soul, multiplied a
thousand-fold, and made eternal, would not yet
come up to the joy which the soul of one single

beatified infant tastes in Heaven in the space of a
short hour, for the simple reason that the knowledge and love on which those joys are founded
are altogether of a lower order than the knowledge
and love which give birth to the joy of which we
are speaking.

4. It is but little that we can say by way of an
attempt at describing the subject-matter of the joys
of Heaven, and yet it is well, as a help to meditation, to set down the chief heads under which
that subject-matter can be ranged. In the first
place, as the Blessed know and possess God, their
joy is founded on the goods which belong to God.
The intrinsic goods, so to speak, of God, are His
Own Ineffably Perfect Essence and Attributes,
which have more than once been spoken of in
these chapters. There is a second class of goods
external to His Divine Essence—the glory which
accrues to God from the Sacred Humanity of our
Lord, the Hypostatic Union, the grace of Jesus
Christ, His Virtues and Works in the world, the
Blessed Sacrament, and the like, and again, from
the Immaculate Mother of God, the Saints and
Angels, and their incessant praises before His
throne, the wonderful kingdom of the Militant
Church on earth, its structure, mission, powers,
government, the Providence which guides it, and
the "healing of the nations" by its means. And
among these goods of God must be reckoned also
the Kingdom of His Justice, in which His enemies
suffer for their rebellion against Him, or those who
are to live for ever in His Presence are prepared

for it.   Then again, the Blessed in Heaven rejoice over another class of goods, which may be said to be their own.   The Beatific Vision of God begets in them a sort of participation in the glory and felicity of God Himself, as if, according to the words of the Psalmist, as quoted by our Lord,* they became, in a manner, gods.   Again, the joy which the Beatific Vision creates in them would be ineffable, if it lasted but for a moment, but it is much increased and perfected by the fixity and eternity of that vision.   The Blessed rejoice, moreover, in the extreme splendour of virtue in which they are, as it were, clothed, when they enter Heaven, in the clear knowledge of all things which they possess, and the delight with which the beauty and sweetness of all the works of God fill them. Even the past is full of delight to them, because they see all the dangers from which they have been guarded, and the eternal pains from which the mercy of God has saved them.   And, if each one of those blessed citizens of Heaven is flooded with delight for the goods which are thus his own, not less is it true that this delight is reflected on all and multiplied in each soul, as it were, by the joy with which they rejoice in the goods which others possess, for they know each other perfectly, and all that God has done for and given to each, and each one rejoices in this as if it were his own.

5. And now, it must be added that all these causes of joy in the Blessed in Heaven are known to and undersood by the Holy Souls in Purgatory,

* St. John x. 34 ; Psalm lxxxi. 6.

not indeed with that clearness and intensity which are to be found only in Heaven, but still with a clearness and intensity which far surpass any that we can have on earth. They know that they ought to be enjoying all these ineffable delights, and thanking God with the gratitude which corresponds to His mercies and gifts in their regard, and that they are unable to do this on account of their own fault. They are like guests bidden to a most exquisite banquet, for which they yearn with an ineffable hunger, who are yet, for their disrespect to the King Who has invited them, made to sit by it with their hands tied behind them, unable to taste it except in desire—a desire which is stimulated but never satisfied by their having to gaze upon it. How gladly would they turn to us and pray us to help them to their release! How gladly would they warn us to practise ourselves in thoughts concerning the eternal goods of Heaven, and in holy desires and aspirations of longing for them—knowing that, in many cases, their detention from the possession of this ineffable joy of which we have been speaking is the punishment of nothing more than a neglect to think of God, and to desire and long for the eternal possession of Himself which He has prepared for His children!

CHAPTER XXXIV.

The Pain of Loss. IV. Causes of Sorrow to the Holy Souls.

(THE CURE OF THE MAN WITH THE DROPSY.)

St. Luke xiv. 1—6.

1. IN the last chapter the Holy Souls of Purgatory were spoken of as guests at a most excellent banquet, who were forced to sit and gaze upon it with their hands fastened behind their backs, and altogether unable to satisfy their hunger upon it. We may conclude the subject of the pain of loss which these Holy Souls suffer, by some other considerations concerning it which may be connected with the next miracle of our Lord, which, like the last, is related by St. Luke alone. It is another of the miracles wrought on the Sabbath day; but it was not in the synagogue, but at one of the feasts which it was customary, as it seems, to connect with the Sabbath. "And it came to pass, when Jesus went into the house of one of the chief of the Pharisees on the Sabbath day to eat bread, that they watched Him. And behold, there was a certain man before Him who had the dropsy. And Jesus answering, spoke to the lawyers and Pharisees, saying, Is it lawful to heal on the Sabbath day? But they held their peace. But

He taking him, healed him, and sent him away, and answering them, said, Which of you shall have an ass or an ox fall into a pit, and will not immediately draw him out on the Sabbath day? But they could not answer Him to these things."

2. The Holy Souls in Purgatory, in regard to the blessings of Heaven to which they are heirs, are very like this poor man, who was healed by our Lord, and then sent away from the banquet. His dismissal, however, did not imply any reproach or blame, for he was not among the invited guests, and had no right to be admitted to their company. The Holy Souls, on the other hand, are excluded from it through their own fault, like the foolish virgins, as has been said, though only for a time. The last chapters have shown us, in some measure, the outlines of the good of which they have deprived themselves, and it seems natural to follow these with a few considerations as to the method in which the forfeiture has been incurred. This is a subject supplementary to that of the pain of loss in itself. And we cannot doubt that this is a subject constantly present to the minds of the holy sufferers of whom we speak, inasmuch as it is directly connected with the pain of loss as a cause with its effect, although the fault which may have been involved in it has been already forgiven.

3. The chief heads of the sorrow of which we are now speaking are referred to, more or less, in various chapters of this work, so that we are not under any necessity of dwelling on them here at any great length. We may imagine that a Holy

Soul, in the midst of its pain at its banishment from the sight of God, and the subsequent delay of its entering on that life of love and joy which belongs to those who are in His presence, might ask itself, how it had come about that it incurred this banishment? It would remember in the first place, how often it had rejected or turned away from the grace of God, the holy inspirations, suggestions, promptings, warnings, with which its most loving Father had so frequently, as it were, wooed it to greater carefulness and exactness in His service. The light in which it is now able to see the character of God, His immense dignity, the wonderful condescension and love which are implied in every suggestion of grace addressed to His poor creatures, will make its grief for the rejection of any single such suggestion very poignant indeed, especially when it adds to such considerations those of the relationship to God to which it had undeservedly been raised, and the immense debt of gratitude which binds it to Him. In the same way the consideration of the truth as to the beauty and worth of sanctifying grace, of which it had made so little, will produce the same effect on the mind. Sanctifying grace is called by theologians, following the language of Scripture, a "partaking of the Divine Nature:" it is the infusion and presence of the Holy Ghost in the soul, making us act and live as the children of God, His friends, His Spouses. The more clearly the Divine character of sanctifying grace is allowed to dawn upon the soul, the more miserable, sorrowful, and shameful does the neglect of it appear. That neglect is a sort of contempt of God, as our Father, our Lover, our Friend, and this it is which has brought about the exclusion of so many thousands of souls from His sight for ever, and of so many thousands more from His sight for a time.

4. The same considerations may easily be formed in regard of sin, in the light in which the Holy Souls now regard it. All these sins are perfectly forgiven as to their guilt; but this does not prevent the memory of the causes of their exclusion from Heaven from abiding in the minds of these blessed prisoners as a part of their pain. They know now what sin is, or rather they knew it before, and there is nothing to intervene to prevent them from attentively contemplating and comprehending it, and they love God intensely, Who is injured by sin. Sin is a wrong and a harm done to God, and the more His Majesty is understood and His love esteemed, the greater must be the sorrow that He has been offended. There is nothing on earth that is loathsome and disgraceful and monstrous, which is so loathsome and so disgraceful and so monstrous as sin is seen to be by the Holy Souls. They see that they have lifted their hands against God, in a manner which, in mortal sin, implies a readiness to kill and destroy Him if such a thing were possible, to crucify our Lord over again, and drive away the Holy Ghost. They understand how far they have gone towards depriving themselves of the dignity of sons of God, towards renouncing their Heavenly inherit-

ance, and even towards incurring, at the hands of God's justice, the extreme degradation and misery of eternal damnation. This sentence has been actually incurred in the case of every single mortal sin, and an approach towards deserving it has been made by every wilful sin of a lighter kind. Other heads of sorrow may be added to these, which may help us to estimate as it ought to be estimated this pain of loss. One is that of the grief with which the Holy Souls regard their own neglect to make satisfaction for their faults, while satisfaction was as yet so easy, by almsdeeds, by prayer, by fasting, and other works of penance; or again, to obtain the benefit of that satisfaction which is to be had by means of the sacraments, especially by the Sacrament of Penance, by hearing Mass, by gaining Indulgences and the like.

5. If these thoughts be added to the other considerations which have been suggested in the three preceding chapters concerning the pain of loss, we shall find it easier to set before our minds some kind of image of what that pain is. We may add to them, however, a few more reflections concerning points as to the detention of the Holy Souls which have been left unnoticed in other parts of this work. Such is the thought that Purgatory is uniformly represented to us as a prison, not merely an abode or resting-place, but a place of detention and confinement. This element in their condition is all the more felt by these Holy Souls, not only because they would so gladly fly at once to their home in the presence of God, but because of the

natural activity of spiritual existence, and the intense vitality and energy which belong to it in such a state as theirs. It is useful to remind ourselves of what holy writers have told us of the place of Purgatory, lest we should get unconsciously to think of it as something less real and true than it is. It is well to remember that it is a place of pain and punishment and torment, even if it be not, as many writers think, close to Hell itself, and within reach of the sights and sounds and company which are there. It is well to remember that to this sad and penal abode the Holy Souls are bound by chains far more stringent than any material fetters. These circumstances all belong to the subject on which we have been engaged, as well as the privation of the Beatific Vision, the delay of the time when their love for God and their joy are to be made perfect, and their grief for the causes which have led to their detention there.

CHAPTER XXXV.

Visits to the Blessed Sacrament for the Holy Souls.

(THE HEALING OF THE TEN LEPERS.)

St. Luke xvii. 11—19.

1. ST. LUKE tells us that in one of our Lord's journeys at this time of His Ministry, He passed along the confines of Galilee and Samaria, and that at the entrance of a certain town He was accosted by a company of lepers, who "stood afar off, and lifted up their voices, saying, Jesus, Master, have mercy on us." These poor sufferers were banished from their homes on account of their dreadful disease, and so were fain to consort together. They were afraid to approach our Lord and His little band of followers, and so called to Him from a distance. "Whom when He saw, He said, Go show yourselves to the priests. And it came to pass, as they went, they were made clean. And one of them, when he saw that he was made clean, went back, with a loud voice glorifying God. And he fell on his face before His feet, giving thanks, and this was a Samaritan." It may be that, as a Samaritan, he would not have been received and examined by the Jewish priests; but he found his way to the one true Priest, and, at all events, he did not fail in the fulfilment of the

great paramount duty of thanksgiving. "And Jesus answering, said, Were not ten made clean, and where are the nine? There is no one found to return and give glory to God but this stranger. And He said to him, Arise, go thy way, for thy faith hath made thee whole."

2. It is easy to see that the point in this miracle which gives to it a particular character, is the incident of the thanksgiving of the restored leper, and of our Lord's remark on the absence of such thanksgiving in the others, from whom it might, perhaps, have been expected rather than from him. Our Lord speaks, as if He were pained and hurt at their ingratitude. This point may serve us as a guide in our application of this miracle to the state of the Holy Souls in Purgatory. The reflections which we have lately been making on the subject of the pain of loss, and all that is contained in it and connected therewith, naturally suggest the further thought of the immense and burning devotion which they must feel to the Sacred Humanity of our Blessed Lord. It is by means of that Sacred Humanity alone that they have had the prospect of the Beatific Vision opened to them, that it has become possible for them ever to glow with the ecstatic love of Heaven and to lose themselves in its joys. It is by means of that Humanity alone that the treasures of sanctifying grace have been laid open to them, that they have had the capacity of propitiating God for their offences and shortcomings by prayer, fasting, and almsdeeds, and that the satisfactions stored up

v

in the sacraments, and in such means of grace as Indulgences, have been placed within their reach. Every thought of grief or self-reproach which has arisen within them on account of the losses, temporal or eternal, which they have incurred, on account of the sins, mortal or venial, with which they have been stained, is a thought which brings our Lord Jesus Christ home to them, as their Master, Friend, Ransomer, Lover, and Eternal Reward. Everything reminds them of their ingratitude to Him, and of the wounds which they have inflicted on His loving Heart. Closely as they are united with Him, they are detained from His Personal Presence; they cannot see His face, though it has shone upon them at the moment of their judgment with a light of love, but still of displeasure, nor have they now that Sacramental Presence of His to be their consolation and resource, which they had the opportunity of enjoying while they were members of the Militant Church. It may be that they have to reproach themselves with this among other things—that they have been wanting in gratitude to our Lord in His sacramental love. This may be a special cause of sorrow to them, now that they are deprived of the opportunities of which they have thought so little.

3. We have already spoken of the marvellous blessings which we possess in the Sacrifice of the Altar and in Holy Communion. It seems natural, therefore, that we should find a place in this work to speak of the third great display of our Lord's

love to us in the Blessed Sacrament, which consists in His continual residence among us in the sacred Tabernacle. We have in that Presence of His a blessing which turns earth into Heaven, if we would but know it. The perpetuity of His abiding there, and the circumstances and manner of that abiding, the silence, the confinement, the solitude, the neglect, often the irreverence, and ill-treatment to which they expose Him, are all so many proofs of His immense love as shown in this mystery, because it must be thought that He could not submit to so much, except for the purpose of gaining a very great good indeed—a very great good, not to Himself, certainly, but to our poor souls, for whom all this is endured. In nothing is our Lord exposed to so much negligence or ingratitude—His Church, His Priests, His Grace, are all His, but they are not Himself, as is the Blessed Sacrament. Holy Mass passes away in half an hour, Holy Communion is over in a few minutes, but the dwelling of our Lord in the Tabernacle goes on hour after hour, day after day, week after week. Here we have His Presence, which the Blessed in Heaven have in another way, but which the Holy Souls in Purgatory have not. It is a Presence the condescension of which it would overtask the tongues of all the saints and angels to declare, and in order to secure which for us He has to work more stupendous miracles than we can give an account of. It is a Presence which imparts blessings to the Church, to the world, and to His faithiul worshippers in particular, as many as the sands on the sea-shore and more glorious in their effect than the stars of the heavens. And this may be said to be the very chief of all the uncomprehended and most disregarded mercies of God to us in our present state: more so, when the immensity of the graces which might be won by it is considered, than the guardianship of the angels, of which we think so little, or the practical benefits which flow from our membership of the Church, or from the prayers and protection of the Saints, or even from the mightiness and power and vigilant tenderness of the motherly care of Mary herself. Each one of these indicates a great ocean of blessings, in which we float, as in the air which we breathe, with scarcely the consciousness of its existence and of what we owe to it. But all taken together are as little when compared to the Personal Presence of our Lord in the sacred Tabernacle.

4. As the Holy Souls are now deprived of this ineffable blessing, it would certainly be a thing very highly consoling and refreshing to them in their indigence if we connect our prayers for them, as far as possible, with some special honour done to our Lord by way of gratitude for His sacramental love. As we hear or say Mass for them, or endeavour to refresh or aid them by receiving Holy Communion, we may add to these devout practices that of frequently visiting the Blessed Sacrament for their intention, or to perform an act of religion which may help to their deliverance. The time which we thus spend in thus

honouring our Lord may be used for any holy purpose whatever, for meditation, examination of conscience, imploring pardon for sin or strength against temptation or increase in virtue or in any other such way. But it seems very natural indeed that it should be in part spent in special exercises of adoration, praise, thanksgiving, and intercession, and these, both on our part and on the part of the whole Church, and on the part of the Holy Souls. If we give ourselves earnestly and thoroughly to the devotion to Purgatory of which this little volume treats, we shall be able to say to ourselves after a time, that though we cannot ourselves worship and praise and thank God as the saints and angels worship and praise and thank Him in Heaven, still we have contributed something towards sending into His adorable Presence at least some souls, who might otherwise have not been so soon delivered from Purgatory, who may praise and thank Him in our stead. And in the same way, when we kneel before the Tabernacle, and take with us, as far as is in our power, the Holy Souls to be the companions of our adoration, we can give them the satisfaction that, if they cannot worship the Blessed Sacrament themselves, they are at all events not unrepresented before the throne of His infinite condescension.

CHAPTER XXXVI

Purgatory and the Glory of God.

(THE RAISING OF LAZARUS.)

St. John xi. 1—44.

1. WE are now drawing near to the end of the glorious cycle of the miracles of our Lord, and it will be necessary to adapt the few remaining subjects which are usually handled in treatises about Purgatory to the narratives which have yet to be considered. The next miracle in point of time is that most stupendous work of the raising from the dead of our Lord's intimate friend Lazarus, after he had been laid in the grave for more than four full days. The incidents of the history are so familiar to all, that it will not be necessary to repeat them. Our Lord, at the time of the dangerous illness of Lazarus, was at some distance from Bethany, but not too far for the holy sisters, Martha and Mary, to send to tell Him, and, by telling Him, to implore Him to come to the relief of their brother. Our Lord remained in the place where He was for two days, after answering the message of the sisters by the implicit promise, " This sickness is not unto death, but for the glory of God, that the Son of God may be glorified by it." He afterwards, as St. John men-

tions, referred to this message, as containing an assurance from Him that the sisters were not to be deprived of their brother. Our Lord, after the lapse of the two days already spoken of, proposed to His disciples to return into the land of Judæa, the neighbourhood of Jerusalem, from which He had lately withdrawn on account of the attempts made by the ecclesiastical rulers to put Him to death. This proposal was objected to by the Apostles, and when our Lord persisted in his intention, St. Thomas uttered those memorable words of affectionate devotion, "Let us also go, that we may die with Him." When He came near to Bethany, His coming became known first to Martha and then to Mary Magdalene her sister, each of whom went forth in turn to meet our Lord. Mary's movement to meet Him was mistaken by the Jews who had come to mourn with and comfort the sisters, who thought she was going to indulge her feelings of grief by weeping at the grave, and thus they followed her. Each of the sisters addressed our Lord in the loving words, "Lord, if Thou hadst been here, my brother had not died." Martha was led on by our Lord to a formal profession of faith in Him, very like to that which was so much commended by Him in St. Peter: "I have believed that Thou art the Christ, the Son of the Living God, Who art come into this world." But this did not prevent her, when they had come to the sepulchre, and our Lord bade the bystanders take away the stone, from remonstrating on account of the length of time during which the corpse had laid in the grave. Our Lord answered her, " Did I not say to thee, that if thou believe, thou shalt see the glory of God ? " And when the stone had been removed, He lifted up His eyes and gave thanks before them all to His Father for hearing Him, before He called Lazarus forth. Thus, all through the narrative of the Evangelist, we have the thought of the glory of God constantly recurring, as the end and object of our Lord in working this great miracle.

2. The sequel of the history shows how true and how prophetic were these words of our Blessed Lord. The glory of God and of His Son was greatly advanced by the death of Lazarus, inasmuch as that death gave our Lord the occasion of raising His friend from the dead. And although the immediate consequence of the miracle was the determination of the Jewish rulers to take away our Lord's life, a resolution which was carried out in His Passion a few weeks later, still that also conduced in the most wonderful manner to the glory of God and of our Lord, because the redemption of the world and the foundation of His eternal Kingdom came about as the fruit of the Passion. Thus God permitted a calamity to befall the household which was so dear to our Lord, in order that their sufferings and faith might give an opportunity for the exercise of His miraculous power in the most stupendous instance which is recorded for us in the Gospels. And He also allowed the enormous sin of the judicial murder of

our Lord, in order that, by means of that sin, He might be glorified as the Redeemer of mankind. We have here, then, set before us the principle of God's government which is exemplified whenever He does or allows anything which may be, on certain grounds, undesirable or strange, apparently contrary to His mercy or love or to some other of His attributes, but which is not so in truth, or which illustrates other parts of His all-perfect character, such as His justice or His love of purity. This thought will be enough to occupy us profitably with regard to His permission that the Souls whom He loves so tenderly should suffer in the flames of Purgatory.

3. It is most true, as we shall see, that the existence of Purgatory is a great witness to the glory of God in many different ways, so that, if there were no Purgatory, the glory of God would be less than we know it to be. So that, putting aside any direct decree of God, by which He might provide for His glory in the same degree in some other manner, it may be said that souls in love with the glory of God might wish that, if Purgatory did not exist, it might be created. Let us consider a few of the reasons which may be given for this truth. In the first place, it may be said that as God is glorified by anything in His Kingdom and the arrangements of His government which displays either His Wisdom or His Mercy, so also He is glorified by anything therein that displays in a striking way His Justice and Holiness. Now there is perhaps nothing in the whole range

of the Kingdom of God which more clearly
displays His justice, than the punishments which
are inflicted in Purgatory. For this reason God
desires and allows those punishments, because they
are due to His justice. The souls who are there
imprisoned are very dear to Him and confirmed in
His grace, but they are not sufficiently purified to
stand in the presence of His infinite holiness.
God does not inflict the sufferings of Purgatory
because they torment and afflict the souls that
suffer there, nor does He take delight in their
sufferings, as such, but because they are just and
conduce to His honour in the first place, and
because they are of immense profit to the souls in
the second place. His ineffable goodness cannot
allow any good work or service done to Him, however trifling it may seem, to go without its reward.
As in the same way, His ineffable justice cannot
allow any fault to go without its punishment. But
if there were no Purgatory, many evils would
remain unpunished, unless, indeed, as some of His
enemies have imagined, He were to punish all sins
alike by the eternal pains of Hell. The perfect
equity of His rule requires that the soul that has
despised Him, the highest good, and postponed
Him to the lowest kind of good, or rather, to the
false good, of pleasure and sin, should in its turn
be placed in subjection and captivity, as it were,
under the dominion of pain. Every sin contains
in itself three things, for it is an offence against
His Divine Majesty, it is an injury to the Holy
Church, and it defaces and deforms the Divine

Image in the soul itself. The offence requires punishment, the loss to the Church requires satisfaction, and the defacement of the soul requires purification. These three things may be wrought out here on earth and during this life. But if they are not, they remain to be accomplished hereafter, and the place in which they are accomplished is Purgatory. It is there, then, that the honour of God is avenged, the injury to the Church repaired, and deformity of the soul done away. That so it should be, is a great triumph due to the most pure and holy justice of God.

4. And again, it is a great triumph to the mercy of God that He should have made a place where His justice can be satisfied, and yet, after all, His mercy have its way. No doubt, the great feeling which dominates the souls of these holy sufferers, is that they are very leniently dealt with, even though they are in the hands of God's justice. After all the opportunities of grace and penance and satisfaction which they have neglected, it is a great mark of mercy that God should take into His own hands the purification of their souls as far as the punishment of sin is concerned, the inflicting of which on themselves is the most difficult task, it may be said, which our poor nature had to undertake. Moreover, the realm of Purgatory is full of alleviations, all of which are granted by God in His mercy, as when the prayers of the saints and angels and of Christians on earth are heard for the Holy Souls.

5. We know that God is His own end, and that

He can do nothing at all for anything less worthy of Him than His own honour. The Psalmist says: "Mercy and judgment will I sing to Thee, O Lord."* And in another place, "Holiness becometh Thy house, O Lord, for length of days." This idea of what is becoming and worthy of God is used by St. Paul as an argument about the Passion, where he says that it "became Him for Whom are all things, and by Whom are all things, Who was bringing many children to glory, to make perfect the Author of their salvation by His Passion."† Thus we may say that it became God, in the great work of calling millions of spirits whom He had created free for that purpose, to share His own eternal glory and blessedness in Heaven, to show Himself bountiful as well as wise, and just as well as merciful. It is becoming to Him Who has redeemed the world by the Incarnation and Death of His Son, to give the free gift of eternal life for His sake to an immense number of souls who have never themselves toiled and struggled for it. Such as are the souls of Christian children saved by their baptism, and who have never lived to the age of reason. It is also becoming to Him, that in the case of millions of others, the crown which is awarded them, through the merits of our Lord, should be, as St. Paul calls it, a crown of justice, won by their own faithfulness and exertion, by their successful struggle, in their weak human flesh, against all the snares and dangers by which they were surrounded in the

* Psalm ci. 1.   † Heb. ii. 10.

world, against the malice of their invisible foes
and against the traitorous suggestions of their
fallen nature. It became Him also that there
should be in His Kingdom another class of
redeemed souls, which have not passed through
the battle of life unscarthed, and who have yet, by
means of His abundant provisions of grace, been
able to reach the shore of Heaven in all the
holiness and purity which that abode of bliss
requires in its inmates, and who have yet not left
one farthing of their debt to the ineffable justice of
God unpaid. It is becoming that nothing in the
slightest degree impure or imperfect should approach
the realm of the Divine light, and present itself
before the all-searching eyes of the Holiest of
Holies. And as so great a number of the souls
for whom our Lord died would pass out of this
world not perfectly pure enough for His sight for
ever, it became Him to provide at once for the
dignity of His dwelling and for the purposes of
His loving condescension, to satisfy alike the
claims of His justice and the demands of His
mercy, to fill his banquet with guests, according to
the parable of our Lord, and yet to see that no
one entered there without a wedding garment.
And this He has done most perfectly and beautifully
by the institution of the sacred prison of Purgatory,
without which these things could not be brought
about.

6. Again, Purgatory, and the sufferings which
are there endured, add not a little to the glory of
God in His character of our Redeemer as well as

in that of our Sovereign and our Judge. Just as it
adds to the honour of our Lord that there should
be so many souls in Heaven who are there through
His merits alone, and without any working of their
own by way of correspondence—for they have
never, as has been said, reached the age of reason
so as to be capable of sin or merit—so it is greatly
to His glory that there should be many saved by
means of His sacramental grace alone, after they
have lived to offend Him. And this is the case of
those who have received the Sacrament of Penance
duly at the point of death, without having that full
and perfect contrition which would have reconciled
them to Him even without that sacrament, if it
had not been in their power to receive it. Such
persons are often burthened with a large debt to
the justice of God, which can only be paid in
Purgatory, but being reconciled to God at the
last, they are confirmed in grace at the moment of
death, and so are made capable of the salutary
sufferings of Purgatory. Their number may be
very great, and thus a large portion of the Holy
Souls may witness in this special manner to the
efficacy of the grace which He has left behind
Him in the Church.

7. Again, God is glorified not only in the
institutions and arrangements of His wisdom and
mercy, but in the manner in which they call forth
from those who belong to Him the exercise of the
virtues which reflect His own perfect character.
In this way our Lord is glorified by the patience,
and resignation, and zeal for His honour, which

make the Holy Souls willing sufferers, desirous rather to see His justice vindicated in their regard than to appear before Him unfit for His presence. They love His justice, though it has to be wreaked upon themselves, and the knowledge that it is His will that they should suffer as they do, is enough to stifle in them all murmuring and repining. Their state also calls forth great and intense compassion and sympathy in the Saints, whose charity is kindled by the sight of so many souls who are destined to share their own glories and blessedness, and whom they know to be left by the Providence of God to their intercessions and to those of the Church upon earth for the shortening of their period of banishment. In the same way is the charity of the Church Militant excited, and aroused to activity and exertion, by the state of the Holy Souls, and in this way also God's glory is advanced. He is honoured by the urgency of prayer, which has its efficacy through the Incarnation and the Communion of Saints; He is honoured by the labours of charity, which afflicts and puts itself to pain out of love for Him and those who belong to Him; He is honoured by the offering of the Holy Sacrifice and of the works of satisfaction or mercy for the Holy Souls. He is honoured again by the tenderness with which the Holy Angels, as we shall see, pray for or relieve, according to what is permitted to them, the sufferers on whom the hand of His justice is heavy for a time, but whom He intends throughout all eternity to praise and adore Him along with those

Holy Angels, and to thank them also for their charity, and to give thanks to Him for His mercy and love towards them. In these and in other similar ways we may see how true it is that the holy prison of Purgatory gives glory to God for His mercy and wisdom, as well as for His justice.

———

CHAPTER XXXVII.

Diligence in Relieving the Holy Souls.

(THE CURE OF THE BLIND MEN AT JERICHO.)

St. Matt. xx. 29—34 ; St. Mark x. 46—52 ; St. Luke xviii. 35 ; xix. 1.

1. THE miracles of which we are now to speak are almost the very last which our Lord wrought before His Passion of which we have any detailed account, and it is perhaps for some reason connected with this that they are related by the Evangelists. St. Matthew, in his summary manner, puts them together, but St. Luke and St. Mark seem carefully to distinguish two several cases, and the lesson which we may learn from them is much enhanced in its importance and force if we take the whole narrative together. Our Lord was on His way to Jerusalem from Peræa, that part of the Holy Land on the farther side of the Jordan, and He was accompanied in His progress by a large multitude, partly from Peræa, and partly, as it seems, made

up of the crowds of devout Galilæans who were going up to the feast at Jerusalem, and whose ordinary route lay along the farther side of the Jordan valley, in order that they might avoid passing through the schismatic and hostile country of the Samaritans. Jericho was the great town between the ford of the Jordan and Jerusalem through which the line of march lay; and the two miracles before us took place, one at the entrance of the city towards the Jordan, the other just outside the gate which led towards Jerusalem. It was naturally at the gates of the city that beggars and suppliants of all sorts took their posts on such occasions as the passing of the great caravans of pilgrims towards the holy city. Thus it was that on this occasion our Lord's progress was twice stopped, once at each side of the city. At the gate on the Jordan side a blind man was sitting begging, and hearing the footsteps of the large multitude he asked the bystanders what it was, and was told that Jesus of Nazareth was passing by. He began immediately to call on our Lord as the Son of David to have mercy on him. The leaders of the caravan, anxious that there should be no stoppage on the way, especially as they were about to pass through the narrow street of the city, rebuked him, and bade him hold his peace. " But he cried out much more, Son of David, have mercy on me ! And Jesus, standing, commanded him to be brought to Him. And when he was come near, He asked him, saying, What wilt thou that I do for thee ? And he said, Lord, that I may see.

W

And Jesus said to him, Receive thy sight, thy faith hath made thee whole. And immediately he saw, and followed Him, glorifying God. And all the people when they saw it gave praise to God." Our Lord then went on and passed through the city. At the farther gate there was another collection of beggars, and a very similar scene was repeated. Here there was a blind man, who seems afterwards to have been known in the Church, as St. Mark mentions his name, Bartimæus. He too, when he heard Who was passing by, called on Him as the Son of David, and insisted all the more the more he was rebuked. Our Lord again stopped on His way, and bade them bring the blind man to Him. "And they call the blind man, saying to him, Be of better comfort, arise, He calleth thee. Who, casting off his garment, leaped up and came to Him." Our Lord asked him the same questions as in the former case, and received the same answer. "And Jesus saith to him, Go thy way, thy faith hath made thee whole."

2. The most prominent point in this beautiful narrative is the manner in which our Blessed Lord makes everything, as it were, give way to the interest of these blind men. It was, no doubt, a great inconvenience to stop the march of so large a procession of people, for those who were behind would naturally crowd on those in front, up to the point where our Lord was, and those who went before Him would press on unconscious that they were leaving their companions behind. But nothing of this sort had any weight with our Lord, and

He seemed determined to listen, with the utmost patience, to the prayer of each suppliant, and to miss no opportunity of relieving misery such as theirs. He knew how short His time now was, and that He would never again pass along that road to the feast. He seems to teach us in this way the great lesson concerning works of mercy, something like the lesson as to the forgiveness of injuries which is conveyed in His injunction to go on forgiving, not until seven times, but until seventy times seven.* The lesson which is here taught us is that we are never to weary in doing mercy and charity, never to let the trouble which they may cause us hinder us from them, never to let the fact that we have done one act of kindness make us think ourselves dispensed from doing another. In hearts full of charity this lesson is not so much needed. But charity and mercy, beautiful as they are in themselves, and full of comfort and joy to those who practise them, are yet directly against the current of our self-interest and natural indolence, and so they require a fresh impulse of grace and a fresh exertion each time that occasion presents itself. It is very often a slight trouble or fatigue which makes us put off doing a good work, and we very often say to ourselves that we have done enough, and now may rest, whereas it is God's way constantly to send us another call on our charity just after we have put ourselves out for the same purpose. Such calls are in truth rewards for what we have already done,

* St. Matt. xviii. 22.

but our foolish nature does not always recognize the hand and intention of God.

3. The lesson which we thus learn in regard to the assistance which we try to render to the Holy Souls in Purgatory is very obvious and simple. We have already had occasion to speak of the virtue of promptitude in this respect,* and we must now add the perfect diligence and care to miss no opportunity which comes to us for the practice of this great charity, greater than that of giving sight to the blind, inasmuch as the vision of God in Heaven is infinitely more precious than the light of this world. We shall not be thoroughly penetrated with the truths about Purgatory, and about our duties to the Holy Souls, we shall not be altogether filled with the devotion to which those truths lead, or with understanding as to what is God's desire and our own great interest in the matter, till we come to see that the law of charity binds us, not only to occasional and intermittent exertions on their behalf, but to a perpetual and ever-vigilant service, like that of a slave or of a soldier in the field of battle. The sufferings of the Holy Souls are unintermittent, and so must be our labours for them. To have freed one soul is a reason for beginning to toil for the freedom of others, not for resting on our arms ¡in the holy warfare. Thus there may be a great danger of our losing the reward of perfect faithfulness in this respect. We ought to help the Holy Souls every day of our lives, in all the ways we can, and at

* See Chap. vii.

every time that we can. As a general reviews his
forces, or as a merchant looks into his accounts to
see that no part of his capital is allowed to be idle,
no occasion of gain passed over, no market for his
goods neglected, so must we review the means
which God has given us of practising the necessary
work of charity, and endeavour to use all, to use
them always, and to use them in the best possible
way—prayers, vocal and mental, Masses, Communions, visits to the Blessed Sacrament, acts of
corporal and spiritual mercy, mortifications, indulgences, devotions, and penances of every kind.
It ought to be a matter of scruple to those who
take up this holy and blessed devotion, to have
left anything undone for the Holy Souls which they
might have done for them.

4. As our Lord so frequently uses the motives
of hope or fear in His exhortations to the practice
of virtue, and not least in His admonitions about
the value of good works and almsdeeds, it may
well be to fortify ourselves from time to time, in
any exertions which we may make for the relief of
the Souls in Purgatory, by reminding ourselves of
the very great blessings which may be obtained in
return for this charity. There can be little doubt
that all who help the Holy Souls must by that
charity render themselves very pleasing to God,
especially if they give away what might otherwise
be applied to themselves by way of satisfaction, as
is done by those who make what is called the
" Heroic Act," and by the good religious to whom
the blessed name of Helpers of the Holy Souls

belongs as by special right, who give up their whole lives to labours which are applied to Purgatory. All the blessings which the promises of Scripture secure to almsdeeds and charity in general, or to them who "preach the good tidings of peace," or "separate the precious from the vile," or "instruct many unto justice," and the like, must surely belong to such persons. Our Lord will certainly acknowledge them as His own, as having carried on His own work, as having suffered, and exposed themselves to suffering, for Him; they will have the blessing of unfailing support, which was given to the widow of Sarepta who fed the prophet, the "good measure, pressed down, and shaken together, and running over," of which our Lord speaks. No trafficking or investing of "pounds and talents" committed to our charge can be more lucrative in eternity than this. It is quite certain that those who are merciful in this way will very easily find mercy for themselves, as their reward will be an increase of grace in this life, which will enable them to merit very great rewards, and lay up against themselves very little of punishment. The charity which they show to the suffering souls will be abundantly repaired by the prayers which they will make, or win from the saints and angels, for those who befriend them. Our Lord will be especially bound by gratitude to them for delivering His servants, His friends, His spouses, His children. Our Lady, the Mother of the Holy Souls, will regard this charity as done to herself. Their guardian angels, patron saints, and

all the dwellers in Heaven, will speedily protect
and pray for them. There are many passages in
the lives and writings of the Saints which bear
witness to this truth. St. Bridget* relates a prayer
which she heard made by the Holy Souls for their
benefactors, " O Lord Jesus Christ, the Just Judge,
send Thy charity to those who have spiritual power
in the world, for then we shall be able to share
more largely than now in their sacred chants and
offices and sacrifices." . . . "O Lord God, give of
Thine incomprehensible goodness an hundredfold
reward to every one in the world, of those who by
their good works raise us up into the light of Thy
Divinity, and the vision of Thy face." St. Catharine
of Bologna said that she had received very many
graces by means of the intercession of the Holy
Souls, graces which in some instances she had not
obtained through the Saints. Anne of St. Bartholomew, the companion of St. Teresa, used to re-
commend promises of Masses to the Holy Souls
as means of securing favours from Heaven. All
the marks of predestination are said by some
writers to be found in those who are strongly
moved to this devotion, nor is it at all unfrequently
found that temporal as well as spiritual blessings
are obtained in this way.

* *Rev.* lib. iv. ch. vii.

CHAPTER XXXVIII.

The Angels and the Holy Souls.

(MIRACLES ON PALM SUNDAY.)

St. Matt. xxi. 14—17.

1. WE have already spoken of the relation in which the Holy Souls of Purgatory stand towards the Church on earth and in Heaven, towards the Saints and the children of the Militant Church, towards our Blessed Lady, their special Queen and Mother, to our Lord Himself, and to God. But one immense multitude of their friends, more than the stars of heaven in number, and more glorious than stars or anything that eye has ever seen or heart imagined, yet remains to be mentioned, both on account of the special love with which they regard them and the commission which they have received concerning them, and also because we have had to mention their spiritual enemies, the devils, who are by nature the same as the mighty and blessed Angels of God, of whom we are now to speak. Innumerable as are the evil spirits who are allowed to beset us and hinder us in our path towards Heaven, they are far inferior in power to the glorious citizens of Heaven, to whom God has given us in charge, and who love us with the most intense love for

His sake, and because we are intended by Him
to take our places among them, and fill up the
gaps made in their ranks by the apostasy of Satan
and his companions in rebellion. The Angels
were in continual attendance upon our Blessed
Lord during His sojourn upon earth, and it was
by their agency, we may suppose, that many of
His marvellous works were wrought. Thus they
are present to the eye of faith in every one of His
miracles, though they are not specially mentioned
by the Evangelists, as afterwards in the history of
the Resurrection, and of certain parts of the Acts
of the Apostles, as in the cases of St. Peter,
St. Paul, and St. Philip. On account of their
constant presence with our Lord, and of their
execution of His behests, the Angels might have
been mentioned in connection with many of the
miracles on which we have already commented.
But we have kept any special consideration of their
interest in the Holy Souls almost to the last.

2. The miracles to which we now come are those
few cures of the lame and the blind in the Temple
at Jerusalem which our Lord wrought on the after-
noon of Palm Sunday, after His triumphant entry
into the Holy City. "There came to Him," says
St. Matthew, "the blind and the lame in the
Temple, and He healed them. And the Chief
Priests and Scribes, seeing the wonderful things
that He did, and the children crying in the
Temple, Hosanna to the Son of David, were moved
with indignation, and said to Him, Hearest thou
what these say? And Jesus said to them, Yea,

have you never read, Out of the mouth of infants
and of sucklings Thou hast perfected praise?"
These miracles of our Lord must have especially
delighted the holy Angels, who dwell with great
love and reverence in the temples consecrated to
God, and to whom the Temple of Jerusalem was
very dear.   For these are the only miracles which
our Lord is recorded to have worked in that Holy
Place.   Indeed, the whole scene of Palm Sunday
brings the Angels before us, as that triumph was
a representation of His triumphant entrance into
Heaven at His Ascension, when the Angels came
forth to meet Him as the crowds on Palm Sunday.
The praise which they render to God in Heaven
has yet to be made complete by the addition of
the countless myriads of redeemed souls who are
to be there, and this the Angels especially desire
in their eagerness for the deliverance of the Holy
Souls.

3. St. Paul says of the holy Angels, that they
are "all ministering spirits, sent to minister to them
who shall receive the inheritance of salvation." *
These few words are enough to remind us of their
relations to the Holy Souls.   The ministering of
the Angels begins with our entrance into the
world, and, as the Apostle implies, is not to cease
until we receive "the inheritance of salvation."
How faithfully and lovingly they watch over us as
long as our period of trial lasts, no tongue can tell,
and it will be one of the great surprises of the next
world to learn.   It is certain, also, that the care of

* Heb. i. 14.

the Angels increases in vigilance, if that be possible, as the last moment of life draws nigh, that they are standing by us in our last conflict, and that they meet us at our entrance into the next world, conveying our soul to the tribunal of the Judge, or rather, as that judgment takes place at the moment of death, being present while it is being made. The Angels rejoice immensely at a good and happy death. The Church bids her ministers commend the soul, as it departs, to their charge. "When thy soul shall depart from thy body, may the resplendent multitude of the Angels meet thee, may the court of the Apostles receive thee," and the rest. And again : "Come to his assistance, all ye Saints of God, meet him, all ye Angels of God, receiving his soul, and offering it in the sight of the Most High. May Christ receive thee, Who hath called thee, and may the Angels conduct thee to Abraham's bosom. Receiving his soul, and offering it in the sight of the Most High." The Angels stand by at the time of judgment, and defend the soul against the charges of the devils, as is found in many of the revelations of the Saints. They tell us also that St. Michael, the Patron of the Catholic Church, exerts his power the more especially in favour of her children, and this is alluded to by the Church in some of the antiphons which are used on his feasts. If the soul be sentenced to Purgatory, the Angels conduct it thither, as St. Thomas teaches ; * and Suarez says that this escorting of the souls to their place of exile is to

* In *Sent.* iv. dist. 11, qu. 1, art. 1.

comfort them, and also to show them honour as the children of God and spouses of Christ. But when once the souls are conveyed to Purgatory, we are told that the Angels, especially their Guardian Angels, visit them and console them frequently. The full enjoyment of the society of the Angels cannot be had until we reach Heaven, but they are not prevented from comforting the suffering Souls in their prison, any more than from suggesting to the living to pray for them and offer for them works of satisfaction or the Holy Sacrifice of the Mass. St. Peter Damian mentions a curious reason for the setting apart of the Monday in each week as a day of special devotion both to the Angels and the Holy Souls. He says* that on Sundays the Holy Souls rest from their sufferings, and that as these begin again on the Monday, the Holy Mass is offered in honour of the Angels, to procure their powerful assistance to them, as also to others who are to die. The opinion about the cessation of suffering on Sunday may be uncertain, but the Saint's words show that the power of the Angels is constantly exerted for the Holy Souls.

4. Catholic writers seem to make no doubt of the truth which has just now been stated, that the holy Angels frequently visit and console the holy suffering Souls. It may be thought that the mere presence of such blessed and glorious beings, which must be far more keenly perceived by the souls separated from the body than is now possible to us, would go far to make that mournful prison

* St. Peter Damian, *Epist.* ii. 14.

bright and joyous with the light of Heaven itself. We cannot tell to what extent the Holy Souls are allowed to enjoy to the full the natural effects of the near presence of the Angels. But we may feel certain that their visits are of ineffable comfort and relief. We may take as an image of this consolation that visit which our Lord condescended to receive from one of the Angels in His Agony in the Garden, a visit which must have been the appointed means of some great strengthening of the Sacred Humanity for the terrible conflict which He was about to pass through, or rather which He had already in great part experienced, for the Agony was itself one of the greatest of our Lord's sufferings. The Angel may be thought to have set before our Lord the will of the Eternal Father as the reason for the chalice which He was to drink, the immense glory to His Father and to Himself which would accrue therefrom, the great fruit which His sufferings would produce in the souls of men, most of all in those of His Saints, and the whole of the marvellous counsel of God in the application of the merits of His Precious Blood. He may be supposed to have set before Him in particular the joy which was to be His in the redemption of each soul, and of the whole company of His elect, as St. Paul tells us that for " the joy that was set before Him He endured the Cross and despised the shame," * which He was to undergo. In the same way we may suppose that the Angels may comfort the Holy Souls by representing to them the decree of

* Heb. xii. 2.

God's justice, which must be so dear to them, in pursuance of which they are for a time to suffer as they do; the glory which accrues to God from their undergoing the sentence of His justice, the blessed issue of their purification, which will open to them the gates of the eternal home of God's children, and the like. We may suppose that as the Angels have so carefully watched every step of the lives of those who have been committed to their charge, they will be able to instruct them in many wonderful ways as to the providence of God in their regard, especially as to the dangers which have been averted from them, mercies of which they have not been conscious, or, again, boons which might have been theirs at the price of greater faithfulness. It appears to be one of the constant and ever-fresh joys of the holy Angels, to watch the marvellous providence of God towards His Church as it unfolds itself age after age and year after year, and in the same way they have rejoiced over His good mercies in the case of each single soul. All this they can reveal to the Holy Souls to explain to them the debt of gratitude which they owe to God, as well as the amount of that other debt which they are to pay to His justice.

5. But it must be the most direct part of the consolation which the holy Angels constantly minister to the Souls in Purgatory, to give them intelligence of the prayers and satisfactions which are offered for them in the Church on earth, and thus to let them know that they are not forgotten,

and that the time of their detention is to be shortened. In this respect they are in truth messengers of good tidings and of peace, which they so much delight to be. Moreover, it is probable that the holy Angels are the sources from whom proceed a thousand suggestions to us to pray for the Holy Souls, sudden remembrances of them, feelings as if they were near and in need of our prayers, and the like. The visions of the Saints reigning in Heaven are ordinarily the works of the Angels, and it may be that, if there be from time to time any similar visions of the souls in Purgatory, the Angels are also the artificers, so to speak, of these. Thus we get some faint idea of the work of the Angels of the Holy Souls, as of a work of active and multifarious charity, carried on with unwearied energy and vigilance, the object of the whole being to procure relief for those sufferers in all the many ways God allows of their being relieved. They pray for them before the throne of God, and, if the Angel of Macedonia could appear to the Apostle and entreat him to come over and help him, it is not wonderful if they now implore the Saints to intercede for the Holy Souls, and also stir up the hearts of the children of the Church on earth for the same objects of charity. And then at length comes the time of intense joy, both to the Angels and to the Holy Souls themselves, when the purification has been accomplished, and nothing now remains but for the souls to be presented to God by their Guardians, at the head of whom the blessed St.

Michael is placed for this solemn act of triumph. It is, then, in our power to rejoice the hearts of the glorious Angels of God by the suffrages which we offer for the Holy Souls, to make them our friends, and secure their advocacy for ourselves, by making them our debtors for the charity which we have shown to those in whom they regard themselves as relieved and succoured by our prayers. Our Lord says some terrible words about those who scandalize one of the little ones who believe in Him, on account of the simple truth that their Angels always see the face of His Father. We may turn the threat which His words convey into a most gracious promise of protection and advocacy on the part of these glorious princes of the Court of God, by praying and suffering faithfully for these Holy Souls whose Angels are always in God's presence, to bear witness to the slightest act of charity which is done for these patient sufferers.

CHAPTER XXXIX.

Fasting and Almsdeeds.

(THE WITHERING OF THE FIG-TREE.)

St. Matt. xxi. 19 ; St. Mark xi. 13, 14, 20.

1. THE miracle of the withering of the barren fig-tree stands by itself among the miracles of our Lord. For it is the only act of destruction for which He used His power, though on one other occasion, that of the entrance of the devils into the herd of swine, He permitted something of the sort. In ordinary cases His miracles were works of mercy, although, as we have seen, He more than once worked them unasked, and for the obvious purpose of proving or illustrating some Divine truth. The case of the withering of the fig-tree is not altogether different from these. For as in other cases our Lord wished to teach a certain truth relating to Himself, so in this instance He appears to have desired to make a kind of prophecy of the future barrenness of the Synagogue, which was represented by the fig-tree. Thus, there was something to be taught as true which it was important should be known, which was set forth by this act of our Lord's power. This is all the more clear, because the

x

season for fruit had not yet come, and therefore it was not natural to expect that this tree should have borne any figs as yet. The miracle, therefore, is a visible parable. It was on the day after His triumphant entry into Jerusalem and the Temple that "when they came out from Bethania, He was hungry. And when He had seen afar off a fig-tree having leaves, He came, if perhaps He might find anything on it. And when He was come to it, He found nothing but leaves, for it was not yet the time for figs. And answering He said to it, May no man hereafter eat fruit of thee any more for ever. And His disciples heard it." Then, as St. Mark tells us, He went on and cleansed the Temple for the second time, arousing thereby afresh the malicious enmity of the Chief Priests and Scribes. "And when evening was come, He went forth out of the city. And when they passed by in the morning, they saw the fig-tree dried up from the roots." It is almost as if the final determination of the Chief Priests to put Him to death, which was quickened into activity by His marvellous display of power on Palm Sunday and the following day, had filled up the measure of the probation of the Synagogue.

2. In these considerations on Purgatory we are dealing with souls which have been to some extent, often to a great extent, barren of the good fruits which our Lord might have expected of them, but which by His mercy have not been "withered up from the roots," nor condemned to perpetual sterility as to the praise and honour which they

are to render to Him in Heaven. We cannot, therefore, find in them anything that resembles the case of the withered fig-tree. But there are two circumstances connected with the miracle which we may use as enabling us to find in this narrative something which may be very useful to our general purpose. In the first place, the circumstance of our Lord's hunger may remind us of His constant fasts, and of the hard treatment to which His Sacred Body was usually subjected, and this will enable us to complete in this chapter the subject which was begun in that on the Cure of the Lunatic Boy. In that miracle our Lord sets before us the peculiar efficacy of prayer and fasting for the obtaining of certain great deliverances. But our space then only allowed of our speaking of prayer. We may now pass on to speak of fasting. In the second place, there is one matter in which we may all of us sometimes be like the fig-tree, in refusing the alms which are sought of us, as our Lord sought from the fig-tree the boon of a little food in His hunger. If any self-reproach of this kind is to be found among the Holy Souls, it will be very much enhanced by the knowledge which they now possess of the immense value of alms-deeds as a work of satisfaction. It can hardly be said that the subject of almsgiving has been hitherto passed over in this volume, for it has frequently been mentioned among other good works, by means of which the Holy Souls may be relieved. But there are still a few remarks to be made more directly on the subject, and these will be included in the present chapter.

3. The power of fasting as a work of satisfaction is so universally recognized in Sacred Scriptures and in the Church that it may seem almost superfluous to insist on it at any great length. Fasting seems to have been connected with devotion for the dead among the Jews, not to speak of other nations, as we see in the fasting which was made for Saul after his death.* The instinct of the Church and of the Saints has always been in the same direction, and if the early Fathers do not mention fasting among the means to be used for the relief of the departed, it is only because they include it under the head of prayer. It has the special direct power of satisfaction, all the more because it is one of the works which are most painful to the body, and it is thus one of the customary penances in all religious bodies in the Church. The lives of the Saints and the chronicles of the religious orders are naturally full of instances in which the Holy Souls have either begged that fasting may be made for them, or have expressed their gratitude when they have had that aid afforded them. In speaking of the satisfactory power of fasting, it is well to join to it the other similar works of penance which are usually reckoned under the same head, such as the affliction of the body by disciplines, hair-shirts, vigils, prostrations, and the like. There is an old story of the great Emperor Otho, who is said to have appeared

* 1 Kings xxxi. 13 ; 2 Kings i. 12.

after his death to a near relation of his own, who
was the Superior in a convent of nuns, begging
the aid of her religious to free him from Purgatory.
The petition which he made would startle many
of those who think very lightly of the pains of
Purgatory. He prayed the abbess to send letters
to various monasteries in order that a great amount
of penance might be done for him—ten thousand
psalters, with ten strokes of a discipline at each
psalm, during which the *De profundis* was to be
recited, and a *Pater noster* and *Ave Maria* were
to be added at each verse. And the historian adds
that this was required for an emperor who had
during his lifetime been a great benefactor of the
Church and of the poor. There is an anecdote
in the life of the famous Catharine of Cardona,
who was the contemporary of St. Teresa, to the
same effect. She was made aware of the death
of the well-known Ruy Gomez at the moment
when it happened, and before the news could
reach the part of the country where she was in
the ordinary way. She was so affected by the
knowledge which she received of the great sufferings to which he was subjected, that she immediately disciplined herself so severely that the cell
in which she lived was all sprinkled with her blood.
There are many other such instances. We may
add to such corporal austerities as these the bodily
sufferings which come to us in the course of
God's providence, if they are readily welcomed and
joyfully undergone, and under the same head will
come the afflictions which the servants of God

sometimes are prompted to ask for, in order that they may suffer more for the relief of the Holy Souls. The Saints have sometimes petitioned to be allowed to bear in this life the Purgatory of this or that soul, and the prayer has been heard. The two St. Catharines, of Ricci and Raconigi, were both remarkable for this. Indeed, any suffering, of whatever kind, even though not corporal, such as the patient bearing of dryness and desolation, or, again, charity under some great calumny, has the effect of satisfying largely for sin, and may thus be beneficial to the Holy Souls if offered for them.

4. It is time to say a few words in addition as to the satisfactory power of almsdeeds, although it has been impossible to reserve for one chapter what is so obvious a means of relieving the holy suffering Souls. Nothing can be stronger than the language of Sacred Scripture on the power of almsdeeds to "deliver from death," * to "purge away sin," † and the like. It is compared to the effect of water on fire, ‡ or to that of ransom to the captive, § or to that of a sacrifice, ‖ which propitiates God. It is compared to a second baptism,¶ and is said to be more efficacious even than fasting. It would be well to remember that both almsdeeds and fastings will be more efficacious if they are done with this distinct intention of delivering the Souls of Purgatory, or any particular souls in whom we may be interested. In that case, it is not only

---

* Tobias xii. 9.   † Prov. xv. 27.   ‡ Ecclus. iii. 33.
§ Dan. iv. 26.   ‖ Heb. xiii. 16.   ¶ Ecclus. vii. 46.

the satisfactory power of the good works which is applied to the souls, but the work as a whole, with all its merits of impetration as well as satisfaction. It is a much greater charity to undertake directly to fast, or to afflict ourselves in any other way, for the Holy Souls, than to apply to them the satisfaction of the good works of this kind which we should otherwise do as a matter of course. No one can do the first of these things without being very much in earnest in his desire to relieve the misery of the sufferers in Purgatory.

5. Another item of advice which is found in some writers relates to the question of pious foundations for the benefit of the holy departed, whether they be hospitals or convents or orphanages or colleges for the clergy or of any other kind. It is said that if the object be to benefit some one soul in particular, it is more prudent to give away all that we can in alms or for Masses at once, in order that the soul for whom we are interested may enjoy the benefit of our charity as soon as possible. But if the intention be to benefit the Holy Souls in general, then it is better to found such institutions as those just now mentioned, which may last on from year to year and from generation to generation, and benefit successive numbers of sufferers in Purgatory.

6. Another counsel, with which we may conclude, is found in the revelations of St. Bridget, and has reference to the correspondence of the good works which are done for the benefit of a soul for the faults which he may be known to have committed

in his lifetime. The Saint was careful to give a
great deal by way of alms for the repose of her
husband's soul, and he begged her to sell his plate
and horses, in which he had taken an excessive
delight, for his benefit. In another of her visions *
she heard the soul of a certain noble person cry
"woe" four times, and she was told by an angel
that there might be four kinds of expiation offered
for him. The first of his woes was that he had
loved God but little, and to atone for this thirty
chalices might be offered for him, in which the
Precious Blood might be offered in Holy Mass,
and God thus specially honoured. The second
"woe" was that he had but little fear of God,
and for this thirty devout priests were to be
chosen, each of whom was to say thirty Masses
for him—nine of the Martyrs, nine of the Con-
fessors, nine of All Saints, one of the Angels, one
of our Blessed Lady, and one of the Most Holy
Trinity. The third "woe" which he uttered was
on account of his pride and avarice, and for this
thirty poor persons were to be taken in, clothed
and fed, and their feet washed in humility, and
prayers were to be made to our Lord that, for the
sake of His own humility and His Passion, the sins
of that soul might be forgiven him. The fourth
"woe" was for the pride of the flesh in him, and
this was to be atoned for by sending one virgin to
a convent, and providing for one widow, and for
one marriageable maiden, sufficient for food and
maintenance in each case, and then God was to be

* Lib. iv. c. 9.

prayed to forgive him the punishment due to his sins of the flesh. These and other similar reflections may at least serve to show that, in the best Christian ages, the idea of the debt of punishment which might be due to God in Purgatory was by no means a slight one, and that very great exertions were not thought too much to offer for the deliverance of single souls. We might as well hope to relieve a great city, suffering under famine, by collecting the crumbs of bread after our dinners day by day, or to stop the progress of a mighty epidemic by a few bottles of rosewater, as to relieve the sufferings of the Holy Souls of Purgatory by trifling alms which cost us nothing, or slight penitential exercises which give but little pain.

CHAPTER XL.

Forgiveness of Injuries.

(THE HEALING OF MALCHUS.)

St. Luke xxii. 50, 51.

1. ALL the four Evangelists mention the incident in the apprehension of our Lord in the Garden of Olives, when St. Peter in his fiery zeal drew a sword in defence of his Master, and cut off the ear of one of the servants of the High Priest, who had joined the band sent under the guidance of Judas. St. Luke alone mentions the miracle which our Lord wrought in favour of the poor servant, who may have had no faith in Him, and even have been actuated by the hatred towards Him which would have been natural in one who heard Him so continually censured and spoken against by his own master.   After reproving and warning St. Peter, St. Luke tells us that our Lord, "answering, said, Suffer ye thus far.   And when He had touched his ear, He healed him."   It is as if He asked leave of His enemies to work this miraculous cure, in order that no traces might remain of the intemperate violence of His Apostle.   The miracle may have been wrought partly out of our Lord's unfailing and ineffable tenderness of heart, for He could not bear to see blood flow, except it were

His own, shed for the sins of the world. But it is probable that the chief motive of our Lord was rather to show His entire want of all animosity or anger against His enemies, and to set us an example of that perfect forgiveness of injuries and insults which does not stop short at simple pardon, but adds to that any sort of active kindness or charity of which the case admits. It has been sometimes said of the Saints, that the way to secure the utmost possible kindness from them was to do them some injury, and our Lord in this miracle seems to have acted on the principle thus attributed to the Saints. He went out of His way to heal this poor man, and this is the only instance in which it could have been recorded of Him that He worked a miracle in favour of one who was hostile to Him at the time, and bent on His destruction. At the very moment of the beginning of His Passion, when He was treated with indignities and insults so great, when they were about to put Him in chains and drag Him so cruelly to the tribunals of Annas and Caiaphas, He took occasion to use His miraculous power for the last time before His death, not to serve Himself or even to deliver His Apostles—though the miracle may have had some effect in making the leaders of the armed band listen to His injunction to let them go—but to staunch the wound and restore the lost limb of one of His bitter enemies.

2. This great example of our Lord has many lessons for us in every way, but it helps us

especially with regard to the subject of these chapters by suggesting to us one of the most efficacious means which are in our power of escaping the sufferings of Purgatory. We have not made these means so much a subject of direct study in these chapters as the means by which we may aid the present holy sufferers in Purgatory to a speedy release; but it is, of course, clear that, in general, the same methods, especially of satisfaction, which seem to relieve them, are also available for ourselves. But holy writers on this subject often mention certain practices and virtues as having a particular power in shielding us from the danger of falling ourselves under severe punishments in Purgatory. It will be useful to set down some of these here, and to consider the miracle wrought on Malchus as suggesting them, because it suggests that one of them which has the special promise of our Lord. For He Who has taught us not to pray for the forgiveness of our own sins, except with the qualification that we are to ask to be forgiven as we ourselves forgive, has also promised distinctly that if we forgive we shall also be forgiven. Now, when our Lord speaks of the forgiveness of sins in the Gospel, He speaks of it in the fullest and most complete sense which His words will bear. That is, He speaks of that entire forgiveness as given by God, which not only absolves the sinner from the guilt of sin and from its eternal consequences of separation from Him, but which also remits the temporal punishment due to sin, whether in this world or in the next.

But this remission is that of which we have had to say so much in these chapters on Purgatory. We have His word, therefore, that it is in our power, with the help of His grace, entirely to cancel the debt of satisfaction which we may owe to His justice for our sins, and that the means by which this is to be done is the perfect forgiveness on our part of all the trespasses against ourselves by others of which we have to complain. It is very clear that our forgiveness of others must be as ample and unreserved and ungrudging as we wish that to be which we ourselves desire to receive from God. It is often the case, that we can forgive an injury, or a harsh and insulting word, or even a grave act of injustice and wrong, so far as is absolutely necessary in order not to lose the grace of God ourselves. That is, we do not bear malice or wish the person who has injured us any wrong, while yet we are unable to show him any greater marks of charity than are the absolute rights of one Christian from another. We are not ready to exert ourselves for him, as our Lord exerted Himself for Malchus, or to do for him any extraordinary and unusual charity. Such forgiveness may be enough to satisfy the commandment of God, but it is not enough to win the abundant and overwhelming grace which is in store for those who can from their hearts love those who have injured them, for the sake of our Lord, and as being their own great benefactors. In order to this we have need of very great grace, and it is this kind of forgiveness which has the power of absolutely cancelling the debt of punishment which we may owe for our sins. For those who can with all their heart, in this way, forgive their enemies, must be very closely united to God, and are indeed His true children.

3. There are two other virtues which have the same power, and the same promises, for these are very nearly akin to that of which we have been speaking. These are the virtue of not judging others, and the virtue of perfect contrition. Our Lord has said distinctly, "Judge not, that you may not be judged; for with what judgment you judge, you shall be judged, and with what measure you mete, it shall be measured unto you again."* This is something different from the forgiveness of injuries. In the forgiveness of injuries, there is no question about the fact of the injury; but in abstinence from judging, even the fact is not assumed. The forgiveness of injuries is grounded on our own relation to God and to those who may injure us; the virtue of abstinence from judging is based on the consideration that to God alone belongs the right of judgment, as well as the right of punishment. Other considerations, such as that of our own miseries and faults, which are quite enough to occupy our whole attention, may well come in to aid in the formation of this virtue, which requires the truest humility as its condition. But there are some blessed souls in the Church who have this special grace of always looking on others with the eyes of charity, of

* St. Matt. vii. 1, 2.

turning away from all that is evil so as not to see it, and of interpreting everything well, even when such interpretation is most difficult. Such persons have the promise of our Lord, that they shall not be judged, that is, that they shall either be preserved from all faults in return for their simple and divine charity, or shall at least have all their faults perfectly forgiven. In the case of the virtue of perfect contrition, it must be evident that it contains the perfect love of God, and where the perfect love of God exists, the sorrow which is founded upon it must be so pure and so intense, as altogether to cancel any debt that may be owing to His justice.

4. There are other things which may be mentioned under the head of the means of escaping Purgatory. Some of these may be said rather to be the suffering of Purgatory here. Such is the case of those who undergo some great trial, such as a great calumny against their reputation borne without resentment or repining, or any attempt at justification. Such is the case of those also whom God afflicts with great bodily sufferings and ailments, if they too are endured with perfect resignation and cheerful union with the will of God. Such is the case of those who labour long and assiduously in propagating the faith among the heathen, or who use themselves up entirely in other works of charity for their neighbours, keeping up all the time their union with God and the peace of a good conscience vigilantly guarded. In all these cases, and in others like them, it may be said that Purgatory has been endured before its time.

The same may be said of the satisfactory power of perfect fidelity, even in the least things, to a religious rule, which is a burthen that presses at no time with any great heaviness, but the continuity of which makes it very meritorious in the sight of God. Other means, again, to the same end are to be found in the perfect use of the ordinary means of grace, such as the sacraments. For the Sacraments of Penance and Holy Communion have the power perfectly to purify the soul from the debt of pain as well as from the stain of guilt, and that they do not do this in ordinary cases is not because of their lack of power, but of the imperfect manner in which they are received. Lastly, we may mention the careful and perfect use of Indulgences, and also a very deep and true devotion to the Passion of our Lord.

CHAPTER XLI.

The Treasure of the Church.

(OUR LORD'S LAST MIRACLE ON THE LAKE.)

St. John xxi. 1—19.

1. THE last recorded miracle of our Lord was worked after His Resurrection, during that part of the forty days which He spent with His disciples in Galilee. The narrative is given to us by St. John alone, who was himself present, with six other Apostles, his own brother St. James, St. Peter, St. Thomas, St. Bartholomew or Nathanael, and two others who are not named, but who may be conjectured to have been St. Andrew and St. Philip.* It is not necessary to repeat the story of the fishing of the Apostles during the night—when, as on the former occasion of which we have had to speak, they caught nothing—of our Lord's appearance in the early dawn on the shore, bidding them cast the net on the right side of the boat, then of the marvellous draught of fishes which was immediately enclosed in the net, of St. John's

---

* The four Apostles not included in this list would thus be St. Matthew, who was not a fisherman, and the three who were near relations or connections of our Lord, St. Simon, St. Jude, and St. James the Less. These might probably be with our Lady and the holy women at the time. But it is needless to say, that this is pure conjecture.

Y

discerning our Lord, of St. Peter's leaping into the water to go to Him, and of the meal which was awaiting them when they landed. The points on which we may fasten in this great miracle, and in the conversation which followed on it, are the following—the action of St. Peter, the Prince of the Apostles, in drawing the net to land himself, containing a certain recorded number of large fishes, "one hundred and fifty and three," and the commission which was afterwards so solemnly given to him by our Lord, and repeated thrice, in which, after asking Him thrice whether he loved Him, our Lord bade him, "Feed My lambs," "Feed My sheep." It is generally considered by Catholic commentators on Scripture and by the theologians of the Church that our Lord on this occasion conferred on St. Peter, for himself and for his successors, the authority and commission to rule the Catholic Church which He had before promised to him, when he made his great confession of faith in the Divinity of his Master. Then He had said: "Thou art Peter, and on this rock I will build My Church, and the gates of Hell shall not prevail against it, and I will give unto thee the keys of the Kingdom of Heaven, and whatsoever thou shalt bind on earth it shall be bound also in Heaven, and whatsoever thou shalt loose on earth it shall be loosed also in Heaven."* Now He says, "Simon, son of John, lovest thou Me more than these? . . . Feed My lambs. Feed My lambs. Feed My sheep."

* St. Matt. xvi. 18, 19.

2. It is on this great commission, promised in the first of these passages and conferred in the second, that the vital Catholic doctrine of the prerogatives of St. Peter mainly rests for its Scripture proof, though there are also other texts and incidents in the life of our Lord on which it is based, and though the whole argument from Scripture embraces also the commentary on the acts and sayings of our Lord which is furnished by the history of the Acts of the Apostles and by the Epistles. It is of course not to our present purpose to draw out the whole argument, as we can only have to deal with that part of the power which has been conferred on St. Peter and on his successors which has immediate relation to the subject of Purgatory. That part, however, of St. Peter's power is very important indeed to us, and it may very fitly be made the subject of this our last chapter on the miracles. The power conferred on St. Peter, with regard to this subject, may be connected immediately with the words of St. Matthew which have been quoted in the last paragraph. St. Peter, in the passage of St. John's Gospel before us, is practically ordered by our Lord to use his power in all charity for the benefit of the flock committed to him. That is one meaning at least of the touching question thrice put to him by our Lord, " Lovest thou Me ? " It is as if He had said, " If you love Me, and as you love Me, feed My lambs, feed My sheep." But the power which is thus to be exercised according to the instinct and measure of his love to our Blessed Lord is, as has been said, that which was promised

before in the words which St. Matthew has recorded. That power, then, consists, first, of opening the Kingdom of Heaven, for such is the meaning of the power of the keys; and secondly, it consists in the power of binding and loosing. By this, for the purpose with which we are now concerned, is meant the power of either opening Heaven or not, and of laying down the conditions on which the power of the keys is exercised, in any particular case or under any particular circumstances.

3. It is plain that the power thus conferred on St. Peter of opening the gates of Heaven must mean the power of removing all the impediments which, in any particular case, shut the gates of Heaven and prevent this or that particular soul, or certain classes of souls, from entering there. Now, it has already been said that there are two impediments to entrance to Heaven, original sin unremoved, and actual mortal sin unrepented and uncancelled as to its guilt. Either of these two impediments, while it exists, is enough absolutely to bar the gates of Heaven. The first of these impediments is removed by our Lord Himself, and the application of what He has thus done to particular souls takes place in Holy Baptism. The second impediment, that created by actual sin, is removed by the power of the keys. But this impediment, which is caused by actual sin, is twofold, and consists in the guilt of sin, and in the punishment due to it. If the guilt is not removed, the soul can never enter Heaven, and, even when the guilt is removed, the soul cannot enter Heaven until the punishment has been removed also. · The

guilt of sin, then, is removed by the power of the keys in the Sacrament of Penance, according to those words of our Lord, " Whose sins ye remit, they are remitted." The impediment of the punishment is also removed by the power of the keys, in the concession of Indulgences, according to those other words, " Whatsoever thou shalt loose on earth, it shall be loosed also in Heaven." And it must be said that any idea of the power of the keys which leaves out this remission of the pain due to sin as well as of the guilt of sin itself—when due dispositions exist, and under all due conditions, according to the laws of the Kingdom of our Lord —is absolutely defective and inadequate. It has been said above that any idea of our Lord's Mission as the Redeemer of the world which leaves out His Mission with regard to Purgatory, is defective and inadequate. It represents Him, practically, as not being He Who was to come, and it implies, practically, that we must "look for another." In just the same way, the power of the keys would not be what it ought to be, it would not answer to the largeness and fulness and universality of our Lord's commission to St. Peter, if it did not include, in some way or other, the power of loosing the bonds of pain as well · as the power of loosing the bonds of guilt. Our Lord, as the people in Decapolis said, hath done "all things well," not only "some things ; " *
and the power which He has left behind in the hands of St. Peter and his Successors to be exercised in charity must extend to all the needs of human

* St. Mark vii. 37.

souls waiting at the gates of Heaven.   But it would not so extend, unless it had some provision for the removal of the impediment of pain, as well as for the removal of the impediment of guilt.

4. The provision of which we speak is exactly that which Catholics know as the power of Indulgences.   An Indulgence is a remission of the pain due to sins, of which the guilt has already been forgiven.   This remission is made by the same power which imposes this or that work of penance as an accompaniment of absolution, that is, the power of the keys of which we have just now spoken.   By this power the "treasury," as it is said, of the Church is opened, and the merits of our Lord, the Blessed Virgin, and the Saints are applied in satisfaction to the souls to whom the Indulgence is granted, by the authority of the Chief Pastor of the Church, the Successor of St. Peter, and, to a certain extent, of the Bishops.*   The doctrine of the Church on this point is summed up in the decree of the Council of Trent (Session 25), which declares that the power of Indulgences has been granted by Christ to the Church, and that they are useful and salutary to the faithful.   It would not fall within the scope of the present work to argue the point as to the doctrine of Indulgences against those who deny it.   It is enough to say that it is,

---

* Benedict XIII., *Trigies. II.* Serm. 24, teaches that Archbishops in their provinces and Bishops in their dioceses may grant Indulgences of a year on the dedication of a church, and of forty days at other times.   But he adds that they have greater powers in the private tribunal of penance, in regard to their own subjects.

in principle, contained in the famous passage of
St. Paul about the incestuous Corinthian, whose
penance had been forgiven him by the Church,*
and that there are traces of the practice in the
earliest times, though it is undeniable that the great
use of Indulgences, and particularly of the very
large Indulgences which have been granted in the
late centuries of the Church, is a development
which has grown with the decay of penitential
rigour and, in fact, with that great increase of
human infirmity which characterizes modern times.
The comparative ease with which Indulgences may
now be gained is a great blessing to the faithful of
our times—a great blessing to those who avail
themselves of it largely and diligently, while it may
turn out to be a cause of severe self-reproach to
those who neglect to avail themselves of the
immense benignity of the Church. The causes
for which Indulgences are granted are quite independent of the conditions assigned to them, and it
is not necessary for us to know them,—it is sufficient that the Pope has a reasonable ground, of
which he is the judge. The great reason of all, no
doubt, is the extreme tenderness of the Church,
which desires that we should know her love for her
children, and so be moved to praise the mercifulness of God, and which uses, in these days of
corporal weakness and feeble virtues, an immense
gentleness to the generations which have not the
strength or courage to accomplish the severe penances of the ancient Canons. But at no time was

* 2 Cor. ii. 5—11.

it necessary that the works prescribed for those who are to gain Indulgences should correspond to the latter in importance. For Indulgences rest on the merits of our Lord, and not on those of the person who may gain them.

5. We have hitherto spoken of Indulgences indifferently, without distinguishing between their application to the living and that which is made of them to the dead. The Indulgences which the Church distributes to the living are given to them directly, those which are applied to the dead, only indirectly and by way of suffrage. Hence it follows, that if a living person is truly sorry for all his sins, venial as well as mortal, and if he performs accurately, with all the due dispositions, the works which are enjoined as the conditions of an Indulgence, he cannot fail to gain that Indulgence, our Lord's fidelity, of which St. Paul so often speaks, being pledged to him in the matter. This is what is meant, as it seems, by the theologians who speak of an Indulgence as granted by way of absolution, in which case the Church exercises her jurisdiction over her own direct subjects, that is, the living faithful, granting to them the satisfactions which they require out of the merits of our Lord ; whereas in the case of the departed, they are no longer directly her subjects, and so the Indulgence is granted to them by way of suffrage. And, to return to the former point, a soul in Purgatory cannot perform any of the works which are enjoined as conditions of an Indulgence, and is no longer in a state to merit anything. There is, therefore, no

tie of fidelity on the part of God which may bind Him to grant the Indulgence to such a soul, even though the works prescribed be performed by the living, and though the Indulgence be made by the Church applicable to the holy departed. This application, again, which is an exercise of the power of the keys, cannot be made by any but the Church, and unless she makes it, no one can benefit the Holy Souls by such an explanation.

6. It should also be remembered that the remission of the pain due to sins, which is the fruit of an Indulgence, can only fall on those sins the guilt of which has been already forgiven, that is, on those which have been truly, in some way or other, retracted. This it is which makes a Plenary Indulgence so difficult of perfect acquisition. But it does not follow, because some venial sins may not have been forgiven as to their guilt, that therefore the fruit of an Indulgence is lost, as to other light sins which have been forgiven. Again, it is taught by theologians that light sins committed at the time when a person might be receiving the fruit of an Indulgence, do not hinder the fruit of that Indulgence as to the other venial sins on which it would fall, though it is otherwise with sins committed at the time of performing the works which are exacted as conditions of the Indulgence, if those works are truly vitiated thereby. Again, it must be remembered, with regard to the Indulgences which are applied to the Holy Souls, that their venial sins which may have remained unforgiven before their death, on account of their never

having retracted them, are cancelled as to their guilt at the time of death, by the perfect conversion of the soul to God, which takes place in all who die in a state of grace.   As to the remission of the pain due to these sins, it must be remembered that the effect of Indulgences does not come from the devotion of those who gain them, or from the labour to which they put themselves, or from the alms which they may give as their condition, but from the abundant treasure of the merits of the Church.   Thus St. Thomas teaches that the essential conditions requisite for the fruit of which we speaking, are simply authority on the part of those who grant the Indulgence, piety in the cause for which it is granted, and charity or the state of grace in those who are to receive the benefit thus bestowed.*   Nevertheless, although all the Holy Souls are capable of receiving the fruits of Indulgences, because all are in the grace of God, it remains true that some are more capable of profiting largely in this way than others, because the fruit of this kind is shared by them according to the greater or less degree of their charity.   Thus it may be necessary for some souls that a great many Plenary Indulgences should be gained for them, while others, to whom God allows a single Plenary Indulgence to be applied, may by virtue of that alone be delivered from all the pain which they owe to His justice.

7. It is certain that the blessed provision of Indulgences is one which conduces very greatly

---

* St. Thomas, *in Sent.* iv. dist. 20, qu. 1, art. 3, 2.

to the glory of God. It is surely to His glory that
the abundant treasures of satisfaction which have
been accumulated in the Church should be used,
that piety and religion should be served by their
use, that the rulers of the Church, who succeed to
the throne of St. Peter, should exercise every part
of their mighty prerogative for the good of souls,
that a number of good works should be promoted,
such as visits to the tombs of the Apostles and the
Saints, or the relief of the poor, or the advancement
of missions, and a thousand other good works, by
being made the conditions on which Indulgences
may be gained by those who also approach the
sacraments worthily, and pray for the good of the
Church. All these things are for the glory of God
and of our Lord. All of them belong to the advancement of the great Kingdom of the Incarnation,
and charity, as well as the glory of God in other
respects, is promoted when the faithful are urged
on to them by the holding out of Indulgences so to
be gained. Whenever we practically show our
belief in the powers which God has granted to the
Church, we do Him honour, and our faith is sometimes more displayed when it is exercised on things
which do not meet the sight, and are less easy of
proof; or again, when the points to which it refers
are more questioned and assailed by the unbeliev-
ing world. On this account, if on no other, it
would be our duty to proclaim in the face of the
world our belief in these powers of the Church, and
we might expect a greater blessing from God in
proportion to our boldness and simplicity in this

respect. But in truth, few things would be more
to the glory of God in our generation than a great
increase of devotion to the Holy Souls in Purgatory and to their interests in general, and of diligence and zeal in helping them by means of Indulgences in particular.   When we review all the means
of aiding them which God has put into our hands
—prayers, Masses, Communions, almsdeeds, mortifications, pilgrimages, the Divine Office, the Office
of the Dead or of our Blessed Lady, the holy
Rosary, works of active mercy, the teaching the
Christian doctrine, the attending of funerals, and a
thousand more, we can find none more powerful
in themselves, if the fruit be really gained, none
more honourable to God and to our Lord and to
His Church, than this of holy Indulgences.   And
besides, the mind of the Church is expressed by
the fact that she makes this most loving and beautiful exercise of her prerogative go along with and
accompany all other aid to the Holy Souls.   For
there can hardly be found any one of those named
or alluded to which is not enriched by her with
copious Indulgences, which are thus placed by her
within the reach of all who can do any one of those
other works, while she gives them besides for many
a short prayer or pious practice which requires the
very slightest exertion or expense of time.   And
yet it is not a little thing that we do, or that we
neglect to do, when we either impart to these holy
sufferers a portion, be it large or small, of the in-
expressibly precious merits and satisfactions of our
Lord Jesus Christ and His Saints, or leave them

without that solace and assistance—often, we may fear, because we have not ourselves the intelligent faith to appreciate duly the needs of those who are detained in Purgatory, or the ineffable glory which results to God from the devout and charitable use of the exhaustless treasures of the Church, which He has purchased with His own Blood, and to which He he has left the exercise of the powers in Heaven and on earth which were won by His Passion.

QUARTERLY SERIES.

(The Volumes in Italics are at present out of print.)

1, 4. **The Life and Letters of St. Francis Xavier.** By the Rev. H. J. Coleridge, S.J. Two vols. 10s. 6d.

2. **The Life of St. Jane Frances Fremyot de Chantal.** By Emily Bowles. 5s.

3. **The History of the Sacred Passion.** By Father Luis de la Palma, of the Society of Jesus. Translated from the Spanish. 5s.

5. *Ierne of Armorica:* A Tale of the Time of Chlovis. By J. C. Bateman.

6. **The Life of Dona Louisa de Carvajal.** By Lady Georgiana Fullerton. Small Edition, 3s. 6d.

7. **The Life of St. John Berchmans.** By the Rev. F. Goldie, S.J. 6s.

• 8. *The Life of the Blessed Peter Favre*, of the Society of Jesus; First Companion of St. Ignatius Loyola. From the Italian of Father Guiseppe Boero, of the same Society.

9. **The Dialogues of St. Gregory the Great.** An Old English Version. 6s.

10. **The Life of Anne Catharine Emmerich.** By Helen Ram. 5s.

11. *The Prisoners of the Temple;* or, Discrowned and Crowned. By M. O'Connor Morris (Mrs. Bishop).

13. *The Story of St. Stanislaus Kostka.* Edited by the Rev. H. J. Coleridge, S.J.

15. **The Chronicle of St. Antony of Padua.** "The Eldest Son of St. Francis." Edited by the Rev. H. J. Coleridge, S.J. In Four Books. 5s. 6d.

16. *Life of Pope Pius the Seventh.* By Mary H. Allies.

18. **An English Carmelite.** The Life of Catherine Burton, Mother Mary Xaveria of the Angels, of the English Teresian Convent at Antwerp. Collected from her own writings, and other sources, by Father Thomas Hunter, S.J. 6s.

21. *The Life of Christopher Columbus.* By the Rev. A. G. Knight, S.J.

22. **The Suppression of the Society of Jesus in the Portuguese Dominions.** From documents hitherto unpublished. By the Rev. Alfred Weld, S.J. 7s. 6d.

23. **The Christian Reformed in Mind and Manners.** By Benedict Rogacci, S.J. The translation edited by the Rev. H. J. Coleridge, S.J. 7s. 6d.

24. **The Sufferings of the Church in Brittany during the Great Revolution.** By Edward Healy Thompson. 6s. 6d.

25. **The Life of Margaret Mostyn** (Mother Margaret of Jesus), Religious of the Reformed Order of Our Blessed Lady of Mount Carmel (1625-1679). By the Very Rev. Edmund Bedingfield. 6s.

26. **The Life of Henrietta D'Osseville** (in Religion, Mother Ste. Marie), Foundress of the Institute of the Faithful Virgin. Arranged and Edited by the Rev. John George MacLeod, S.J. 5s. 6d.

28. **Three Catholic Reformers of the Fifteenth Century** (St. Vincent Ferrer, St. Bernardine of Siena, St. John Capistran). By Mary H. Allies. 6s.

29. *A Gracious Life* (1556-1618) ; being the Life of Madame Acarie (Blessed Mary of the Incarnation), of the Reformed Order of Our Blessed Lady of Mount Carmel. By Emily Bowles.

30. **The Life of St. Thomas of Hereford.** By Father L'Estrange. 6s.

32. **The Life of King Alfred the Great.** By the Rev. A. G. Knight, S.J. 6s.

33. **The Life of Mother Frances Mary Teresa Ball**, Foundress in Ireland of the Institute of the Blessed Virgin Mary. By the Rev. H. J. Coleridge, S.J. With Portrait. 6s. 6d.

34, 58, 67. **The Life and Letters of St. Teresa.** 3 vols. By the Rev. H. J. Coleridge, S.J. 7s. 6d. each.

35, 52. **The Life of Mary Ward.** By Mary Catherine Elizabeth Chambers, of the Institute of the Blessed Virgin. Edited by the Rev. H. J. Coleridge, S.J. Two vols. 15s.

38. **The Return of the King.** Discourses on the Latter Days. By the Rev. H. J. Coleridge, S.J. 7s. 6d.

39. **Pious Affections towards God and the Saints.** Meditations for Every Day in the Year, and for the principal Festivals. From the Latin of the Ven. Nicolas Lancicius, S.J. 7s. 6d.

40. **The Life of the Ven. Claude de la Colombiere.** Abridged from the French Life by Eugene Sequin, S.J. 5s.

41, 42. **The Life and Teaching of Jesus Christ** in Meditations for Every Day in the Year. By Father Nicolas Avancino, S.J. Two vols. 10s. 6d.

43. **The Life of Lady Falkland.** By Lady G. Fullerton. 5s.

44. **The Baptism of the King.** Considerations on the Sacred Passion. By the Rev. H. J. Coleridge, S.J. 7s. 6d.

47. **Gaston de Segur.** A Biography. Condensed from the French Memoir by the Marquis de Segur, by F. J. M. A. Partridge. 3s. 6d.

48. **The Tribunal of Conscience.** By Father Gaspar Druzbicki, S.J. 3s. 6d.

50. **Of Adoration in Spirit and Truth.** By Father J. Eusebius Nieremberg. With a Preface by the Rev. P. Gallwey, S.J. 6s. 6d.

55. **The Mother of the King.** Mary during the Life of our Lord. By the Rev. H. J. Coleridge, S.J. 7s. 6d.

56. **During the Persecution.** Autobiography of Father John Gerard, S.J. Translated from the original Latin by the Rev. G. R. Kingdon, S.J. 5s.

59. **The Hours of the Passion.** Taken from the *Life of Christ* by Ludolph the Saxon. 7s. 6d.

60. **The Mother of the Church.** Mary during the first Apostolic Age. By the Rev. H. J. Coleridge, S.J. 6s.

61. **St. Mary's Convent, Micklegate Bar,** York. A History of the Convent. 7s. 6d.

62. **The Life of Jane Dormer, Duchess of** Feria. By Henry Clifford. Transcribed from the Ancient Manuscript by the late Canon E. E. Estcourt, and edited by the Rev. Joseph Stevenson, S.J. 5s.

65. **The Life of St. Bridget of Sweden.** By the late F. J. M. A. Partridge. 6s.

66. **The Teachings and Counsels of St.** Francis Xavier. From his Letters. 5s.

69. **Garcia Moreno, President of Ecuador.** 1821—1875. From the French of the Rev. P. A. Berthe, C.SS.R. By the Lady Herbert. 7s. 6d.

70. **The Life of St. Alonzo Rodriguez.** By the Rev. Francis Goldie, S.J. 7s. 6d.

71. **Chapters on the Parables.** By the Rev. H. J. Coleridge, S.J. 7s. 6d.

73. **Letters of St. Augustine.** Selected and Translated by Mary H. Allies. Price 6s. 6d.

74. **A Martyr from the Quarter-Deck.** Alexis Clerc, S.J. By The Lady Herbert. Price 5s.

75. **Acts of the English Martyrs,** hitherto unpublished. By the Rev. J. H. Pollen, S.J. With Preface by the Rev. John Morris, S.J. 7s. 6d.

77. **The Life of St. Francis di Geronimo,** of the Society of Jesus. By A. M. Clarke. 6s.

79. 80. **Aquinas Ethicus; or, the Moral** Teaching of St. Thomas. By the Rev. Joseph Rickaby, S.J. Two vols. 12s.

81. **The Spirit of St. Ignatius, Founder of** of the Society of Jesus. Translated from the French of the Rev. Father Xavier de Franciosi, of the same Society. 6s.

82. **Jesus, the All-Beautiful.** A Devotional Treatise on the Character and Actions of our Lord. By the Author of *The Voice of the Sacred Heart* and *The Heart of Jesus of Nazareth.* Edited by the Rev. J. G. MacLeod, S.J. Price 6s. 6d.

Volumes on the Life of our Lord.

BY THE REV. H. J. COLERIDGE, S.J.

INTRODUCTORY VOLUMES.

19, 20. **The Life of our Life.** Introduction and Harmony of the Gospels, with the Introduction rewritten. Two vols. 15s.

36. **The Works and Words of our Saviour,** gathered from the Four Gospels. 7s. 6d.

46. **The Story of the Gospels.** Harmonized for Meditation, 7s. 6d.

THE HOLY INFANCY.

49. **The Preparation of the Incarnation.** 7s. 6d.

53. **The Nine Months.** The Life of our Lord in the Womb. 7s. 6d.

54. **The Thirty Years.** Our Lord's Infancy and Early Life. 7s. 6d.

THE PUBLIC LIFE OF OUR LORD.

12. **The Ministry of St. John Baptist.** 6s. 6d.

14. **The Preaching of the Beatitudes.** 6s. 6d.

17. **The Sermon on the Mount.** To the end of the Lord's Prayer. 6s. 6d.

27. **The Sermon on the Mount.** From the end of the Lord's Prayer. 6s. 6d.

31. **The Training of the Apostles.** Part I. 6s. 6d.

37. **The Training of the Apostles.** Part II. 6s. 6d.

45. **The Training of the Apostles.** Part III. 6s. 6d.

51. **The Training of the Apostles.** Part IV. 6s. 6d.

57. **The Preaching of the Cross.** Part I.
6s. 6d.

63. **The Preaching of the Cross.** Part II.
6s.

64. **The Preaching of the Cross.** Part III.
6s.

THE FIRST DAYS OF HOLY WEEK.

68. **Passiontide.** Part I. 6s. 6d.

72. **Passiontide.** Part II. 6s. 6d.

76. **Passiontide.** Part III. 6s. 6d.

CONCLUDING VOLUME.

78. **The Passage of our Lord to the Father.**
7s. 6d.

The Manna of the Soul. By Father Paul
Segneri. Second Edition, in two volumes. Cloth
lettered, price 12s.

The Adorable Heart of Jesus. By Father
Joseph de Galliffett, S.J. With Preface and Introduction by the Rev. R. F. Clarke, S.J. Price 3s.

The Seven Words on the Cross. By Cardinal
Bellarmine. Translated from the Latin. Second
Edition. 5s.

The Seven Words of Mary. By the Rev.
H. J. Coleridge, S.J. Price 2s.

The Virtues of Mary, the Mother of God.
By Father Francis Arias, S.J. With Preface by
George Porter, S.J., late Archbishop of Bombay. 2s.

The Prisoners of the King. Thoughts on
the Catholic Doctrine of Purgatory. By the Rev. H.
J. Coleridge, S.J. New Edition, 4s.

St. Ignatius Loyola and the Early Jesuits.
By Stewart Rose. With about 100 Illustrations. Handsomely bound in cloth, extra gilt. Price 15s. net.

The Life of St. Ignatius of Loyola. By
Father Genelli, S.J. New Edition (American). 6s.

The Condition of Catholics under James
the First. By the Rev. John Morris, S.J. Second Edition (a few copies). 14s.

The Troubles of our Catholic Forefathers
related by themselves. By the Rev. John Morris, S.J. Series I. (out of print). Series II. demy 8vo, cloth, 14s. Series III. demy 8vo, cloth, 14s. A few copies of Series I. II. III. complete, £2 2s.

The Life of Father John Gerard, S.J. By
the Rev. John Morris, S.J. Third Edition, re-written and enlarged, 14s.

The Letter-Books of Sir Amias Poulet,
Keeper of Mary Queen of Scots. By the Rev. John Morris, S.J. 3s. 6d.

The Life and Martyrdom of St. Thomas
Becket. By the Rev. John Morris, S.J. Second and enlarged edition. In one vol. large post 8vo, 12s. 6d. Or in two volumes, 13s.

The Venerable Sir Adrian Fortescue, Knight
of the Bath, Knight of St. John, Martyr. With Portrait and Autograph. By the Rev. John Morris, S.J. 1s. 6d.

The Devotions of the Lady Lucy Herbert
of Powis, formerly Prioress of the Augustinian Nuns at Bruges. Edited by Father John Morris, S.J. 3s. 6d.

Meditation: An Instruction for Novices. By
the Rev. John Morris, S.J. 6d. net. by post 7d.

Daily Duties: An Instruction for Novices. By
the Rev. John Morris, S.J. 6d. net, by post 7d.

Vocation: or Preparation for the Vows, with a
further Instruction on Mental Prayer. By the Rev. John Morris, S.J. 6d. net, by post 7d.

Theodore Wibaux, Pontifical Zouave and
Jesuit. By Father Du Coetlosquet, S.J. With an Introduction by the Rev. R. F. Clarke, S.J. Crown 8vo, handsomely bound in blue and gold, price 5s.

Thoughts on Apostolic Succession. To help Catholics in Discussion with their Anglican Friends. By the Rev. P. Gallwey, S.J. Price 1s.

Twelve Lectures on Ritualism. Vol. I. Lectures I.—VIII.: Ritualism not blessed by Heaven; not Catholic; entirely opposed to our Lord's plan of one Sheepfold governed by one Shepherd, and to the faith of the Early Church. Vol. II. Lectures IX.—XII.: Anglican Orders, and the Anglican Confessional. By the Rev. P. Gallwey, S.J. Price, two vols., 8s.

The Precious Pearl of Hope in the Mercy of God. Translated from the Italian. 4s. 6d.

An Hour before the Blessed Sacrament: or, With my Crucifix. 4d.

The End of Man. Library Edition. Crown 4to. with four Autotypes after Overbeck, De Vos, Francia, and Fra Angelico. By the Rev. A. J. Christie, S.J. 10s. 6d. Smaller Edition, 2s. 6d. and 1s. 9d.

The Spiritual Exercises of St. Ignatius. Meditations for an Eight Days' Retreat. By the Rev. A. J. Christie, S.J. Cloth, 2s. 6d. The Meditations in loose papers, 2s.

The Text of the Spiritual Exercises. 2s. 6d.

Records of the English Province of the Society of Jesus. By Henry Foley, S.J. Vols. I. to VI. £6 6s. Vol. VII, in Two Parts, price 21s. each.

The Order for the Dedication or Consecration of a Church. Translated from the Roman Pontifical. 1s. 6d.

The Rite of Conferring Orders. Translated, with Annotations, from the Roman Pontifical. 1s. 6d.

———

JAMES STANLEY,

MANRESA PRESS, ROEHAMPTON, LONDON, S.W.